Teaching YA Lit through Differentiated Instruction

Teaching YA Lit through Differentiated Instruction

Susan L. Groenke
University of Tennessee

Lisa Scherff
University of Alabama

NCTE NATIONAL COUNCIL OF TEACHERS OF ENGLISH
1111 W. KENYON ROAD, URBANA, ILLINOIS 61801-1096

Manuscript Editor: Jane M. Curran

Staff Editor: Carol Roehm

Interior Design: Jenny Jensen Greenleaf

Cover Design: Pat Mayer

Cover Images: iStockphoto.com/Lobke Peers and iStockphoto.com/Qweek

NCTE Stock Number: 33705

Library of Congress Cataloging-in-Publication Data

Groenke, Susan L.
  Teaching YA lit through differentiated instruction / Susan L. Groenke, Lisa Scherff.
    p. cm.
  Includes bibliographical references and index.
  ISBN 978-0-8141-3370-5 (pbk)
  1. Young adult literature—Study and teaching (Secondary) 2. Fiction—Study and teaching (Secondary) 3. Young adults—Books and reading. 4. Youth—Books and reading. I. Scherff, Lisa, 1968– II. Title.
  PN1009.A1G76 2010
  808.8'992830712—dc22

                                                                              2010033422

Contents

Foreword

ALAN SITOMER, *California's Teacher of the Year, 2007*

Wow, do I agree with—and *love*—the central premise of this book! To me, it's a no-brainer. Young adult literature needs to be, as the authors boldly claim, "at the *heart* of the English curriculum."

Truly, if I have achieved any success at all in the English classroom as a teacher of teens, it is due to YA lit. (Of this I have no doubt.) There are a few prominent reasons why.

First off, the core curriculum English standards are not text specific. Essentially, this means that our academic objectives as laid out by all the big kahunas at the state and national level do not mandate the teaching of any particular book or text. Therefore, whether I am using Jane Austen, the Holt Reinhart textbook, or Walter Dean Myers in the classroom is of no direct import; what matters is whether I am teaching my students core academic English content-area standards such as figurative language, theme, tone, and so on.

But if you don't think that there's a difference to the wi-fi, hip-hop teen of today when it comes to book selection, you probably don't know the difference between a text message and a telegram. (Or, to get all pun-ny, you're probably living in the Twilight of a Brave Old World.)

See, using contemporary YA lit empowers teachers such as myself to tap into the great power lying within modern-day books. It also recognizes something spectacularly self-evident about today's classroom world: teens today are reading almost in spite of school, not because of it.

Ouch, I know. The truth hurts.

And in a way, I gotta say, who can blame them? I mean, the language arts textbooks are so watered down, so flavorless, so oversized, overweight, and overpriced that it's the rare teens indeed who will buy into the idea that there is absolutely something riveting on page 1127 of the _____ Language Arts Textbook. (You fill in the blank; they are all pretty much egregiously equal in pandering to a one-size-fits all mentality.)

Yet almost every English classroom in America is outfitted with these anthological monstrosities as if they are "the great answer," the holy "we must buy this product" solution to all the challenges of improving modern-day student achievement and literacy.

Hogwash. Kids love real books. They love the variety of authors, they love the variety of titles, and they love the variety of subject areas about which today's YA novelists are writing. Young adult literature has literally exploded this decade . . . and there are no signs of it slowing down. Talk to any publishing executives in the book industry right now, and they will tell you that there is no area hotter than YA literature—and no area poised for more growth over the course of the next decade as well.

And yet, schools, as usual, are the last to recognize and adapt accordingly. I mean, I have heard stories that you would not believe. Stories about how some school districts are even banning the use of novels all together. That's right, they are banning the use of real books in English classrooms. (You just can't make this up.) And why is that?

Because essentially, people who do not work with real kids day in and day out do not understand how real kids work. Today's students love real books. Therefore, as an English teacher, should I not be providing these for them in order to better achieve my educational aspirations?

Don't answer—it's a rhetorical question.

Textbooks are oh-so-twentieth century. The classics, I love them; and when students have the capacity to navigate some of history's most sophisticated and thoughtful texts, they often take great joy from reading these as well. (Trust me, I love the canon, and this book respects its role in the spectrum of the modern-day English classroom—yet that role is no longer exclusive.) However, real books— with real stories, real journeys, and real adventures—are what teens want and are where the world is headed.

Plus, you know what? All the best teachers I know use real books in their classrooms. All of 'em! Almost each and every excellent English teacher I know uses some form of YA lit in their classroom today. Care to guess why?

Well, the text you are about to read will tell you why. It provides the research. It provides the data. It also provides anecdotes, stories, and the strong, confident voice of two literacy experts who certainly make a case that I find to be almost irrefutable. From "how to choose the right books" to addressing "what teachers can do with young adult novels in whole class instruction," this text you are about to read is rich with ideas and insight.

We must bring YA literature into the classroom. By the time you finish *Teaching YA Lit through Differentiated Instruction*, you will certainly see why.

Happy reading!

Introduction

Why We're Fans of Young Adult Literature

Susan's Story

Most people don't believe me when I say I was a C–/borderline D student in my high school English classes. I was an angry, bitter teen—my parents divorced when I was in middle school, my mom later remarried, and I didn't like my new stepfather. As a result, I ran away from home my sophomore year and showed up on my dad's doorstep (his new girlfriend was not amused).

In the eleventh-grade high school English class at my new high school, I just couldn't get motivated to read and discuss "Young Goodman Brown" or *The Scarlet Letter*. My teacher made frequent phone calls home, telling Dad about incomplete work and suspicious absences. He was confused: at home, I read all the time, anything I could get my hands on, from V. C. Andrews's gothic novels, to biographies on Anne Sexton and Sylvia Plath, to Dad's banjo magazines. I was different at school, though. I didn't feel connected to anything there, especially the teachers who didn't seem interested in getting to know me. They thought I was "too quiet," said I needed to "participate more in class." I perceived this to mean I was dumb—I must be, right? To not like (or "get") the literature I was supposed to appreciate in high school—despite the fact that my world had been turned upside down and I was pissed off!

By twelfth grade, I was just coasting through with Cs, making more effort to at least look attentive during lectures on *Beowulf* and Chaucer (Dad's warnings heeded). By sheer luck (and good grades in a summer art program in New York), I got into a local college and floundered around as "Undecided" until I got excited about a creative writing class in the English department. The writing professor told me I had talent (me?), and that one day he would "see [me] in print." I didn't feel so stupid in this class, and I went on to take other English classes and excelled in those, too. I finally decided to major in English and became an A student, wondering what my eleventh-grade English teacher would think of that.

(I sometimes dream about showing up on her doorstep, singing Toby Keith's "How Do You Like Me Now?")

Toward the end of my undergraduate career, as most English majors do, I began thinking about what I would do with an English major after college. I began to think about teaching, wondered if I could do things a little differently than my own English teachers had done. I took a few general education courses and, once hooked, enrolled in a teaching program at the college. There I took an English methods course and read my first young adult novel, Mildred Taylor's (1976) *Roll of Thunder, Hear My Cry*. Then I read another, and another, and wondered why I'd never heard of the genre before.

I wondered why my own teachers hadn't used young adult literature in high school—it featured teenagers, dealing with life on their own terms as best they could. It honored teens' lives and their experiences, showed teens as capable, smart, and multidimensional. I thought maybe if my eleventh- and twelfth-grade teachers had used young adult literature, my own experience during those two years—both in and out of the classroom—might have been better. One thing I did know: when I got the chance, I would use young adult literature to make connections with students, to find out about them—not overlook them—and make them feel important and listened to in my classroom.

Over the course of my fifteen-year teaching career, I have made many connections with students through young adult literature. There was Latanya, my first African American student, who I connected with through Rita Williams-Garcia's (1998) *Like Sisters on the Homefront*. In another classroom, in another time and place, I made another connection with Brett, an angry teen who wrote about drug use in his journal, with Melvin Burgess's (1999) *Smack* and *Go Ask Alice* (Anonymous, 1972). In a college young adult literature course, I made a connection with a lesbian student who had come out in high school through such novels as M. E. Kerr's (1995) *Deliver Us from Evie* and Nancy Garden's (1992) *Annie on My Mind*. This student became a teacher, and we keep in touch to this day.

As a teacher, I knew these connections were important and necessary if I was to engage these students in class. Only when the students felt their lives and voices mattered did they begin to notice and listen to me. In this way, young adult literature can be a powerful, motivational tool in the English classroom.

Lisa's Story

My story parallels Susan's somewhat: most people would be shocked to connect me, the "professor," with me, the suicidal (yet 4.0 GPA) teenager who later became a lackluster English education student, then finally gained confidence to enter the profession after my master's thesis adviser told me I was indeed a good teacher. (See what the encouragement from just one conscientious teacher can do?)

While I taught high school English for six years, and struggled to engage students with canonical works (the only books in the book room), it is a recent return to the classroom that exemplifies why I continue to be a fan of young adult literature. From January through May of 2010, I returned to a ninth-grade high school English classroom to co-teach with two interns and the classroom teacher. My goal in returning to the secondary classroom was threefold: to get a better sense of teaching in today's "test-crazed" climate in order to improve how I prepare English teachers; to go beyond the one intern/one teacher model, especially in "struggling" schools; and to provide a classroom teacher with three more sets of hands and eyes. Going into the project, I left my rose-colored glasses at home. I had returned once before to the high school classroom, in 2004, and had been a high school English teacher as recently as 2002. However, all of my past classroom experiences did not prepare me for some of the hurdles I would face, including the intense, tunnel vision focus on test preparation and the lack of resources necessary to teach equitably (books, technology, unlimited photocopies, etc.). Nonetheless, one key pedagogical tenet became a thread throughout the semester-long project: listening to students and using students' backgrounds and interests to engage them with the curriculum was absolutely necessary to fostering positive attitudes toward reading.

During my first week in the classroom, two male students refused to select library books and read during independent reading time. I realized this would be the tipping point for the rest of the semester. How I handled this situation would set the tone for the remaining time I was there. Rather than force the students to read something from the library, allow them to do nothing, or send them out of the room, I engaged them in one-on-one conversations. It took some prodding, but I managed to learn that one of the students liked to write rap lyrics. I was almost certain that if I brought in Tupac Shakur's (2009) *The Rose That Grew from Concrete* I would score some points (for listening), and he might read. Turns out I was right on both accounts. This student soon became the most prolific reader in the class, reading three to four novels per week! He read a range of titles, too, from R. A. Nelson's (2005) *Teach Me* to Coe Booth's (2007) *Tyrell* and (2008) *Kendra* to *Always Running: La Vida Loca: Gang Days in L.A.* (2005) by Luis J. Rodriguez, which he later said was his favorite book.

And once he started reading, other students followed suit.

I began to bring in title after title from my personal young adult novel library and, at least in my opinion, daily silent reading became the students' favorite part of the class. Students who did little or no work any other time during class were reading book after book during class, ignoring all other instructional activities. (This was one of those moments where the classroom teacher and I had to decide whether to let them continue reading or make them put their books down—we went for option one. Some may not agree with our decision, but we learned that if they put the books down, their heads would soon follow.)

Two female students read their way through Sarah Dessen's entire collection. Another student read the Make Lemonade trilogy by Virginia Euwer Wolff (in addition to ten other novels). Suzanne Collins's (2008) *Hunger Games* and its sequel, *Catching Fire* (2009), became favorites, crossing gender, race, cultural, and socioeconomic lines. So, too, did Paul Volponi's books (*Rikers High* [2010], *The Rooftop* [2007], *Hurricane Song* [2008], and *Black and White* [2006]). I have seen what young adult literature can do in the classroom—it can motivate even the most reluctant readers to read, and it can help to build important interpersonal bridges between teachers and their students.

Rationale for This Book

Our stories serve as testament to our belief that when adolescents have the opportunity to make choices about what they read, access to young adult literature, and time to read, *they will read*. So we certainly value the importance of independent reading time in the classroom, and much has been written about using young adult literature in this way (see Teri Lesesne's [2003] *Making the Match: The Right Book for the Right Reader at the Right Time* and Janet Allen's [1995] *It's Never Too Late: Leading Adolescents to Lifelong Literacy*). But, beyond individual connection making and independent reading, less has been written about using young adult novels in whole-class instruction.

It's time to move young adult literature to the center of high school English instruction. The quality of much young adult literature published today will surprise English teachers who continue to pooh-pooh the genre. The genre deserves careful literary study. Thus, this book serves as a guide for choosing young adult literature for whole-class instruction and teaching it through differentiated reading instruction. We hope it will inspire English teachers to see young adult literature—and adolescents—with new eyes. Young adult literature is not just for independent reading anymore.

Centering Young Adult Literature in the High School English Curriculum through Differentiated Instruction

Young adult literature has come of age in the twenty-first century. Sales of young adult novels are up (despite claims that teens aren't reading), and some say the genre is experiencing a second golden age (Reno, 2008). Young adult novels now top annual best book lists and win prestigious awards. Yet the genre continues to have "stepchild" status in the high school English classroom, due partly to misconceptions about it.

One misconception is that young adult literature is for struggling, reluctant readers *only*, rather than sophisticated, already-motivated readers. Books like Janet Allen's (1995) *It's Never Too Late* and Marilyn Reynolds's (2004) *I Won't Read and You Can't Make Me: Reaching Reluctant Teen Readers* reinforce this idea. In addition, many English teachers do not consider young adult literature "good literature" and see its use as "lowering the bar" and accommodating students' desires for entertainment and quick consumption. NCTE president Carol Jago (2004) has suggested that young adult literature is useful only when entertainment and pleasure—rather than careful literary study—are instructional goals (p. 4).

Due to these misconceptions, when young adult literature can be found in schools, it is usually in remedial reading classes, in the school library, or on teachers' personal classroom library shelves, where students can check young adult novels out for independent, silent reading. Some teachers use excerpts from young adult novels as a bridge or "complement" to the classics (Kaywell, 1993), but rarely is a contemporary young adult novel centered as a core text for whole-class instruction.

Research shows that the novels high school English teachers currently use for whole-class instruction are the same classic, canonical works they used more than a decade ago—texts like *The Scarlet Letter*, *Romeo and Juliet*, and *The Great Gatsby* (Applebee, 1993; Stallworth, Gibbons, & Fauber, 2006). As Applebee (1993) explains, "These are the texts at the heart of the English curriculum and thus [they] receive the most time and attention . . . [and] other selections are often organized and introduced [around them]" (p. 234).

We're fans of classic texts, and believe *all* students—and not just those in honors or advanced placement (AP) classes—should have opportunities to read them. But we also believe, as Teri Lesesne (2008) exhorts in her "Young Adult Reader's Bill of Rights," that adolescents have the "right to demand changes in the literary canon for the 21st century." Respecting this right means today's English teachers should consider centering high-quality young adult literature at the *heart* of the English curriculum, as we know the following from decades of classroom-based reading research:

- Adolescent engagement with reading and motivation to read *increases* when adolescents read young adult novels (Ivey & Broaddus, 2001; Pflaum & Bishop, 2004; Worthy, Moorman, & Turner, 1999).
- Adolescent literature has the potential to broaden adolescents' vision of self and the world, providing an avenue for reflection and a means for personal development (Bean & Harper, 2006; Glasgow, 2001; Landt, 2006).
- Adolescents choose to read adolescent novels over more canonical works when given opportunities to choose (Cole, 2009).

We know adolescents like young adult novels because, unlike classical, canonical works, these novels have been written *about* adolescents, *with adolescent readers in mind*. It is these books that teachers should use in the classroom if today's adolescents are to see school as relevant to their lives and experiences.

Speaking at the Assembly on Literature for Adolescents of NCTE conference at the 2007 NCTE Annual Convention, young adult author Chris Crutcher said that when we omit young adult literature from our classrooms, we say to students that the kids in those books—and their lives—don't matter. Teenagers' reading habits and their out-of-school lives *must* matter in today's classrooms if we don't want to further students' disengagement with school. Until young adult novels become the "curriculum heart" of secondary English programs, the genre—like adolescents' lives and adolescent literacies—will continue to remain at the margins of school curricula (Cole, 2009).

We're fortunate because much of the young adult literature being published today is high-quality literature that deserves teachers' attention and consideration for whole-class instruction—for struggling and advanced readers alike. In *Classics in the Classroom*, Carol Jago (2004) insists that "good" literature is literature requiring careful study, often guided by a teacher, and we think quality young adult literature fits this description. The best young adult literature possesses themes that merit and reward examination and commentary, and most standardized test and curriculum requirements about literary elements and devices can be taught with a young adult novel.

Choosing young adult novels for whole-class instruction can be difficult, though, because while high-quality books for young adults abound, so, too, do those that promote quick indulgence and gratuitously portray some of the most troubling representations of adolescence circulating in popular culture today—promiscuous sex, drug and alcohol abuse, indifference to adults and society's ills, to name a few.

Cecily von Ziegesar's (2001) Gossip Girl series serves as example. The novels that constitute this series—twelve at last count—have sold in the millions, predominantly to teenage girls. The books are sold in large retail bookstores, as well as retail chains like Target and Wal-Mart. A *Gossip Girl* website (www.gossip girl.net) exists, and in fall 2007, the *Gossip Girl* TV series premiered on the CW, a broadcast network owned by Warner Brothers and CBS (http://www.cwtv. com/thecw/about-the-cw). Despite their popularity, however, the novel series and TV show have been challenged by teachers and parents for their portrayals of drug and alcohol abuse, sexual content, and offensive language.

In our work with preservice and classroom teachers, and as teachers of young adult literature courses, we stay away from judging young adult literature as simply "good" or "bad," because we know readers read for multiple reasons and purposes, and even our most sophisticated readers may choose to read novels like *Gossip Girl* independently. We also know that reading serial novels helps develop fluency and prediction skills in struggling readers. Some reading researchers say serial novels appeal to teens because of the "comfort of the familiar" and readers' desires to "be a part of a community of readers who share delight in particular stories, characters, or language" (McGill-Franzen, 2009, p. 57). Ross (1995) explains reading is more often than not a "social activity" and "series books have the cachet of something precious, to be collected, hoarded, and discussed" (p. 226).

In addition, even though we don't like books like *Gossip Girl* because they contribute to the misconception that all young adult literature is "low-brow fluff" (among other reasons), we don't think it's a bad idea to use *Gossip Girl* in the high school classroom *if* instructional goals include helping adolescents navigate the popular culture discourses on teenage sexuality and consumption present in the work, and skilled facilitators are present (see Ashcraft, 2006; Glenn, 2008; Groenke, 2007).

What we're trying to say is we believe every young adult novel has its place in the high school English classroom, which marks the usefulness and versatility of the genre. Some young adult novels are better served in silent, sustained independent reading, while others should be considered for whole-class instruction. But which ones? How can teachers make the distinction among young adult novels to use for whole-class instruction versus independent reading?

Choosing High-Quality Young Adult Literature for Whole-Class Instruction

The *ALAN Review* coeditor Steven Bickmore (2008) explains, "Choosing YA literature does not have to mean providing a text of inferior quality, but it does mean that more of us should explain the craftsmanship in these novels" (p. 77). We couldn't agree more. Thus, one objective of this book is to provide secondary teachers with some criteria they can use to select high-quality young adult novels for whole-class instruction versus novels that might be better suited for independent reading.

In *Classics in the Classroom* (2004) Carol Jago writes, "There is an art to choosing books for students. First I look for literary merit. Without this, the novel will not stand up to close scrutiny or be worth the investment of classroom time" (p. 47). She goes on to list six additional criteria she considers before selecting a text for whole-class study. Such works:

1. are written in language that is perfectly suited to the author's purpose;

2. expose readers to complex human dilemmas;

3. include compelling, disconcerting characters;

4. explore universal themes that combine different periods and cultures;

5. challenge readers to reexamine their beliefs; and

6. tell a good story with places for laughing and places for crying. (p. 47)

While Jago is referring to the use of classic texts (e.g., *Romeo and Juliet*, *The Odyssey*, *My Ántonia*), these same criteria can and, in our view, *should be* applied when choosing young adult novels for whole-class study. Because we want to emphasize the literary merit of many of the young adult novels published today, and because we believe young adult literature deserves careful attention and study from students and their teachers, we have applied Jago's criteria to the selection and evaluation of the young adult titles we describe and feature in this book.

Many of these titles—all published since 2000—have won prestigious awards, are featured on "Best of" lists (e.g., Nilsen & Donelson, 2009), and, perhaps most important, are popular with teen readers, if teen polls like the ones published annually by the Young Adult Library Services Association (YALSA), and *Journal of Adolescent and Adult Literacy* are any indication. Many of these titles we teach in our young adult literature courses. Some have been recommended by long-time teachers and former students. Some we have found by attending librarian and teacher conferences (e.g., NCTE, ALAN, ALA), frequenting local book-stores, and reading young adult book lovers' blogs (thank you, Teri Lesesne, aka Goddess of YA Lit!). Some we discovered by sheer luck. All of them, we think, merit teachers' attention and consideration for whole-class instruction.

But we understand selecting titles for instruction is only part of teachers' work. What can teachers do with young adult novels in whole-class instruction? How can teachers use young adult novels in whole-class instruction to address the needs of diverse readers in the classroom?

Teaching Young Adult Novels to the Whole Class through Differentiated Reading Instruction

Differentiated reading instruction is an excellent way to teach young adult lit-erature to a whole class of mixed-ability learners. The high-quality young adult novel lends itself well to differentiated instruction as it has broad appeal and allows for various levels of interpretations in line with the various levels of stu-dents' abilities in the high school English classroom. A second objective of this book, then, is to provide teaching strategies for whole-class, differentiated read-ing instruction of the young adult novels featured in this work. We know that all classrooms—even honors and AP classes—are populated by readers at various perceived ability levels, with varying reading interests and habits. Katie Dredg-er, a former high school AP English teacher, suggests that instead of asking if students are in the "correct placement" when we recognize reading differences, we should instead ask, "What circumstances will be the most effective catalyst for this student's development?" (2008, p. 30).

In this book, we take very seriously the latest research numbers that tell us only 3 percent of all eighth graders read at the advanced level and nearly one-third of all ninth graders are two or more years behind the average level of reading achievement and need extra help (Balfanz, McPartland, & Shaw, 2002; Perie, Grigg, & Donahue, 2005). We also consider what current reading research has to say about adolescents' reading development and provide differentiation strategies for helping all the readers in your classroom engage in meaningful ways with characters in stories, develop prosody (or reading with expression) fluency skills, and develop inference and prediction-making skills. We also pro-vide ideas for matching theme-related books with different levels of readers. We have used differentiated reading instruction (DRI) successfully with both striving and sophisticated readers, and we can attest to the high student engagement and motivation that occur with all students when their individual reading abilities and needs are attended to in the high school English classroom.

Differentiated Reading Instruction Defined

Defining differentiated reading instruction is not a simple task, but there *is* one simple principle that constitutes our understanding and use of DRI in the secondary English classroom: *the belief in the potential of every student to become a capable, confident, engaged, skillful reader.* DRI honors this potential by identifying and acting upon adolescent readers' readiness, interests, and learning styles. Key to this process are the following additional integrated principles of DRI.

Proactive, Recursive, Student-Centered Learning

DRI begins with individual students. What are individual students' reading levels when they enter our classrooms? What are their entry-level reading skills? What literacy strengths, abilities, and resources do our students bring to our classrooms? What weaknesses? Are our students voluntary readers outside of school? If not, why not? What do our students like to read? What are they currently reading? What have their past experiences with reading been? Teachers who practice DRI begin with these questions and, once they get answers, begin developing or modifying reading instruction accordingly. With DRI, curricular goals come first, but DRI is an ongoing, recursive process, always anticipating and responding to students' needs. This anticipation and responsiveness result in differentiation of *curricular content, learning process,* or *assessment product* for individual students so they can achieve curricular goals.

Ongoing Pre- and Post-Assessment

Central to centering student learning in DRI is ongoing pre- and post-assessment. At the simplest level, differentiating reading instruction requires English teachers to acknowledge that all students do not read and comprehend texts in the same way, and then to plan and deliver instruction accordingly. As Barbara King-Shaver and Alyce Hunter (2003) explain in their book *Differentiated Instruction in the English Classroom: Content, Process, Product, and Assessment*: "Recognizing that one size doesn't fit all, differentiated instruction asks that each learner and his or her uniqueness be considered, embraced, and celebrated. Differentiated instruction asks teachers to diagnose students as well as analyze content and skills, to know their needs, interests, and learning styles, and to relate to students with a cognitive empathy" (p. 2).

Diagnosing students' reading abilities involves ongoing, formative assessment with which teachers identify students' strengths and areas of need so they can assess students where they are and help them move forward. Knowing students' needs, interests, and learning styles requires that teachers acknowledge and embrace the diversity that exists among our students in their levels of experience and expertise with texts. But how do we assess our students? How do we know "where they are" when they come to us?

Carol Tomlinson (1999)—considered by many the "inventor" of differentiated instruction—suggests the first step in differentiating reading instruction is to assess a student's individual *readiness*, or capabilities as a reader; *interests/attitudes*, or how a student feels about reading, and what a student likes to read; and *reading habits*, or how a student reads. This is a crucial first step in the differentiation process, because if teachers don't know who their readers are and what their needs are, differentiated curriculum may end up looking like "dumbed-down" work for some and "more work" for others. This is not authentic differentiated instruction. A variety of resources is available to assess who your students are as readers when they come to your classroom. We list some of our favorite resources for assessing student reading readiness, their reading attitudes and interests, and their reading habits at the end of this chapter.

Tomlinson explains that understanding these three things about individual students as readers can help teachers make decisions about differentiating reading instruction in three ways: by *content*, or what a student is to learn (e.g., literary terms; understanding of character's motives); *process*, how a student is to learn the content (e.g., whole-class instruction; small group reading); and *product*, or how a student displays what he or she has learned (e.g., tests; skits). In this book, we show teachers how to differentiate for *content*, *process*, or *product* depending on readers' needs.

Appropriate, Blended Instruction

As King-Shaver and Hunter (2009) explain in *Adolescent Literacy and Differentiated Instruction*, the teacher's role in DRI is matching individual learners to appropriate instruction. Thus, rather than solely a "teacher-in-the-front-of-the-class" model of instruction, DRI requires that teachers use varying and various instructional strategies to differentiate learning by *content*, *process*, or *product* for individual learners. To differentiate content, teachers may use classic differentiation strategies such as "jigsaw," in which students work in small groups on a reading activity (groups designated by student readiness and interest) and then reassemble in a second, larger group to share content and skills learned during the first group task. Or teachers may use another classic differentiation strategy called "tiered assignments." Tiered assignments cluster students according to pre-assessed readiness levels to complete a task designed for a certain level of content and skill understanding (more on this later). While students work in such arrangements, the teacher moves from group to group or works one-on-one with various students.

Tomlinson explains that in DRI "everyone gets some of [the teacher] in some configuration smaller than the class-as-a whole" (in King-Shaver & Hunter, 2009, p. vii). In addition to small-group work and independent study, the DRI teacher might also blend instructional styles and strategies, calling students together at various times for whole-class instruction and skills practice. Tomlinson likens differentiated instruction to a "flow" process that moves back and forth among whole-class exploration of topics and concepts, independent skills practice and study, and small-group work (2001, p. 6).

Appropriate Texts

We believe the teacher's role in DRI is also matching individual learners to appropriate texts. We know in many secondary English classrooms, student reading readiness can stretch from first grade to college level. We also know students' reading interests vary widely. Some students may be avid online fan fiction or e-book readers but never pick up a book. Others may love nonfiction or how-to manuals, while still others can't get enough vampire lore. While we believe—like Delia DeCourcy, Lyn Fairchild, and Robin Follet, authors of *Teaching* Romeo and Juliet: *A Differentiated Approach* (2007)—that "all students should have access to Shakespeare" (p. 1), we also know that the esoteric language, need for intensive teacher guidance and explanation, and seeming lack of relevance to today's popular culture are reasons why adolescent readers struggle to engage with classic texts.

We also know young adult authors such as Alan Gratz, Caroline Cooney, Lisa Klein, Sharon Draper, and Walter Dean Myers provide contemporary, relevant updates on classic texts. Choice is key here. When teachers teach thematically in DRI, they can give the student who loves or wants the challenge of Shakespeare a Shakespearean play or sonnet to read, but give other students other options. Not all the time—we understand. Good DRI honors the integration of self-selected books with whole-class instruction of teacher-selected texts.

Let us say a bit more about the importance of choice in DRI. NCTE's 2007 Policy Research Brief explains that "meaningful choice" in the classroom is a powerful motivator for adolescents. Teachers who practice DRI build choice into reading assignments because they know DRI is about promoting independent, lifelong reading. This means our students have to learn to read without us, and therefore they have to know there are books (and other texts) out there that they like to—and can—read. This doesn't mean the teacher becomes obsolete—the teacher must work hard in DRI, both behind the scenes and front and center to (1) pre-assess student readiness and skill levels; (2) find appropriate book options that match learner interests and readiness levels; (3) plan and implement whole-class, small-group, and independent instruction; (4) structure class time to accommodate differentiated instruction; and (5) manage student behavior.

We understand why Tomlinson's description of differentiated instruction as a "flow" process can oftentimes feel like an oncoming flood for teachers—over-whelming and out of control. But DRI doesn't have to happen every day, in every class. We understand DRI takes a lot of time and energy, but we also believe in its potential and success to help all adolescents become confident, engaged readers.

We highly recommend Kathie F. Nunley's (2005) book *Differentiating the High School Classroom: Solution Strategies for 18 Common Obstacles* if you are new to differentiated instruction or are trying to help other teachers new to the concept consider its implementation in the classroom. Nunley suggests that for teachers new to differentiated instruction, the easiest place to start is with independent seatwork. In other words, teachers can divide a class period into two sections: one that includes some type of whole-class instruction and another that involves some type of independent seatwork. Allow some variety and choice in the seat-work. For example, offer a choice to work solo or in a group. Offer a choice between reading silently or listening to a book on tape, or reading with a part-ner (or teacher). This, in essence, is differentiating *content* and *process*. Add an accountability piece (the *product*), and you're on your way to differentiating! We provide more specific how-to information for differentiating reading instruction with young adult literature in this book.

Reading Is Tied to Identity

Another key principle underlying DRI is the understanding that students are different kinds of readers in different contexts, and students' reading practices in school can be performances of identities they may wish others to see in them (Jones, Clarke, & Enriquez, 2010). We see identity play out every day in the classroom when we look out at the sea of faces (and clothes, and gadgets) and see "goths" in one corner, while the "slackers" or "preps" or "jocks" or (insert your own term here) congregate in others. We also see identity at work when the boys in class pick up only books that have footballs or baseballs on the covers, while the girls' picks tend to have what Susan calls "cocktail-colored" covers or the words *boyfriend* and *girlfriend* or *summer love* in them.

We must be careful, though, because adolescent identities are usually in flux. As readers, adolescents probably cross multiple categories in terms of what they like to (and can) read, and how they read. We must keep in mind, too, that today's adolescents inhabit multiple and varied textual and social worlds, and thus "read" and comprehend texts in cyberspace and the popular media (e.g., TV, film) all the time. While your students may not seem to be good readers in your classrooms, their out-of-school reading skills may surprise you. If we get to know what these out-of-school interests and skills are, we can find ways to capitalize on them in the classroom.

Finally, as Jones, Clarke, and Enriquez (2010) suggest, we must pay attention to who we call "good" or "struggling" readers in our classrooms and must not make assumptions about students as readers. In doing so, we can work to reposition students who might be on the margins of reading "success." Differentiated reading instruction is thus also a way to help adolescents construct positive reading identities.

Everyone Improves

The goal for each reader in a differentiated classroom is the same: everyone improves.

It is unrealistic to think we can make every reader a *strong, sophisticated* reader. Remember, the first and foremost premise underlying differentiated reading instruction is to create *capable, confident, engaged, skillful readers*. We can help weaker and average readers become capable, confident, skilled readers, but this does not mean they will be the best readers in class at year's or semester's end (or who knows—maybe they will be!). The goal here is to remember that every reader can get better and more skilled. Everyone, regardless of ability, works toward the same goal: improvement.

Organization of This Book

Each chapter that follows opens with an introduction to and description of a different, popular genre or award category of young adult literature (e.g., realistic teen fiction, nonfiction, etc.). Chapters 2 through 4 focus on realistic teen issues, historical fiction, and the verse novel, a new trend in young adult literature. In Chapter 5 we focus on memoir and reader response, and then move from reader response to critical literacy with multicultural young adult literature in Chapter 6. Chapter 7 focuses on the graphic novel, a popular genre with today's teens. The last two chapters, 8 and 9, focus on what reading researchers deem the two most popular genres with today's adolescents, adventure/mystery and science fiction/fantasy and the supernatural, respectively.

In each chapter, we describe young adult novels published since 2000 that we would use in differentiated whole-class reading instruction. In some chapters, we use Jago's criteria to describe both a book we would use in whole-class instruction and one we'd put on the shelf for independent reading. In other chapters, we use Jago's criteria to describe several books we'd use in whole-class, small-group literature circle activities. In still other chapters, we provide lists of books we've measured against Jago's criteria and recommend that teachers seek out on their own. We then present differentiated instructional activities to use with the novel(s) we profile in each chapter. Effective instructional activities used in differentiated instruction include whole-class instruction and small-group work, and lots of student choice. You'll see examples of this throughout the book.

It is our hope that this book can serve as a resource for English teachers who are strapped for time to find good young adult novels, and who need help understanding and seeing what differentiated reading instruction can look like with older adolescent readers. It is also our hope to provide "research-based" evidence for the instructional strategies we describe in this book. An early reviewer of this book said that much of the language and tone of what we write here is too "academic" and not suited for classroom teachers, who would appreciate a more narrative, readable style. We know teachers are increasingly pressured to use "research-based" strategies to raise students' academic reading achievement, but this research base does not always include the voices of researchers, teachers, and teacher-researchers who examine or teach adolescents in classroom settings. All of the researchers, academics, and classroom teachers we draw on throughout this text are people who care about adolescents and their learning, and who spend lots of time in classrooms trying to understand how adolescents read and comprehend texts, and how best to help them develop as readers. We trust the researchers, academics, and classroom teachers we cite throughout this text, and we hope that teachers will follow up on some of the research on their own and add their voices to the research they rely on when making instructional decisions. At the very least, we hope this book serves teachers in their own professional development as they continue to look for ways to help adolescents become the skilled, capable, and confident readers we know they can be.

Resource Guide for Chapter 1

Next, we list some of our favorite resources for assessing students' reading readiness, determining their reading attitudes and interests, and discovering their reading habits.

Determining Students' Reading Readiness

- Ekwall Informal Reading Inventory (in Shanker & Ekwall, 2000). Diagnostic assessments that provide information about students' independent, instructional, and frustrational reading levels.
- Metacognitive Reading Awareness Inventories (Miholic, 1994; Schmitt, 1990). Examine students' understanding of themselves as strategic readers.
- Ask students to read to you. See Allington (2006) for ideas on three-finger rule, informal accuracy records, and recall summaries—all quick, informal assessments teachers can use to gauge accuracy and fluency while students read to them.
- Informal, low-stakes writing (journal entry written in response to reading).
- Standardized test scores; Stanford 9 reading assessment.
- Observe kids reading independently in your classroom.

Janet Allen (1995) offers tips for recognizing disengaged, reluctant, frustrated, or struggling readers in the classroom. These readers may exhibit the following behaviors:

- Have trouble finding ways to respond to what they've read.
- Not like to talk about or share ideas or information about a book.
- Not attempt to try new authors, titles, genres.
- Have difficulty selecting books for independent reading.
- Look up frequently when reading alone.
- Try to disrupt others during reading time.
- Ask to go to the bathroom during reading time.
- Write notes or do other things during reading time.
- Hold a book close to the face.

- Lip read; subvocalize; finger-stab.
- Turn page infrequently, if at all.
- Check the clock often.
- Frequently change books for new books.

Determining Students' Reading Attitudes and Interests

- Activity ranking sheet (in *"Reading Don't Fix No Chevys,"* Smith & Wilhelm, 2002). Asks students to rank-order specific activities, such as reading or watching TV, from the most favorite to least favorite activity.
- Adolescent Motivation to Read Profile (Pitcher et al., 2007).
- Informal reading survey (in *In the Middle,* Atwell, 1998).
- "Who Are You?" questionnaire (in *Fires in the Bathroom,* Cushman, 2003).
- "Things That Make Me Want to/Not Want to Read" T-chart (in *It's Never Too Late,* Allen, 1995).

Discovering Students' Reading Habits

- Reading survey: What, Why, How, and When Do You Read? (in *Reading Reminders,* Burke, 2000).
- Reading inventories (Atwell, 1998).
- Learning styles inventories: Memletics Learning Styles Questionnaire (free, online at http://www.learning-styles-online.com/inventory/questions.asp?cookieset=y). Includes learning styles descriptions and overview.
- Index of Learning Styles Questionnaire (free, online at http://www.engr.ncsu.edu/learningstyles/ilsweb.html).
- Career interest survey (lots of free ones online).

Finally, we recommend Laura Robb's (2009) *Assessments for Differentiating Reading Instruction,* as it provides teachers with tools to assess students' reading comprehension and to monitor students' reading, among other assessments, with all forms provided on the CD included with the book.

2

Getting into Character with the Realistic Young Adult Novel

The first young adult novels may have been Louisa May Alcott's (1868/2004) *Little Women* or Maureen Daly's (1942/1985) *Seventeenth Summer*, but it's the gritty realism of young adult novels published in the 1960s and 1970s that defines (and continues to define) the best of the genre (Cart, 1996; Nilsen & Donelson, 2009).

In contrast to the focus on romance and Mayberry-esque goodness depicted in novels like Alcott's and Daly's, the publication of S. E. Hinton's (1967/1997) *The Outsiders* portrayed teenage boys smoking (gasp!) and the adolescent experience as rife with violence and social class differences. Robert Cormier's (1974/2000) *The Chocolate War* showed readers adolescence can be a lonely, evil place where good doesn't always prevail. Fourteen-year-old Benjie in Alice Childress's (1974/2000) *A Hero Ain't Nothin' but a Sandwich* is a heroin addict, while the teenaged lovers in Judy Blume's *Forever* (1975/2007) have sex and (double gasp!) enjoy it. Blume has said her daughter asked for a story about two nice kids who have sex without either of them having to die (Whitworth, 2008). Clearly the changing social and cultural values in 1960s and 1970s America, influenced perhaps by the Vietnam War and the Civil Rights Movement, no longer reflected earlier, Victorian-influenced expectations or representations of young people (Cole, 2009).

Today's young adult fiction—informed by our own changing cultural times—is just as realistic, chock full of the personal and social issues adolescents experience across socioeconomic, geographic, and ethnic/cultural boundaries. As an example, the adolescent protagonist, Junior, in Sherman Alexie's (2007) award-winning *The Absolutely True Diary of a Part-Time Indian* must deal with the havoc alcoholism has wreaked on his Spokane Indian family, as he struggles to define himself and decide whether to leave the reservation. In Coe Booth's (2007) *Tyrell*, Tyrell and his family are homeless, and Tyrell must learn what it means to "be a man" if he is to keep his younger brother out of an ineffective foster care system. The many different faces of teenage sexuality are portrayed in Sara Zarr's (2008) *Story of a Girl*, John Green and David Levithan's (2010) *Will Grayson, Will Grayson*, and Chris Lynch's (2007) *Inexcusable*. In Jenny Downham's (2007) remarkable *Before I Die*, Tessie battles cancer—the number one disease killer of children from the age of one through adolescence—while Chanda in Alan Stratton's (2004) excellent *Chanda's Secrets* battles AIDS and its stigma in sub-Saharan Africa.

The publication of these sophisticated novels, and others like them, might help explain the fact that young adult literature is experiencing its second golden age (Reno, 2008). A recent Children's Book Council survey reports sales of young adult novels are up more than 25 percent in the past few years. Levithan (in Reno, 2008) explains reasons for the genre's popularity, including that teenagers are more "emotionally mature," and librarians and booksellers have finally separated teen books from children's book sections. Cole (2009) cites an exploding teenage population as the reason. Others attribute the genre's success to content: everything from drug addiction to incest to life on the front lines in Iraq.

The Appeal of Realistic Fiction to Adolescents

Why are teenagers drawn to realistic books about addiction, abuse, and war? Many young adult advocates suggest adolescents seek out literature that speaks to the issues, conflicts, and stressors they face, and literature that helps them make sense of these issues. Young adult author and advocate Chris Crutcher suggests teens "[long] for recognition of their losses, the chaos of their lives, the desperation they sometimes feel" (in Cole, 2009, p. 104). Good realistic teen fiction provides this recognition. Maybe, too, teenagers like the use of contemporary, authentic language and dialogue that rings true to adolescent ears. Or maybe teens find it flattering when they and their experiences are respected, when teenagers are portrayed as "strong" and capable people (Reid & Stringer, 1997, n.p.).

We know most teenagers experience "normal" stressors that come with adolescence (e.g., peer and parental pressure). But many teenagers also experience debilitating stressors often trivialized in the media and overlooked or ignored by teachers and school administrators. Consider these statistics:

- The risk of depression peaks at age 13 and 14 (Koplewicz, 2002).
- In 2000, suicide was the third leading cause of death among 15- to 24-year-olds. More teenagers die from suicide than cancer, heart disease, AIDS, pneumonia, stroke, and influenza combined (www.teensuicide.us/).

- Approximately 15,000 teens undergo treatment in the United States for cancer each year (www.teenslivingwithcancer.org).

- 48 percent of US female adolescents and 52 percent of US male adolescents use alcohol; 31 percent of these girls and 34 percent of these boys engage in binge drinking (National Institute on Alcohol Abuse and Alcoholism, 2006).

- A 2002 report from the US Office of Juvenile Justice and Delinquency Prevention estimates there are 1,682,900 homeless and runaway youth, the majority between the ages of 15 and 17 (Molino, 2007; National Coalition for the Homeless, 2008).

- 12.1 million US children are living in families with earnings at or below the conservative income poverty line ($17,601 or less for a family of four, according to the US Census Bureau's 2001 guidelines) (Fauth, Brady-Smith, & Brooks-Gunn, 2002).

- 1,760 youth died in 2007 from child abuse and neglect (www.childwelfare.gov).

- Of US high school students in grades 9–12, 47 percent have had sex and 14 percent have had four or more partners (Kaiser Family Foundation, 2005).

- 9.1 million adolescents contract sexually transmitted diseases each year.

- Research shows that more than 90 percent of those who have eating disorders are adolescent girls (www.nami.org).

- 44 percent of women raped in the United States are under age 18, and 15 percent are under age 12; two-thirds of teen sexual abuse is committed by known assailants (e.g., friends, intimate partners, relatives) (Rape, Abuse, and Incest National Network, n.d.).

- In 2006, 1.9 million Americans age 12 and older had abused methamphetamine at least once in the year prior to being surveyed (National Survey on Drug Use and Health, http://www.oas.samhsa.gov/nhsda.htm).

- More than 64 percent of LGBT students say they feel unsafe at school because of their sexual orientation (GLSEN 2003 National School Climate Survey).

- Harrassment and bullying have been linked to 75 percent of school-shooting incidents (US Secret Service Report, 2002).

It is no wonder, then, that for many teenagers the realistic young adult novel provides therapeutic value, an opportunity to see they are not alone. As Reid and Stringer (1997) explain, "Young adult literature can fill this need for many students, reducing their isolation by telling a story that they can relate to, that sounds familiar enough to reassure them of their normality" (n.p.).

Whatever the reason, teenagers *like* realistic young adult fiction enough to buy it, read it voluntarily, and pass it along to their friends, and this is reason enough for English teachers to use the realistic YA novel in whole-class instruction. But other reasons are just as compelling. Crutcher says realistic young adult novels offer us a chance as educators to "open lines of communication across the generations, to hook our lives to the lives of adolescents" (Crutcher qtd. in Cole, 2009, p. 105). But which realistic novels should English teachers consider using in whole-class instruction?

Choosing Realistic Young Adult Literature for Whole-Class Instruction

Michael Cart (1996) suggests that what makes a realistic young adult novel *bad* is a too-narrow focus on a problem, issue, or social concern, rather than a focus on the adolescent characters who populate the novel. Adolescent characters are overshadowed in some realistic teen fiction, and Cart suggests such overshadowing can result in didactic, moral instruction (which teens resist). Reno (2008) explains realistic young adult novels are not popular with teens when they are "self-righteous, based on fear, . . . cautionary and sermon-like . . . [telling] kids how to behave in a 'just say no' fashion." In contrast, sophisticated realistic young adult literature "[does] not pander or talk down to [the teenage] audience. . . . [Today's popular young adult authors] would rather present drugs as a miserable existence and show what it's like to live through this experience than to preach" (Reno, 2008).

A good realistic young adult novel is also usually multi-themed, with several layers of character and plot development for readers to mine. Nilsen and Donelson (2009) explain that "in the best of the problem novels authors take the space to develop various strands of their stories" (p. 115). As an example, Chris Crutcher's sports novels are never just about sports—there's always a life lesson (usually more) to be learned both on and off the football field. For this and the other reasons mentioned earlier, we'd pick Crutcher's (2007) recent *Deadline* to use in whole-class differentiated instruction over a similarly styled book, John Coy's (2007) *Crackback*.

Both are YALSA "Quick Picks for Reluctant Young Adult Readers," but *Deadline* resonates with us in ways that *Crackback* doesn't. In what follows (see Figure 2.1), we apply Carol Jago's criteria for choosing a novel worthy of whole-class

	Deadline by Chris Crutcher 2008 ALA Quick Pick for Reluctant Young Adult Readers	*Crackback* by John Coy 2006 ALA Quick Pick for Reluctant Young Adult Readers
Summary	In August, when the book opens, eighteen-year-old Ben Wolf is dreaming about his senior year and leaving the "Pluto that is Trout, Idaho," when he learns he has a rare, aggressive form of leukemia. Given a year to live, he decides his "chances aren't about living, but living well." He refuses treatment and chooses not to tell his parents or his devoted brother. What's more, the scrawny cross-country runner without "the power to tower" tries out for the football team, goes for the girl of his dreams, and becomes an unlikely hero. But can Ben live with the biggest lie of his life?	Miles Manning wants so badly to be recognized for his quick thinking on the football field. But his coach says there is only "act and react"—no thinking—and his dad only criticizes what Miles does wrong. When some of Miles's teammates begin taking steroids, Miles considers it—they would help him be a stronger player. But gradually Miles realizes that nothing he does will impress his arrogant, misguided coach, and his father has his own burdens to bear. When Miles gets to know the second stringers on the team and falls for a smart girl who likes his brains better than his football skills, he realizes there's more to life than winning or losing a game.
Criterion 1: Written in language perfectly suited to the author's purpose	Chris Crutcher is known for giving readers witty, smart, sarcastic adolescent protagonists and vivid sports action scenes. *Deadline* doesn't disappoint. Readers will engage with Ben's first-person, self-deprecating voice and the respectful tone of the narrative. Crutcher is a master at balancing exposition and dialogue—he has an ear for timing—and, like a photographer, knows when to widen and narrow the narrative lens. Use of racy language in places rings authentic and true, and Crutcher's treatment of teens' sexual experiences is tastefully—not gratuitously—done.	This is a football player's book about football. The language is dizzying in places, as Coy takes the reader into the middle of block tackles and game-winning (and losing) plays. Experienced football players may not get lost in the language, but other readers might. Overall, the language is short, staccato-like, simple, and sometimes repetitive (may be good for struggling or less advanced readers). Coy might have been wanting to move the story forward quickly, help struggling readers along, or mimic action on the football field, but the overall effect is distracting, if not annoying. The language falls flat on occasion and can be coarse (and weird) in places: "I soap myself and piss. It's a small release after all the bad news."
Criterion 2: Exposes readers to complex human dilemmas	Typical of Crutcher's oeuvre, you'll find alcoholic/abusive parents and bigoted teachers in *Deadline*—characters that serve to hit the point home: everyone's got secrets. Ben's got a big one, and thinks he has good reasons: he wants "a regular life where people treat you regular." It doesn't take him long to realize, however, the truth in his girlfriend's words: "Secrecy's okay with the general public, but you'd better not be doing it with people you care about. It ruins everything." Is she right? What is truth? Why does it matter? Why do we keep secrets? Does Ben have the right to keep his impending death a secret? Are there negative effects or consequences for keeping a secret? These questions will certainly fuel classroom discussion.	One of the "problem issues" in *Crackback* is steroid use by young athletes. Coy handles the issue well at first, not letting it distract from the characters, but rather embedding it within a larger compelling story about family and relationships (while also communicating the harmful side effects and life-threatening consequences of steroid use). But Coy lets the issue fizzle, reminiscent of the media's fad-like treatment of it as a topic of concern only during major sports events (e.g., the Tour de France). Part of the problem, too, is the book is chock full of other issues: slavery, immigration, homophobic parents, etc., and when Miles finds out his brother—whom he never knew—died of SIDS as a baby, and *that's* why his dad is such a jerk, well, it's just a little too much to handle. Coy seems to want to throw everything into the book so it's not just a "football book," but unlike Crutcher—who uses such problem issues to nuance his characters and problematize quick character judgments—Coy could learn to edit.
Criterion 3: Includes compelling, disconcerting characters	"I've begun jerking awake in the middle of the night, sweating in the wake of unremembered dreams, getting up to touch my stuff—running shoes and CDs, my leather jacket, my beaded Indian belt—sitting on the end of my bed in the dark trying to wrap my imagination around the fact that in a relatively short time I will simply be gone." Ben puts forth a good poker face—joking about his impending death—but readers will appreciate the moments when Ben expresses his paralyzing fears and gut-level realizations of what death will really mean for him, his family, and friends. Other compelling characters include Dallas, Ben's girlfriend, and his football coach, or Dad #2.	Coy tells this story through Miles's first-person point of view, and readers will appreciate getting inside his head to see how he struggles with his need for approval, acceptance, and recognition from an angry father, an arrogant coach, and steroid-using friends and fellow teammates. While the father, coach, and other football player characters seem a bit unrealistic and stereotypical, Miles is an authentic, well-developed character who is blocking tackles on one page and finding library books on the Middle Passage and the history of American slavery the next. *continued on next page*

FIGURE 2.1. Reviews of *Deadline* by Chris Crutcher and *Crackback* by John Coy, based on Carol Jago's criteria for selecting a whole-class novel.

FIGURE 2.1. Continued

Criterion 4: Explores universal themes that combine different periods and cultures	The tag line on the cover of *Deadline* reads: "What if you only had one year to live ... and you knew it?" What would you do? What would you say (or not say) to loved ones? Death comes to all, but rarely do readers get a chance to live through it with a character, and the mixed emotions it brings—incredible sadness, indifference, anxiety, freedom. Readers will be encouraged to consider and reaffirm their own lives.	Understanding and accepting your family members and figuring out what matters in life are certainly universal and timeless coming-of-age themes for adolescents. But they get wrapped up too neatly and happily in *Crackback* for adolescents to continue to think about them long after the book is finished.
Criterion 5: Challenges readers to reexamine their beliefs	Just as Ben is challenged to reexamine his beliefs about Rudy, the town drunk, and his girlfriend Dallas—who harbors her own secrets—readers will learn there's always more to people than meets the eye, and maybe they deserve a second glance. Ben certainly encourages readers to challenge their teachers and to learn, or unlearn, their own histories, no matter how ugly or painful they might be. Ben's final words will resonate with readers long after they put the book down: "Remember you can keep us alive on Earth with the acts you perform in our names. Decide for yourselves how to do that."	Athlete readers considering steroid use may reexamine the idea, as well as the idea that life = football. But Miles's beliefs about most of the controversial issues in the novel don't change. Miles does begin to see his father differently, so adolescents might be inspired to reexamine their relationships with their parents.
Criterion 6: Tells a good story with places for laughing and crying	Lots of laughing in this book—Ben is so-o-o-o funny, you're going to wish you had a friend just like him. But be warned: because you come to care about—and *like*—Ben, you're going to cry when you notice the shortness in his breath and the fear underlying his humor. This is one you'll need to RWT: read with tissues.	The story is compelling, although the writing is distracting in places. Readers will be happy when Miles struts his stuff on the football field and gets the girl. No need for tissues.

instruction to *Deadline* and *Crackback*, paying special attention to how realistic, "problem" issues are treated in each novel (see criterion 2), how characters are portrayed (criterion 3), and thematic focus in each (criterion 4). Ultimately, we'd teach *Deadline* to a whole class of mixed-ability learners, while we'd put *Crackback* on the shelf for independent reading.

We recommend using *Deadline* with high school seniors, who will soon be embarking on a new chapter in their own lives and might be contemplating this next stage with excitement, anxiety, or dread. High school seniors are usually thinking, "What am I going to do with my life?" or "How can I make my life meaningful?" But English teachers may be asking, "How do I teach *Deadline* to a mixed-ability class of seniors? On what should I focus?" We provide some ideas in the next section.

Focus on Characterization in Realistic YA Literature

Reading researchers suggest characterization is one of the most powerful literary elements (Norton, Norton, & McClure, 2003). Galda and Cullinan (2002) call characterization the "soul of great literature" (p. 183). Roser, Martinez, Fuhrken, and McDonnold (2007) explain:

> the "care-actors" in stories cause us to care about what happens to them. But the best characters may do even more: They may cause us to occupy their world a bit longer. And while we linger—reflecting on their traits, mulling their relationships, gauging their development, or even weighing their goals—we find ourselves reading more deeply. The characters we pause to consider can guide us through their stories, helping us to understand plots and ponder themes: characters can make us better comprehenders. (p. 548)

We think realistic or problem young adult novels like *Deadline*—in which the characters are rich and believable and change over time—can help adolescent readers become "better comprehenders." Lukens (1999) argues that the closer a character is to the story's conflict, the more important it is to understand that character, and in realistic young adult novels, characters are always close to the conflict. Reading *Deadline,* readers will come to care about Ben as his character "comes alive" and the story's conflict forces readers to think about life and death, trust, and relationships.

But as reading researchers suggest, and good teachers know, readers often vary in their abilities to comprehend characters, and thus the role of characterization in literary works. In his study of fifty-one eighth- and tenth-grade readers' reading processes, Thomson (1987) found readers at six different reading stages or levels, with variations of sophistication in understanding characterization within each level, which are described in the next section.

Thomson's Reading Process Stages and Understanding of Characters and Characterization

Stage 1: Unreflective Interest in Action
- Characters are solely objects in the action—little interest in, or imaginative insight into, character feelings and motivations.
- Readers can identify characters and describe external attributes.

Stage 2: Empathizing
- Readers can identify and describe characters' internal attributes.
- Readers relate their personal behaviors to the behavior of fictional characters and are emotionally involved with characters.

Stage 3: Analogizing

- Readers gain a heightened awareness of themselves and their own identities through the personal connections they make with fictional characters—this requires understanding of characters' motives, relationships with others, and ability or inability to change.

Stage 4: Reflecting on Significance of Events (Theme) and Character Behavior

- Readers make generalizations about theme and show an awareness of the significance and implications of characters' actions and behavior; what motivates characters; how characters' relationships with others affect them, and how characters change (or don't).
- Readers understand stories holistically (e.g., characterization is connected to plot, setting, or theme).
- Readers question the text more, modify expectations, and understand literary conventions (e.g., adolescent literature involves coming-of-age themes, thus change in character; the beginning of a work is significant for its ending; a mystery will be solved by book's end; qualities of mythic literature).
- Readers begin to have a distanced evaluation of characters.

Stage 5: Reviewing the Whole Work as the Author's Creation

- Readers understand writers to be "pattern-makers" who "[communicate] a personal . . . interpretation of the human condition" (pp. 209–210).
- Readers at this stage tend to have read a number of works by one author or have a wider literary repertoire to draw on.

Stage 6: Consciously Considering Relationship with the Author, Textual Ideology, and Understanding of One's Own Reading Processes (e.g., How Author Manipulates Reader's Emotions)

- Readers understand literary works to be constructions and understand that authors act on readers to identify or emotionally relate to some characters and not others.
- Readers consider both the implications of text constructedness and the personal significance of their textual interpretations (e.g., what readers' own responses reveal about themselves personally).

According to Thomson, at stage 1, readers can identify characters and describe them physically but may not understand that physical descriptions communicate attitudes about characters. At stage 1, Thomson suggests, readers are more interested in action and plot than characters. At stage 2, readers can relate their personal behaviors to the behavior of fictional characters and are "emotionally involved" with characters (p. 194). At stage 3, readers understand that external character attributes (e.g., physical description, age, gender) communicate attitudes about characters. Readers at this level can generate expectations about characters' motives and feelings. At stage 4, Thomson believes readers "see literature as making complex statements about the human condition and they recognize that these statements can only be understood by considering literary works as wholes" (p. 203). At this stage, readers question the text more, develop and modify long-term expectations, and understand literary conventions (e.g., the beginning of a work is significant for its ending; a mystery will be solved by book's end; qualities of a genre).

For Thomson, the most sophisticated readers operate at stages 5 and 6. At these levels, readers understand writers to be "pattern-makers" who "[communicate] a personal . . . interpretation of the human condition" (pp. 209–210). Thomson found that few readers in his study reached these stages, and those that did had read a number of works by one author or had a wider literary repertoire to draw on.

More recent reading research suggests that less-advanced readers tend to focus on external attributes of characters (e.g., age, gender, physical characteristics) and characters' actions, rather than characters' internal qualities (e.g., personality traits, feelings, values), or what Roser et al. (2007) call the "character's core" (e.g., what motivates the character; important relationships; how the character changes).

In *Fresh Takes on Teaching Literary Elements: How to Teach What Really Matters about Character, Setting, Point of View, and Theme*, Michael Smith and Jeffrey Wilhelm (2010) suggest that both external and internal attributes are important to understanding a "character's core," as both help readers create a general impression of the character in their minds. Smith and Wilhelm explain that the process of understanding character involves making and testing these general impressions while reading. We know strong readers make judgments about characters and characters' actions as they read, and ultimately modify or confirm their first opinions of character as they begin to understand the character more deeply.

The ultimate goal, then, for all readers in our classrooms is to be able to make and reflect on ongoing impressions, judgments, and assessments about characters. But not every reader is ready to do that. Some readers, as Thomson and Roser et al. describe, need help "seeing" and engaging with the characters in a story before they are ready to talk about character motivation or change.

Whole-class differentiated reading instruction assumes teachers meet the reading needs of all students. If we take the time to assess our students' reading habits, styles, and interests (see resource guide at end of Chapter 1), then we know what kinds of readers and character comprehenders we have in our classroom. Now it's time to teach them.

In what follows we lay out a differentiated instructional lesson plan for use with Crutcher's *Deadline* that uses dramatization as a tool for helping all the readers in your classroom "get into story" by "getting into character." We feature dramatization here because it is an instructional tool that supports literacy development, fosters students' imaginative capabilities, and helps students try on characters' perspectives—an important part of understanding characterization in literature. Smith and Wilhelm (2010) explain that dramas "allow students to use their tacit understandings of human behavior as a way to understand the characters about whom they read," and "provide [students] with a concrete experience to think with and abstract from" (p. 55). Ultimately, dramatization in the secondary English classroom can generate excitement and engagement and provide collaborative opportunities for meaning making (Schneider & Jackson, 2000; Wilhelm & Edmiston, 1998).

The lesson plan we outline next assumes that three levels of readers and character comprehenders populate your classroom:

1. *Instructional:* those stage 1–2 readers least adept at entering the story world and "getting into the story" and engaging with characters on their own. These readers may require more modeling and direct instruction, but can work successfully in groups with teacher attention.

2. *Independent:* those stage 3–4 readers who can engage with the character and identify a character's external attributes (e.g., gender, age, etc.), but who may need a push toward identifying the character's internal attributes (e.g., values, feelings, etc.) and "inner core" to better understand the significance and implications of characters' actions and behavior; what motivates characters; how characters' relationships with others affect them, and how characters change (or don't). These readers can work independently on their own and in groups.

3. *Advanced:* those readers who can talk confidently about how characterization relates to theme and other literary elements or how texts operate as authorial constructions. We have included two advanced group activity options in the plan—one for stage 4 readers and one for stage 5–6 readers. These readers may require teacher attention but can work independently on their own and in groups.

Lesson Plan: Differentiating for Characterization in a Senior College Prep English Class

Source: (adapted from King-Shaver & Hunter, 2003)
Text: Deadline, by Chris Crutcher (first four chapters)
Timeline for this lesson: 3–4 days
Themes: secrecy vs. truth; individual vs. family responsibilities; what kind of life is worth living?

Guiding Questions

- What if you had only one year to live . . . and you knew it?
- What would you do?
- What would you say (or not say) to loved ones?
- How would you live your last year?
- What would you want to be remembered for or as?
- What would you do differently?
- What kind of person do you want to be?
- What is truth?
- Why does it matter?
- Why do we keep secrets?
- Does Ben have the right to keep his impending death a secret?

Knowledge and Skills

Students will be able to do the following:

- Develop understandings of character and characterization
- Connect understandings about character to larger themes

Modes of Differentiation Used

We differentiate content, process, and product in our plan in the following ways:

Content: All students engage with the same content (*Deadline*) and learner goals, which include developing sophisticated understandings of character and characterization in the novel through reflection, analysis, and synthesis.

Process: All students participate in the same process: dramatizing understandings.

Product: Products are different, as different groups will present different dramatizations based on their readiness levels.

Frontloading

Opitz and Ford (2008) suggest that differentiated reading instruction should begin with "frontloading," in which teachers generate interest in a text, activate text schema, and develop background knowledge of the text *with the whole class* prior to students moving into individual, small-group activities.

To frontload with *Deadline,* we suggest teachers either read aloud the first four chapters to the class over a period of days, play aloud the first four chapters on audiotape, or ask for strong student readers to read aloud.

Prior to reading, teachers may ask students to journal about the title of the book, *Deadline.*

- What does the word *deadline* make you think of?
- What things have deadlines?
- Who typically assigns deadlines?
- Have you ever been given a deadline for something? Did you meet it? Why or why not? What happened?
- Are deadlines a good thing?
- Why is the word *dead* in deadline? What is the word's origin or history?

During reading, the teacher may stop intermittently to ask students to do journal quick-writes or write journal responses on their *choice* of the following questions (various question types are included here so that readers at all levels in the classroom should feel confident answering ones they choose):

Chapter 1
- How old is Ben?
- What time of year is it when the story starts?
- Where is Idaho? What do you know about Idaho?
- Describe one personality trait of Ben (e.g., brave, smart-aleck, unique, smart, athletic, ambitious). What makes you think this?

- What does Ben value (e.g., knowledge, truth, justice, family, critical thinking, open-mindedness)? How do you know?

- What does Ben's room look like?

- Ben makes reference to Don Quixote. Who/what was Don Quixote and what point is Ben making with this allusion?

- Ben decides not to tell anyone that he has a year to live. Why does he make this decision? Do you agree with it? Why or why not?

- Ben says "I'd rather be a flash than a slowly-cooling ember" (p. 10). What does this mean? Fill in the blanks with your own words: I'd rather be a _____ than a _____.

- One role Ben plays in the story is that of family mediator, or "translator." He says telling his parents his news "would break the fragile symmetry of our lives" (p. 6). What does this mean? What do you know about Ben based on this information?

- Listen to the song Ben listens to on his iPod when he runs, "Too Old to Die Young" by Ann Savoy and Linda Ronstadt (Crutcher, 2009, p. 7). What is the tone of the song? Does this seem like a song Ben would listen to? Would you have it in your music library? What might Crutcher be trying to communicate through including this song? What sad songs do you like?

- Define *foreshadowing*. Do you think Crutcher is foreshadowing things to come in the novel? Explain. Make a prediction about what you think will happen in the next chapter.

Chapter 2

- What are Ben's high school colors? What is the school mascot?

- Describe or illustrate Ben physically.

- What contemporary or pop-culture figure resembles Ben?

- Fill in the blank with a figurative representation: Ben is a _____ or Ben is like a _____. Explain your reasoning.

- Describe one personality trait of Coach Banks, or describe something he values.

- Agree or disagree with this statement: People should have the right to die however they choose.

Chapter 3

- How is Ben feeling about his decision not to tell anyone his secret?
- If you knew you had only a year to live, how would you live it? What would you do, or do differently?
- Ben says he treats Coach Banks's truck like a "place of worship." Read Stephen Dunn's poem "The Sacred." What is a sacred place or space for you? What places do you consider "places of worship"?
- Ben's psychiatrist makes reference to Carl Jung. Who was Carl Jung?

Chapter 4

- Provide one personality trait, physical description, *or* value for the following: Mr. Lambeer, Dallas Suzuki, Sooner Cowans.
- Who is Ben talking to in his dreams? Do you have a Higher Power? What would you ask a Higher Power if he/she/it visited you in your dreams?
- How do you want people to remember you when you're gone?
- Read W. S. Merwin's poem "For the Anniversary of My Death" and connect it to Ben's plan for his last year of life.

Small-Group Differentiated Instruction

After reading the first four chapters with students and discussing students' journal responses, the teacher assigns students to groups based on teacher determination of student engagement with the story world and thus understanding of character and characterization. Students work in groups to prepare a dramatic presentation.

Instructional Group: Hotseating

The following activities for the instructional group are adapted from Wilhelm (2002).

1. Teacher models sitting in the hot seat as a character from text that students have already read.
2. Teacher starts with a prepared monologue, describing the character to audience.
3. Teacher asks students to write questions they want to ask the character.
4. Students ask questions and teacher responds. If teacher has trouble answering a question, teacher asks a group of students to play his or her

brain and advise. If teacher makes a response he or she can't justify, teacher can "rewind" and "replay" answer.

5. After modeling this activity, teacher explains to students that someone in their group will be chosen at random to sit in the hot seat when their group makes their presentation to the class and will field questions from the class.

6. Teacher helps group get started on completion of planning guide (see Figure 2.2). Teacher may want to assign character (Ben), since students may not have enough information at this point about other characters.

Get Ready for the Hot Seat: A Planning Guide

As a group, you must agree on the following information about Ben in *Deadline* so that any one of you could go to the hot seat and answer questions from the class. If the required information is not in the story, you will have to *infer* or make an educated guess about it.

Name of character: _____

1. Age and physical appearance: _____
2. Where character lives: _____
3. List one adjective about this character:_____
   What character actions help support your choice? _____
   _____

   What character words/dialogue help support your choice? _____
   _____

4. List another adjective about this character: _____
   What character actions help support your choice? _____
   _____

   What character words/dialogue help support your choice? _____
   _____

5. Character's main goal: _____
6. Character's biggest obstacles or problems: _____
7. Character's biggest influences: _____
8. List one quotation from the book that reveals who the character is and what the character is about: _____
   _____

Now prepare an opening monologue to introduce the character to the audience. It can be in the form of soliloquy, rap, poem, etc.

Someone in your group will sit in the hot seat for your class presentation. Members of your group not being hotseated will get to ask the first two questions. What will these questions be? And how will your character respond? How do you know that these responses are good ones? Prepare a list of questions in advance and provide answers.

FIGURE 2.2. Get Ready for the Hot Seat: A planning guide handout sheet. Source: Adapted from *Action Strategies for Deepening Comprehension*, by J. D. Wilhelm, 2002, New York: Scholastic Professional Books.

7. Teacher helps students brainstorm questions other students in the class might ask of Ben and other characters.

Independent Group: Good Angel/Bad Angel

The following activities for the independent group are adapted from Smith and Wilhelm, 2010.

1. Pick one person in the group to be Ben.

2. Determine who in the group will be "good angels" and who will be "bad angels."

3. The person playing Ben will prepare a monologue explaining what moral decision he has to make (whether to tell his family he has one year to live). Group members identified as "good angels" must prepare statements and use appeals to persuade Ben to tell his family. Group members identified as "bad angels" will prepare statements and use appeals to persuade Ben not to tell his family. Group members should use textual support but should also anticipate one another's appeals and prepare accordingly.

4. To present, Ben will sit in a chair in front of the room, while "good angels" and "bad angels" alternate providing appeals.

Advanced Group A: Tableaux

The following activity for the advanced group is adapted from Wilhelm (2002).

Create a "slide show" tableaux of gestures or expressions that summarize the relationship Ben has thus far with the following people:

- His father
- His mother
- His brother
- Coach Banks
- Hey-soos
- His therapist and/or Doc Wagner
- Others (group choices)

The slide show should depict multiple relationships.

To get started, students are given the following suggestions:

1. Discuss what each tableau should communicate about the relationship.

2. Determine how the characters (people) will move and what they will do visually to depict important details, emotions, aspects, and the significance of what you are presenting.

3. Create, act out, and freeze the scene into a tableau, as if you were suddenly made into statues, at the high point or most illuminating juncture of your scene or depiction. You might also consider unfreezing characters so they can say what they are thinking and feeling.

4. Rehearse and perform. Your complete presentation of several tableaux and commentary should last three to five minutes.

Another option for the tableaux activity (to make it more abstract) is to ask students to do the same dramatizations, but with the following concepts/ideas/themes:

- Mortality
- Fear
- Congruence
- Religion, spirituality
- Human connectedness
- Individual versus team
- Others (group choices)

Advanced Group B: Author Role-Play or Interview/Panel

The following activity is adapted from Mellor, O'Neill, and Patterson (2000) and Wilhelm (2002).

Based on their reading of *Deadline,* group members make predictions about Chris Crutcher's oeuvre. Group members determine the following *prior to* reading another novel by Chris Crutcher:

- What kinds of characters can you expect to see in Crutcher's works?
- How will Crutcher construct his characters? (What narrative techniques will be used? What "types" of characters will Crutcher feature?)
- Based on your reading of *Deadline,* how does Crutcher make readers care about his characters? Why do you come to care about Ben?
- What point of view will Crutcher use? Why? What is the effect of this point of view?

- What is the tone of Crutcher's story in *Deadline*? What attitude does Crutcher take toward Ben? How does Crutcher encourage readers to share his attitude?
- What kind of structure does Crutcher use to make the story interesting, convincing, or persuasive? (How does Crutcher order the story? What emphasis does Crutcher give to the story's various elements?)
- What will be the main events of Crutcher's story? What will be the climax of the story? How will the story end?
- What will be the theme of Crutcher's works? Will death and dying be a recurring motif?

If time permits, group members will also conduct biographical research on Chris Crutcher, using the following questions as guidelines:

- Where was Crutcher born? Where has he spent most of his life? How has place influenced Crutcher's life and writing?
- What are Crutcher's most significant personality traits?
- What is Crutcher's most famous work? Why?
- Who was Crutcher's most important influence as a writer?
- What awards has Crutcher won?
- What does the author say about why he writes the kinds of novels he writes? Where does he get his ideas? Are Crutcher's characters based on real people? Himself? What topics seem important to Crutcher? What kinds of people? What aspects of Crutcher's experiences seem to be in his books?

After group members determine or find this information, they will read other Crutcher works independently over one to two days and regroup during class time to discuss predictions, expectations, and findings. Students will present the author to the class through their choice of role-playing (e.g., author panel presentation, press conference, Terri Gross NPR interview, *Saturday Night Live* skit).

Teachers might also consider "hotseating" for this presentation or using this hot seat group in conjunction with the other group's hot seat presentation. Wilhelm describes an "Inside/Outside" technique in which students form two circles, with one hot seat group in the inner circle, as the character, and one hot seat group in the outer circle, as the author. Students in the outer circle pose questions to students in the inner circle, and vice versa.

Charting Character Change

The activities previously described are suggested for classroom use early in the reading of the novel to help struggling readers get into the story and focus on Ben, and to help more advanced readers to consider Ben's values, beliefs, and motivations, or Chris Crutcher's oeuvre as an author. Ultimately, though, we want all readers to begin to consider how Ben changes throughout the novel as a result of his decisions and relationships with others.

As Smith and Wilhelm (2010) suggest, understanding character is a process of "making . . . a series of inferences that we must keep categorically tentative as we get new information, so we have to connect more dots that give us a fuller and more complex picture" (p. 24). This process relies first and foremost on understanding a character's external and internal attributes and forming a general, first impression of the character. The dramatization activities described previously should help students develop these impressions and understandings.

Once the dramatization activities are completed, teachers can draw on several resources to help students chart the inferences and ongoing judgments they make about Ben and other characters as they continue to read *Deadline*. We especially like Larry Johannessen, Elizabeth Kahn, and Carolyn Calhoun Walter's ideas in *Writing about Literature* (2009), one of which is an "analyzing values" activity in which students consider a list of values that includes "family," "having fun," and "honesty," and select the ones they value most and least. Using this list, students then do the same for characters in the book. Another activity in the same book, "character analysis," asks students to use the "values" list to chart the character's most and least important values early in the work and at or near the end of the work and to provide reasons and evidence for their choices.

We also like Smith and Wilhelm's (2010) "character response sheet," which asks students to list their initial impressions of characters based on character actions, language, body language, and so on, and then to complete character "check points" along the way to gauge how their initial impressions of characters are (or aren't) changing. We also like Kelly Gallagher's (2004) "character shift charts" in his book *Deeper Reading*. Here, students write adjectives describing the character early in the novel, provide supporting passages from the text with page numbers, and then—after the character has undergone significant change—choose different adjectives to describe the character. In the center of the chart, they note what caused the change to occur in the character.

Finally, we like the idea of using a prereading anticipation guide that students revisit once they have finished the book. As an example, teachers could use the anticipation guide we feature in Figure 2.3 to help students consider

Anticipation Guide for *Deadline* by Chris Crutcher

Before reading the book, place an X on the "Agree/Disagree" continuum that indicates where you stand in regard to the statement that follows. Be prepared to explain your beliefs. After reading the book, compare your postreading opinions with your prereading opinions. What changed? Why?

Disagree---------------------------Agree. 1. It is wrong to keep secrets in any/every situation. Only the truth will set you free.

Disagree---------------------------Agree. 2. You have the right to die the way you choose, even if it means foregoing treatment that might save your life.

Disagree---------------------------Agree. 3. Keeping secrets does not negatively affect the people who keep them.

Disagree---------------------------Agree. 4. Few teenagers die from cancer.

Disagree---------------------------Agree. 5. Life is short, so you should do what you want, no matter the consequences.

Disagree---------------------------Agree. 6. It is OK to keep a secret if the truth will hurt someone.

Disagree---------------------------Agree. 7. There is a "higher power."

Disagree---------------------------Agree. 8. Teens can always rely on their family members when things get tough.

Disagree---------------------------Agree. 9. Your parents/guardian should have the final say in how you live your life.

Disagree---------------------------Agree. 10. You are the pilot of your own life. There is no greater force determining the outcome.

FIGURE 2.3. Anticipation guide for *Deadline* by Chris Crutcher. Adapted from activity posted by the Greece Central School District, http://www.greece.k12.ny.us.

how their own understandings of and feelings about Ben and his decision not to tell anyone about his cancer change over the course of reading the novel.

We think all of these activities can help teachers help readers at all ability levels connect with the characters in young adult literature and begin to develop deeper understandings about the role characters play in literary understanding and appreciation.

3

Historical Fiction: Connecting to Critical Theories

Defining Young Adult Historical Fiction

While it's realistic fiction that teens like to read, we feature historical fiction in this next chapter because there's just too much good stuff going on in this genre to stick this chapter at the back of the book. Jacqueline Kelly's sophisticated (2009) *The Evolution of Calpurnia Tate* will have readers wanting to read about some guy named Darwin. Sharon Draper's (2008) *Copper Sun* will—as one of our preservice teachers put it—make you "know" the horrors of slavery, and Sherri Smith's (2009) *Flygirl* will have readers rooting for Ida Mae Jones—an African American girl who longs to fly planes in the 1940s.

Young adult historical fiction gets adolescents *feeling* the past as they live through the experiences of characters. In addition, as Pam Cole (2009) explains in *Young Adult Literature in the 21st Century*, historical fiction "puts the humanity back into history" (p. 237). The genre adds dimension to historical events and people, helps students understand human problems and relationships in light of historical events, and shows how some themes and needs (e.g., love, hate, freedom) remain constant throughout time (Harmon, 1998).

We think the genre lends itself to whole-class differentiated instruction because it affords opportunities for teachers to provide the crucial social context and scaffolding surrounding literary works that readers at all ability levels need in order to engage with and comprehend texts. Belinda Louie (2005) has shown that adolescents can develop understandings of historical events and empathy for people in different time periods and cultures when teachers scaffold instruction with multiple texts and activities.

Young adult historical fiction can also lend itself to updating the canon in its own right. As we show in this chapter, Mattie Gokey in Jennifer Donnelly's (2004) *A Northern Light* can tell today's adolescent readers as much about women's historical struggles to follow their dreams and find a "room" and voice of their own as Virginia Woolf, Kate Chopin, or Willa Cather can. Too often the stories of these women's lives are lost in the outdated language and unspecified social codes or mores that students don't understand when asked to read more canonical texts (as in *The Scarlet Letter*). Young adult historical fiction—while historical—still offers adolescents the voice, attitude, and experience of teenage protagonists. This might be why the genre proves popular with students.

But what exactly is historical fiction? While, in general, young adult historical novels focus on the past, just how far back must one go to make a book "historical"? In general, historical fiction is defined as fictional works that take place during a specific, often prominent, time period in history, which are written from the perspective of those who lived during that time. Historical fiction can also include (and incorporate qualities of) subgenres, such as mystery, comedy, adventure, fantasy, and even realistic problem stories (Nilsen & Donelson, 2009).

Selecting Young Adult Historical Fiction for Whole-Class Instruction

Nilsen and Donelson (2009) provide some excellent suggestions for evaluating historical young adult fiction. In their opinion, good historical fiction has the following qualities:

- A setting that is integral to the story;
- An authentic rendition of the time, place, and people being featured;
- An author who is so thoroughly steeped in the history of the period that he or she can be comfortably creative without making mistakes;
- Believable characters with whom young readers can identify;
- Evidence that even across great time spans people share similar emotions;
- References to well-known events or people or other clues through which the reader can place the happenings in their correct historic framework; and,
- Readers who come away with the feeling that they know a time or place better. It is as if they have lived in it for at least a few hours (p. 244).

In Figure 3.1, we apply Jago's criteria to two award-winning young adult historical fiction novels—Jennifer Donnelly's *A Northern Light* and Aidan Chambers's *Postcards from No Man's Land*. While we deeply enjoyed reading both books, ultimately aspects of how history is told (criterion 1), how readers experience and understand historical dilemmas (criterion 2), and how readers relate to the characters (criterion 3) make *A Northern Light* a novel we would teach to the whole class and *Postcards from No Man's Land* a text we'd use for small-group or independent reading.

	A Northern Light by Jennifer Donnelly 2004 ALA Top 10 Best Books for Young Adults 2004 ALA Michael L. Printz Honor Book	*Postcards from No Man's Land* by Aidan Chambers 2003 ALA Best Books for Young Adults 2003 ALA Michael L. Printz Award Winner
Summary	It is the early twentieth century, and sixteen-year-old Mattie Gokey is torn between honoring a promise to her dying mother and following her dreams. She could stay in the North Woods, marry Royal Loomis, help run his farm, and honor a promise to her mother. Or she could go to New York City, go to college, become a writer, and stay true to her dreams. Either way, she wins and loses. The events that influence her decision are set against the real-life murder that inspired Theodore Dreiser's *An American Tragedy*.	Seventeen-year-old Jacob Todd, at the request of his grandmother, travels to Amsterdam to visit the family that took care of his grandfather after he was wounded during World War II. While in Amsterdam, Jacob meets Geertrui and discovers that she and his grandfather had a passionate affair while her family was caring for him. During the trip to Amsterdam, Jacob is also forced to examine his own sexual identity as well. *Postcards* took nine years to write, and Chambers spared no details in its creation.
Criterion 1: Written in language perfectly suited to the author's purpose	Donnelly's writing is breathtaking. Mattie's voice rings true to the time and her age. Each of the present-day chapters is initiated by a vocabulary word that is somehow threaded into the action."No one had so much as hugged me since my mamma died. I wished I had the words to describe how I felt. My word of the day, augur, which means to foretell things from omens, had nothing to do with it as far as I could see. I felt warm in his arms. Warm and hungry and blind" (p. 191). The events of Mattie's life are juxtaposed with those surrounding the murder of Grace Brown. Despite the shift from past to present throughout the book, Donnelly makes it easy for readers to follow, incorporating excerpts from Brown's letters to guide them. While the book is lengthy, it reads very easily, and students should have no problems getting through it.	*Postcards* is narrated from two perspectives—Jacob's and Geertrui's—and the switching back and forth between perspectives might be challenging for some students. However, this same structural format would be a wonderful tool to use to discuss various literary techniques, such as point of view. While the book is written at a seventh-grade level, because so much of the action takes place more than fifty years ago and in a foreign country, students might have difficulty distinguishing where and when the action takes place.
Criterion 2: Exposes readers to complex human dilemmas	Mattie, much like Edna Pontellier in *The Awakening*, finds herself torn between two lives: the first, an expected and traditional one as a wife and mother, and the second, a chance to go to college and live out her personal dreams. She is forced to make a choice when doing so means that every person she cares about will get hurt no matter her decision. Trying to live up to others' expectations and pursue one's own interests is a dilemma that is timeless. Beyond Mattie's personal struggle, she has to decide whether to tell authorities that she is in possession of letters that would help solve the Grace Brown murder. Given today's "no snitching" rule that many teens and adults seem to follow, this predicament is timely. *A Northern Light* promises to initiate rich classroom discussions on these two important conflicts.	Chambers presents a new take on the World War II era by having a present-day teenager travel to revisit someone else's past. In a foreign country, Jacob is forced to confront dilemmas to work through, namely his grandfather's infidelity and a person's right to die. In the flashbacks to Geertrui, we see other complex choices: Does breaking the marriage vows count during a time of war when perhaps someone won't see his or her spouse ever again? Is there really a "right" decision? This last question is one Geertrui faces when she discovers that she is pregnant with the grandfather's child. Concurrent with his historical questions, Jacob is also confronting issues regarding his sexual preference, a topic that might turn off some teen readers. continued on next page

FIGURE 3.1. Reviews of *A Northern Light* by Jennifer Donnelly and *Postcards from No Man's Land* by Aidan Chambers, based on Carol Jago's criteria for selecting a whole-class novel.

FIGURE 3.1. Continued

Criterion 3: Includes compelling, disconcerting characters	Each of the main characters—Mattie, Royal and his family, Weaver, Mattie's father—is both compelling and disconcerting. Through Mattie, we see how dreams can be crushed and revived again, although even through following her dream, she loses much. While Royal and his family appear, on the surface, to be doing well because of their farm, here, too, are cracks in their facade. Mrs. Loomis is mean and bitter, suffering through her husband's affair with a local woman. Royal, living in this situation, has suffered, too. Weaver, as a black teenager, doesn't have the same choices as Mattie. His chances of getting out of the North Woods and working at the Glenmont Hotel seem rather slim. And then there is Mattie's father, heartbroken over his wife's death, trying to raise a houseful of young girls. He can't see beyond his own loss to be any help to daughters who yearn for different things.	As main characters, both Jacob and Geertrui are complex and disconcerting. Geertrui becomes a woman, physically, psychologically, and emotionally, during the war and through her experiences with Jacob's grandfather, and she grows even more in her old age through her interactions with Jacob. In turn, Jacob also grows in his maturity and sense of self through his trip to Amsterdam. However, as complex as the main characters are, some readers might find it hard to connect with Jacob or Geertrui.
Criterion 4: Explores universal themes that combine different periods and cultures	As historical fiction, *A Northern Light* is naturally set in a different time period and culture. Donnelly is able to transport readers to that time and place and make the action and events real. Even though the book is set a hundred years ago, its themes are important today: choice versus duty, coming of age, first love, individuality versus conformity, racism and sexism, and telling the truth. This novel could easily be paired with and taught alongside classic works such as *The Awakening* or *My Ántonia*.	*Postcards* provides an alternate look at the World War II era. Rather than focusing on the Holocaust, it presents the stories of a present-day teen's journey into history and the narrative of a woman who formed a bond with an American soldier. Also, Jacob's near obsession with Anne Frank and her story might make the novel a good complement to the study of *The Diary of Anne Frank*.
Criterion 5: Challenges readers to reexamine their beliefs	Donnelly's book may not challenge present-day readers to reexamine their beliefs on the issues and themes presented, but there is ample opportunity to examine the issues from the perspective of someone living in the early twentieth century. Readers could also compare and contrast society's views then versus those of today.	Geertrui's decision to have an assisted death might challenge assumptions about euthanasia and people's reasons for choosing to end their lives this way. Readers' beliefs about sex outside of marriage might be challenged as they read the stories of two people at a certain point in time and what conditions might have influenced their choices.
Criterion 6: Tells a good story with places for laughing and crying	*A Northern Light* flawlessly balances sadness and humor while telling a captivating story. We can feel Mattie's pain over the choice she is forced to make; we feel for Weaver and his mother, having to endure racist comments and actions; we hate that Royal is so ignorant and selfish. We also smile at the subtle humor Donnelly injects: "'Watch out for table six, Matt. He's at it again,' Fran whispers as she passes by. That's our name for Mr. Maxwell, a guest who always takes table six in the dining room because it's in a dark corner. He has trouble keeping his hand, and his other bits, to himself" (p. 43).	*Postcards* tells a good story, even if it doesn't force readers to extremes of laughing and crying. For some students, Geertrui's story will be more moving than present-day Jacob's. She faced a lot in her life: World War II, the threat of death, falling in love with a married man, nearly having a child out of wedlock, and the weight of her secret story. Other readers might connect to Jacob's insecurities and questions.

Differentiating Instruction for Jennifer Donnelly's *A Northern Light*

Joanne Brown (1998) raises some important points that teachers should consider when selecting historical fiction for classroom instruction:

> When we select historical fiction for classroom reading and studying, we often do so with the assumption that the fictitious work has a certain authenticity, or that it conveys the "truth" about a particular period. Yet we must realize that writers of

historical fiction must also contend with another problem: the fine line between historicizing fiction and fictionalizing history. What is the "truth" of historical fiction? …[F]or both the novelist and historian, meaning lies not in a chain of events themselves but in the writer's interpretation of what occurred. As teachers, we can use this view of historical texts to lead students into intriguing activities that require purposeful research, critical analysis, and synthesis of information. We can encourage students to explore the connect ons they establish with the settings, characters, and situations that they encounter in historical fiction. (para. 6)

We believe that Donnelly's *A Northern Light* can encourage students to explore connections between and among setting, character, and situation, and students at all levels, both struggling and advanced, can benefit from the suggested activities that follow.

A Northern Light lends itself to differentiation of *content* (see Chapter 1). At the novel's most basic level is a character, Mattie, whom all readers will like and care about. Her struggles to move away from her family—both physically and symbolically—and the societal expectations of the time will resonate with adolescent readers at all levels of readiness. At a more challenging level, teachers can introduce feminist theory as a lens for reading and understanding the novel and ask students to complete the Major Works Data Sheet to analyze the book more deeply (see Tiered Assignments section in this chapter). *A Northern Light* also lends itself to differentiation of *process* and *product,* as we show in the following examples of differentiated literature instruction: a modified jigsaw/small-group literature circles activity and tiered assignments.

Modified Jigsaw/Literature Circle Roles Activity

Jigsaw is a cooperative learning strategy that divides the material to be studied, usually large sections of a text, into sections and makes individual or groups responsible for learning and then teaching their section to the other students. Literature circles typically make use of multiple texts, and students are assigned roles to fulfill in facilitation of discussion about the text (see Daniels [1994] for more on literature circles).

We combined both activities into a modified jigsaw/literature circle roles activity that focuses on one text—*A Northern Light*—to accommodate students' individual interests, abilities, and readiness as readers. Thus, all students read the same text, and all students are responsible for fulfilling a role (e.g., literary luminary, illustrator) for the section to be discussed at a particular time designated by the teacher. The roles we describe in this chapter have each been differentiated by task complexity so students have multiple options to choose from for fulfilling each role. Teachers can assign roles to students or let students pick which roles they want. Teachers can let students know when discussion about a certain section will be held, and students can sign up to fulfill their roles on certain days. We share some examples of the roles from students in Susan's young adult literature course next. (All roles are adapted from Ammons, Bonds, & Figgs [1999] and Daniels [1994].)

Role 1: Summarizer

Do one of the following:

1. Write a fifty-word, a twenty-five-word, and a one-sentence précis that summarizes today's reading. Then choose a word and finally a symbol that represent the key point of today's selection.
2. Prepare a fifty-word and twenty-five-word précis on today's reading selection.
3. Construct an outline that depicts the plot events of today's reading selection.
4. Complete a sequence chain of the plot events in today's reading selection.

Lindsey Smith, a beginning English teacher, modified option 1—basing her response on the entire novel—and wrote the following:

Fifty-Word Précis:

A Northern Light follows Mattie Gokey's 1906 summer journey as she makes important discoveries about the people in her life and herself. Through tragedy, inspiration, love, and exploration, *A Northern Light* is a coming-of-age story that encourages Mattie to define the most important word of all—herself.

Twenty-Five-Word Précis:

Encourage. Educate. Family. Farm. Literature. Marriage. Decisions. Regret. Hope. Promises. Friendship. Work. Humor. Sickness. Murder. Pregnancy. Table Six. Kitchen. Stove. Hungry. Less Fortunate. Independence. Secrets.

One Sentence:

A Northern Light is an empowering story about Mattie Gokey—an adolescent woman who uncovers what it means to grow up surrounded by constraining gender roles, expectations, and disappointments.

One Word:

Liberation. I chose this word because the story follows the ups and downs of Mattie's battle to become her own woman.

Symbol:

I chose Rosie the Riveter because she is the ultimate symbol of changing gender roles and is an inspiration to women searching for liberation. Mattie longs to go to college and is willing to work and do whatever it takes to make her dreams come true.

Role 2: Illustrator
Do one of the following:

1. Select a piece of published artwork that embodies the same feelings and emotions evoked from the setting and mood of today's selection. Prepare a rationale for your choice of artwork.
2. Create an original piece of artwork that depicts the feelings or emotions evoked from today's selection.
3. Create a storyboard or illustrated sequence outlining the events that occur in today's selection.

Natalie Connors fulfilled this role by sharing a PowerPoint presentation of Andrew Wyeth's paintings. She focused on one in particular, *Wind from the Sea*. Next are excerpts from her rationale:

This painting evokes the same kind of emotional isolation as the book. The world Mattie and the other characters live in is one of extreme poverty. The rich and privileged vacation at Big Moose Lake, and come to be served by the poor and unrecognized. Meanwhile, back on the Gokey farm, if the milk isn't sold or something happens to the crops, the family will barely survive the winter. Being cold is one thing. Being cold and hungry is quite another. Mattie, the main character, wants nothing more than to escape her surroundings and go to college in New York. Faced with not having the funds to go and almost without thinking agreeing to marry local farmer Royal Loomis, Mattie feels as if she is going to stay where she is forever, " … like an ant in pitch."

In Wyeth's painting, there is a dirt road that leads away from the house. The road, which represents a means of exit, of escape, seems to lead toward the ocean, which is typically symbolic of freedom. However, the road itself seems to get lost in the grass and eventually covered over. Even if you start down the path, there's no guarantee you will arrive at your intended destination.

The house Mattie lives in with her sisters and abusive father is ramshackle, especially since Mattie's mother died and her brother left home to be a boat pilot. It is a sad house, full of crushed dreams, veiled threats, and words that can't be taken back. Even though it is busy and filled with people, in many ways, Mattie's house is completely empty. The house in the painting is also completely empty. You can tell by the yellow film on the sheers that blow in the wind.

Because there is no sign of life anywhere in the painting, it seems that the window was left open accidentally. It feels like no one will bother returning to the house and the window will never be pulled shut again.

An empty house holds promise that soon, people will be living there, enjoying themselves and each other. An abandoned house, on the other hand, holds no such promise—only decay and loneliness. Wyeth's abandoned house reflects the lonely lives led by the characters in *A Northern Light*, lives fueled by little more than the animal need to survive. Mattie, of course, dreams for more, but still finds herself playing the role that is expected of her. The wind blows curtains in the house, but there is no one there to feel it.

Role 3: Literary Luminary

Do one of the following:

1. Select a passage that supports one of the underlying themes in the novel that we've been discussing in class. In addition, choose one passage that is a negative or opposite representation of the underlying theme. Explain your passage choices and support them with textual references.

2. Select two passages that *most* help us understand the theme of the selection. Defend why you chose these two passages.

3. Locate five controversial or thought-provoking passages from the text. Discuss how the passages support the theme of the story.

4. Locate five surprising or humorous passages from the text that help develop the main idea. Explain why you chose these passages.

Next are three examples of thought-provoking passages (option 3) that Megan Carmichael, a high school AP English teacher, chose, with explanations describing how she felt they supported some of the feminist themes at work in the story:

Passage One: "I knew then why they didn't marry. Emily and Jane and Louisa. I knew and it scared me. I also knew what being lonely was and I didn't want to be lonely my whole life. I didn't want to give up my words. I didn't want to choose one over the other" (p. 274).

In this passage, the main character, Mattie, struggles with the stereotypical expectations of women in the early 1900s. With literary contemporaries such as Emily Dickinson and Jane Austen revolutionizing the traditional role of women, Mattie finds herself caught between two worlds—love and freedom—and the consequences that come with both. Donnelly uses Mattie's situation to mimic how women seemingly must choose one lifestyle over the other, exemplifying that women who choose career over family usually become socially ostracized. And even though this specific situation is set in the early 1900s, it continues to rile controversy well into the 21st century: What is a woman's place?

Passage Two: "[He] smiled and put his arm around me. It was the nicest feeling. Lucky and safe. . . . I nestled against him and imagined what it would feel like to lie next to him in a pine bed in the dark, and suddenly nothing else mattered" (p. 275).

In this passage, Mattie finds comfort and safety in the arms of her love interest, Royal Loomis. Donnelly uses this specific scene to show how easily Mattie's dreams of becoming a writer are overshadowed by her romantic expectations of love, security, and status. Donnelly uses Mattie's temptations to follow the expected road to marriage, a road that would seemingly have fewer bumps along the way, to represent the difficulties many women find when challenging a societal norm.

Passage Three: "I touch her hand. It is smooth and cold. I know it is a bad thing to break a promise, but I think now that it is a worse thing to let a promise break you" (p. 374).

Donnelly uses Mattie's epiphany about the promise she made to her mother to unite the different storylines in the text. Whether it is the broken promise of faithfulness Mr. Loomis made to his wife; the broken promise Uncle Fifty makes to Mattie to send her to school; or the broken promise Chester makes to Grace—Mattie continually encounters people who are not true to their word. And despite others' inability to keep promises, Mattie strives to keep the promises she has made to others in the past. However, as she stares at the murdered Grace, whose death is a result of a promise kept, Mattie realizes her promise to herself is much more important.

Role 4: Character Creator

Do one of the following:

1. Pick a character in the novel and explain how a contemporary pop-culture figure embodies the same characteristics of this character.

2. Develop and illustrate an extended metaphor that represents attributes, values, beliefs, etc., of a central character.

3. Step inside the mind of a character and create a sensory study by describing his or her thoughts, dreams, values, relationships, perceptions, feelings, and journeys, based on today's reading selection. Consider the following questions: What does the character think and dream about? What are his or her perceptions? How is he or she perceived by others? How does the character feel about certain people or issues? What special relationships has the character established? What journeys do you foresee for your character? What journeys has he or she already taken?

Sandra Van Belkom created two different versions of a character study for Mattie, which are shown in Figure 3.2.

Mattie Gokey (farm girl and Glenmore worker)	Mattie Gokey (aspiring writer and college student)
Thoughts and Dreams: Dreams of being married to Royal Loomis and becoming a good wife, like her own mother.	*Thoughts and Dreams:* Dreams of becoming a writer and going to college to learn more about the world beyond her family's farm. She thinks about words.
Values: Integrity; her mother's ability to take care of the family.	*Values:* Mattie loves her family, but also values education. She studies with Weaver so she can pass her finals.
Relationships: Romantic with Royal; friends with Weaver, Minnie, Tommy; strained relationship with Pa.	*Relationships:* Friends with Miss Wilcox, who advises her to pursue her dreams.
Perceptions: She perceives farm life as drudgery. Perceives life with Royal to be romantic.	*Perceptions:* Mattie feels torn between two worlds, but perceives life as a writer to be the ultimate career.
Feelings: Torn between things she has and things she wants. Feels like she must keep promise she made to her mother. Doesn't know how to feel about Grace's letters in her pocket.	*Feelings:* Confused, but driven. Mattie feels guilty for leaving family behind, but excited to see what the world has to offer a smart, capable young woman.
Journeys: Horse rides with Royal; traveling to the Glenmore to work and save money for the future; reading Grace's letters.	*Journeys:* Mattie leaves the farm behind for college life in New York City.

FIGURE 3.2. Two versions of a character study for Mattie in *A Northern Light* by Jennifer Donnelly.

Tiered Assignments

A tiered assignment is one where "overarching understandings" and "core skills" are the same, but the complexity levels of the tasks might differ (King-Shaver & Hunter, 2003, p. 76). An example of a tiered assignment is the Major Works Data Sheet (MWDS). For Advanced Placement (AP) teachers, the MWDS is a familiar sight. Students complete the form for novels they read in order to better understand an author's craft, critically analyze a text, and learn how to compose a well-written analytic essay. Although the form has traditionally been used with AP literature classes, there is no reason why it has to be applied to only "AP literature" or reserved solely for AP students. With proper modeling, scaffolding, and practice, all students can complete the MWDS for the literary works read in class (and outside of class).

Like the previous modified jigsaw/literature circle assignment, the MWDS can be an activity completed individually, in pairs, in small groups, or jigsawed out—each student/group completing a different section or page, depending on ability (differentiated *process*), but with the same text (*content*). We have slightly altered the standard template (Figure 3.3), removing the "Old AP Questions" section and adding a spot for literary theory(ies) that can be applied to the work. (Numerous templates for the four-page standard form can be found on the Internet; we have condensed ours here to fit the format of the book.)

From what students fill out on the MWDS (either alone, in pairs or small groups, or at learning stations), they have not only a beginning point for understanding better how all the parts of the novel work together but also a starting point for writing several different types of literary analysis papers: from symbols and themes in the novel to the importance of the parallel stories. These writing assignments (*product*) can be differentiated according to students' ability, both in terms of the writing prompt and the evaluation criteria or rubric. The main point is that all students are provided the opportunity to show what they learned through the writing assignment—the end product is not reserved for only the "highest level" students.

Title: *A Northern Light*	Biographical information about the author:
Author: Jennifer Donnelly Publication Date: 2003 Genre: Historical Fiction	Jennifer Donnelly was born in 1963 in Port Chester, New York. She attended the University of Rochester and majored in English literature and European history. Donnelly lives in both Brooklyn and Tivoli, New York. She is married and has a daughter and two rescued greyhounds (source, http://en.wikipedia.org/wiki/Jennifer_Donnelly). See also: http://www.jenniferdonnelly.com/

Historical or contextual information:
A Northern Light is based on the real murder that inspired Theodore Dreiser's *An American Tragedy*. Detailed information on the real case can be found at http://www.nycourts.gov/history/gillette.htm.

Plot summary:
In 1906, Mattie Gokey is a sixteen-year-old girl who lives with her father and three sisters (ages five, eleven, and fourteen) in rural New York. She is torn between honoring a promise to her dying mother and following her dreams. She promised to stay and help out the family. That would mean marrying Royal Loomis and helping to run his farm. Or she could go to New York City and go to college, staying true to her dreams. Either way, she wins and loses at the same time.

The events of the novel alternate between what goes on at home and with Royal (such as helping around the house, the tense relationship between Mattie and her father, attending school, and Royal's insensitivity toward her) and what occurs while she is working at the Glenmore Hotel (the apparent murder of a woman named Grace Brown).

Mattie must choose between the North Woods and New York City. In the end, she chooses the big city and going to college.

Describe the author's style:	An example that demonstrates style:
Rich description and real-to-life dialogue. Donnelly alternates between Mattie's time at the Glenmore and the time she spends with her family and Royal. Figurative language permeates the novel with personification, similes, and metaphors on nearly every page. She also incorporates allusions to numerous works of literature. Each non-Glenmore chapter is headed by a word of the day—and that word comes to relate to that action in that chapter.	"Things you can't see. A sigh trapped in a corner. Memories tangled in the curtains. A sob fluttering against the windowpane like a bird that flew in and can't get back out. I can feel these things. They dart and crouch and whisper" (pp. 134–135) "His smile was as warm as fresh biscuits on a winter morning" (p. 163)

Memorable Quotes	
Quote	Significance
"I wanted to ask her about promises, too, and see if she thought you always had to keep the ones you made just the way you made them, or if it was all right to alter them a bit" (Mattie, p. 88)	This quote is important because it is the first time that we understand how torn Mattie is over her promise to her mother.
"No, they're not, Mattie, they're books. And a hundred times more dangerous" (Emily Wilcox/Baxter, p. 204)	Although there was a hint of it earlier, this quote really foreshadows the sad events to come regarding Miss Wilcox—Mattie's teacher—who turns out to be a censored famous poet. *continued on next page*

FIGURE 3.3. Sample Major Works Data Sheet for *A Northern Light* by Jennifer Donnelly.

FIGURE 3.3. Continued

"I wondered if he was supposed to have said he loved me when he told me about the ring. Or maybe that came later" (Mattie, p. 226)	Royal offers to give her a ring, but he doesn't tell her that he loves her. Mattie knows deep down that he would never be enough for her, but she also wants what all the other local girls have.
"She looked small to me. Small and fragile and defenseless. She had not looked that way when I'd arrived" (Mattie, p. 311)	This is how Mattie describes Miss Wilcox after they say goodbye—Miss Wilcox's true identity was found out and she was fired. Her husband is coming for her and if he finds her, she will be sent to a sanatorium. Instead, she is running away to Paris in order to be free. But Mattie sees how men and society can knock down a once strong woman.

Characters			
Name	Role in the story	Significance	Adjectives
Mattie Gokey	Main character	Narrator—must choose between her heart and her head.	Smart, witty, soulful, inquisitive
Michael Gokey	Mattie's father	He works hard but is an absent father, caught up in grief over his wife's death.	Sad, disengaged, disconnected
Ada, Lou, and Abby Gokey	Mattie's younger sisters	Each has her own personality but none really understands Mattie.	Rough, oblivious, caring
Royal Loomis	Asks Mattie to marry him	We are never sure whether he really loves/respects Mattie or just wants to marry her so he can get part of her land.	Unaware, rough around the edges, not formally educated
Emily Wilcox/ Baxter	Mattie's teacher	Famous banned poet hiding from her husband.	Strong, devoted, clever, caring
Weaver Smith	Mattie's friend; only black boy in the area	He struggles with outright racism and has the same dream as Mattie—to go to college in New York City.	Angry, smart, witty, caring, devoted
Grace Brown	Woman who drowns; gave Mattie a set of letters to destroy	Her letters provide another level to the story; she was murdered because she was pregnant with Carl Graham's child.	Mysterious, sad, weak
Carl Graham/ Chester Gillette	Man that Grace Brown was last seen with	Carl Graham took Grace out on the boat in order to kill her; then he ran off.	Evil, selfish, criminal
Aunt Josephine	Mattie's aunt (her mother's sister)	She is the stereotypical town gossip and is more concerned with herself and her money than anyone else; she has the potential to be "good" to everyone in the story.	Hypocritical, selfish, mean, self-important
			continued on next page

FIGURE 3.3. Continued

Setting	Significance of the Opening Scene
The setting is the North Woods part of New York (Adirondacks) in the year 1906. Specifically, most of the action takes place during the summer. Some events take place at the Glenmore Hotel, while others take place on the Gokey farm.	The opening scene—July 12, 1906, at the Glenmore—not only introduces the reader to Mattie, but it also sets up the two storylines: the murder of Grace Brown and Mattie's conflict over the pursuit of knowledge or the pursuit of "love"; at that time in history, women could rarely have both.
Symbols	**Significance of the Ending/Closing Scene**
Grace Brown—becomes a symbol of how investing too much in a man can ruin a woman. The robin (p. 211) is a symbol of how close Mattie feels she came to realizing her dream. Emily Wilcox represents all that Mattie thinks she wants in terms of a learned life; Minnie represents the traditional, ideal for women at the time—both sides appeal to Mattie. The fountain pen, a gift from her uncle, symbolizes her dream of going to college and writing. Daisy the cow—at times she symbolizes Mattie in how she wails for the Loomis's bull, just like Mattie swoons over Royal Loomis (the bull is on one side of the fence and Daisy is on the other, so the fence can become a symbol, too).	As Mattie writes it, "To New York City. To my future. My life." Leaving without an in-person goodbye is the only way that Mattie is able to leave the North Woods and pursue her dream—departing just like Emily Wilcox/Baxter. The significance is that Mattie made her choice: college over what she promised her mother and what was expected of her. Also significant is that she had to choose one—she could not have both.
Possible Themes	**Literary Theory(ies)**
Coming of age—In 1906 coming of age for girls often meant marriage and children. Mattie confronts that and coming of age in terms of pursuing dreams. The role of women—Mattie is looked down upon by her father and Royal for wanting to read and learn new things.	Feminism is the most prominent theme to explore in the novel. Readers can study the expectations for women versus what Mattie wants. Questions to consider include: • What differences between men and women appear to be highlighted in the novel? • How do boys and girls perceive the older men and women in the novel? • Which characters have more power in the novel and which do not? Why? • Do the actions of the men and women appear to be stereotypical? In what ways? • Does the author challenge stereotypes? If so, how? • How does the novel portray boys/men and the effects they have on the girls'/women's lives?

4 The Verse Novel and Fluency Development for Older Adolescent Readers

Defining the Verse Novel

Is it poetry? Or prose? Both? Neither? Since the early 1990s, when the verse novel first came on the young adult literary scene, the genre has vexed librarians, teachers, and literary critics alike. Works in this genre typically consist of interconnected free verse poems that, when taken together, create a cohesive narrative. Therefore, the genre has been dubbed "novels in verse" and "poetry–novel hybrids." To complicate matters, however, some verse novelists resist the label of "poetry" for their works. Virginia Euwer Wolff, considered by many the pioneer of the verse novel, has said, "Writing my prose in funny-shaped lines does not render it poetry" (Sutton, 2001, p. 613). Yet other verse novelists are published poets, like Kirsten Smith (*The Geography of Girlhood*). We're back where we started, then, in a never-ending loop where definitions elude us. No wonder some critics describe the verse novel as a "function of postmodernism" (Van Sickle, 2006).

Certainly everything old is made new again. Pam Cole (2009) explains prose novels were popular during the Romantic period, and Vardell (2007) describes today's verse novel as the "contemporary offshoot of the ancient epic poem, a lineage including Chaucer's *Canterbury Tales* and even Tennyson's *Idylls of the King*" (n.p.). Yet, while the verse novel draws on traditional narrative verse forms and the oral tradition of storytelling, rhythms of ordinary speech take the place of formal metric patterns in today's YA verse novels. In addition, today's YA verse novel mimics the short scenic structures found in more contemporary storytelling media forms like TV shows (Michaels, n.d.). The effect is cinematic, and this may explain the appeal of the genre for adolescents. Glasgow (2002) explains, "Young readers in a digital age are more open to experiments in style and format and to books whose designs are influenced by the media" (p. 41). Adolescents may also like the provocative themes, strong sense of voice, voyeuristic perspective, intense emotion, and concentrated narratives that are hallmarks of the genre (Sullivan, 2003, p. 44).

On a more practical note, the verse novel—even long, 600-pagers like Ellen Hopkins's (2004) popular *Crank*, are shorter and faster to read than traditional narratives. Sullivan (2003) suggests the substantial white space on the pages of verse novels appeals to reluctant readers. Indeed, Wolff has suggested she had reluctant, struggling readers—and single teenage mothers—in mind when she wrote *Make Lemonade* (1994), a story in which Jolly, a seventeen-year-old down-trodden, single parent of two, begins to imagine a different life when the four-teen-year-old main character, LaVaughn, comes to her aid. Wolff says, "I wanted young girls in Jolly's situation, maybe pregnant or with babies, and maybe going back to school, to be able to say, 'I read two chapters!' In the amount of time they had, with the amount of concentration they could muster, I wanted them to be able to get through the book" (qtd. in Sutton, 2001, p. 282). Wolff says she used the verse novel format because she wanted the "friendliness of white space on a page" (p. 282). She says, "I myself am intimidated by huge pages of gray without any white space. I wanted the white space to thread through the story and give it room to breathe" (p. 282).

Struggling readers may appreciate the breathing room afforded in verse novels, but advanced readers have reasons to appreciate the genre, as well. At the very least, verse novels require that readers be attuned to the elements of poetry and consider the function of poetic elements in their interpretative, meaning-making processes. In addition, verse novels featuring multiple narrators and multiple voices, like Karen Hesse's (2003) *Witness* and Stephanie Hemphill's (2007) tribute to Sylvia Plath, *Your Own, Sylvia*, are very complex, sophisticat-ed works that draw readers into many different minds and emotions and thus encourage the consideration of many "truths." Teachers can make connections to Faulkner's use of multiple characters and Whitman's and Twain's beliefs that everyone should have a voice through the use of verse novels featuring multiple narrators (Sutton, 2001).

We think the time is right for teachers to explore verse novels with today's adolescents. The verse novel can be an appealing introduction to poetry or a contemporary addition to a poetry/writing unit. The verse novel also provides teachers with opportunities to read and discuss new, postmodern texts with adolescents and thus bridge out-of-school literacies with literacy work in the classroom (Alvermann, 2002). As we show in this chapter, the verse novel also affords opportunities to develop reading fluency, textual and genre awareness, and understandings of poetic elements within larger thematic units of study.

Selecting Quality Verse Novels for Classroom Instruction

It was difficult for us to pick one verse novel to highlight in this chapter, as the genre has taken on many shapes and sizes—as well as varying kinds of content—since its debut in the early 1990s. Put simply: there isn't just *one* kind of verse novel. As our resource guide near the end of this chapter shows, in recent years the verse novel genre has evolved to feature multiple narrators and thus multiple points of view, and diverse kinds of content—including historical fiction, biography, and poetic forms themselves.

But as we emphasize in Chapter 2, young adult novels tend to appeal to adolescents because they feature strong teenage characters going through emotional events they must ultimately live through and learn from. For this reason we wanted to highlight a verse novel that features an adolescent character readers may recognize, connect with, and trust.

But we also wanted to feature a verse novel that uses the free verse format effectively. The "verse" of the verse novel matters: in bad verse novels, the language can be stale, melodramatic, even distracting, and the plot superficially handled. As Sutton (2001) suggests, bad verse novels employ the verse form "in empty ways" (p. 282). By contrast, in the best verse novels, language is condensed (or compressed) and lines are shaped to enhance sense, while the use of figurative language supports multiple layers of meaning and unifies the story. In the best verse novels, the poetry is there for a reason—it *does* something to the story, to us as readers. Form and function go hand-in-hand, or as Virginia Euwer Wolff explains, "form is . . . an extension of content" (Sutton, p. 283).

For these reasons, we chose to feature in this chapter a verse novel that effectively matches the free verse *form* to the *function* of effectively depicting adolescent life. In what follows (see Figure 4.1), using Jago's criteria as guide, we share reasons why we'd use Ann Burg's (2009) *All the Broken Pieces* in whole-class instruction and put Kirsten Smith's (2006) novel *The Geography of Girlhood* on the classroom library shelf as an independent reading selection.

Teaching *All the Broken Pieces* to the Whole Class: Focus on Fluency and Interpretation

We envision high school English teachers using Burg's verse novel in an eleventh-grade American literature class of mixed-ability readers (ideally, in a team-taught, interdisciplinary American lit/American history context). The book could be a good introduction to a unit focused on the unintended

	All the Broken Pieces **by Ann Burg**	**The Geography of Girlhood** **by Kirsten Smith**
Summary	It is 1977. The Bee Gees' "Stayin' Alive" is on the radio, Jimmy Carter is in the White House, and the Cold War continues. But Matt Pin can't forget another war that almost killed his younger brother and got Matt airlifted out of Vietnam, away from his family and childhood home. Now Matt lives with a loving, adopted American family. He is learning to play piano and excelling as pitcher on his baseball team. But memories of his past, and present prejudices, continue to haunt him, and Matt must ultimately learn how to heal "all the broken pieces" inside him.	Ninth-grade year is almost over for fourteen-year-old Penny Morrow. Penny's mother abandoned the family long ago, Penny's older sister is staying out all night with her hunk boyfriend, and Penny's single father is driving everyone stir-crazy. Penny wants to "go somewhere real, do something great, and be someone wonderful," but her friends and family are let-downs in the guidance department, and she has to navigate first love, puberty, crushes, death, changing friendships, high school, and a new stepbrother all on her own. Leaving town sounds like a good idea, until it isn't.
Criterion 1: Written in language perfectly suited to the author's purpose	Matt's life is fragmented—he is caught between the pretty Vietnam presented in fairy tales his English language teacher reads and the war-torn Vietnam he remembers: "tanks lumbered / in the roads / like drunken elephants, / and bombs fell / from the sky / like dead crows" (pp. 19–20). Matt is caught between his "then" family—a mutilated brother and abandoned mother—and his "now" family. Matt wants to move forward, but he continues to "stumble / going back" (p. 38). The verse novel format supports Matt's fragmented, "broken" sense of self and identity, and Burg's spare, but intense, free verse poems and figurative language take us into Matt's head and help us see with his eyes and heart.	While there are some sharp, startling images here (kissed lips look like "bruised plums"), much of the language doesn't ring true. Penny likens being fourteen to "rotten candy" (p. 4). This image didn't work for us, nor does Penny's description of her sister's breasts "lodged high / like tea cakes / on her powdery skin" (p. 5). Lettermen's jackets glow "like blue diamonds pulled from the bottom of the bay" (p. 35). Huh? Also, Smith moves back and forth between free verse and prose paragraphs, and if you rearrange the line breaks of the free verse poems into paragraphs, it doesn't feel like anything is lost. Not clear what distinction Smith is making in the change of forms. Many of Smith's free verse poems provide melodramatic punch lines at the end. We struggled to get through this one, as the form is distracting and tedious in places.
Criterion 2: Exposes readers to complex human dilemmas	At the heart of this story is the aftermath of the Vietnam War— what came after for not only the eager American high school boys who returned from Vietnam disillusioned, broken, and unwelcomed, but also for the Vietnamese children who were fathered by American soldiers (then left behind once the war was over), or given by their mothers to American soldiers evacuating Saigon (in hopes the children would survive in America). As Burg's verse novel shows, the individual, personal consequences of wartime acts are deep scars that continue to hurt long after war is over. There are no winners in war. Certainly a timely, complex human dilemma is presented here.	Navigating the unpredictable seas of adolescence—with no compass or map—is the human dilemma presented in this verse novel. Penny's mother left when Penny was six, and Penny's life with an overprotective single dad and an angry, gorgeous big sister ("a walking tiara") has been anything but rosy since. Penny still hopes for her mother's return but begins to understand her mother's restlessness and desire to escape small-town life. The novel follows two years in Penny's life, as Penny ages from fourteen to sixteen and grows wiser about friendship, love, and family.
Criterion 3: Includes compelling, disconcerting characters	Burg's language creates a compelling, disconcerting character in Matt. He is "the dragon / who went beyond the mountain / and never came back" (p. 1); he is "too much fall— / wet brown leaves / under a darkening sky" (p. 8); "an afraid quiet" (p. 42); "Matt-the rat" and "Frog-face" to his teammates; "the coin / you drop in the poor box / at church" (p. 115). As Matt struggles to reconcile his past and present, he must also come to trust the adults in his life, and ultimately himself. Adolescent readers will appreciate Matt's insecurities and lack of self-esteem, as well as his strength and resiliency. Matt's parents and other characters are well developed, too.	We loved Penny's authentic voice and insightfulness, and think adolescent readers will, too. Penny knows her limits (no romantic experience, no hot bod, no normal family to speak of), but it doesn't hurt to daydream and imagine a different kind of life. Even so, Penny's voice stays sharp and wry as she describes friendships that come and go, her changing body, memories of her mother, and a growing desire for her older sister's boyfriend: he has a motorcycle and knows the way out of town.
Criterion 4: Explores universal themes that combine different periods and cultures	"Who am I?" is a universal question that spans age, time, and culture. It is one authors have answered in countless different ways, showing that while the search for identity is universal, what constitutes each person's identity is not. As Matt's plight in Burg's novel shows, our memories shape us—our past informs our present—and identity work includes reconciling our personal histories with our present experience, as well as speaking truth to stereotype.	Adolescence as storm and stress may not be a universal theme for young people all over the world, but it's a popular one in YA literature for American teens. If teachers are looking for young adult novels that characterize adolescence as a rocky, unpredictable journey of discovery (or, at least, an adult author's characterization of adolescence as such), then this book is a good example. *continued on next page*

FIGURE 4.1. Reviews of *All the Broken Pieces* by Ann Burg and *The Geography of Girlhood* by Kirsten Smith, based on Carol Jago's criteria for selecting a whole-class novel.

FIGURE 4.1. Continued

Criterion 5: Challenges readers to reexamine their beliefs	Several American characters make fun of twelve-year-old Matt because he is Vietnamese and blame him for the loss of American soldiers in the Vietnam War. But Matt is fathered by an American soldier (who deserts the family), and the fall of Saigon ultimately results in Matt being sent to the United States by his mother, who hopes he will survive there. In America, Matt is still haunted by guilt and feelings that he abandoned his family. Burg's book lends itself to consideration of multiple "truths" surrounding war. Burg's book also encourages readers to see that we are all connected and affected by war, and that the line between enemy and friend is often blurred.	Smith's book encourages readers to see that adolescence isn't something one ultimately wins or loses—it is a process that one endures, often painfully, as it brings about change, growth, and new insights. Adolescents will see themselves in Penny, but we like this book especially because it portrays an adolescent girl as strong, insightful, and resilient. The book may help adult readers give adolescents more credit for being the very capable, courageous people they are.
Criterion 6: Tells a good story with places for laughing and crying	There are places in the book where we had to stop reading and pause to let the emotional impact of Matt's story settle in. In other words, we had to stop to *deal* with the emotional weight of the story. This isn't something you'll have to do all the time—ultimately Matt's story is a hopeful one—but the weight and tragedy of war is here in Burg's book, and there are places where it stops you cold.	No hearty belly laughs here, or heavy emotional sadness, but Penny's story rings authentic and true nonetheless.

personal and individual consequences of war in general, and how the Vietnam War affected individual people, American and Vietnamese alike, in particular (see the resource guide at the end of the chapter for companion titles). The book could also be a good cross-curricular title for units on the 1960s and 1970s. We like the idea of featuring a verse novel in such a unit because it emphasizes the idea that poetry is something that can be read and studied all year long, not just in April (National Poetry Month) or in the end-of-the-year poetry unit. Using a verse novel in a thematic unit also offers English teachers opportunities to discuss with students why authors choose certain formats and genres in which to tell their stories.

Thematic connections aside for a moment, our focus for whole-class differentiated instruction in this chapter is on fluency development with older adolescent readers.

Defining Fluency

Reading fluency is recognized by many reading researchers as critical to all students' literacy development (Allington, 2009; Rasinski, 2006). Twenty-five years ago, Richard L. Allington—former president of the International Reading Association—called for fluent reading to be a more common instructional goal. More recently, the National Reading Panel (National Institute of Child Health, 2000) includes it as one of five pillars of effective reading instruction.

So what is reading fluency? Reading fluency is typically defined as consisting of three interrelated dimensions: (1) accuracy, or accurate decoding of words in text; (2) speed and automaticity, or the automatic recognition of words in connected text, and (3) prosody, or reading with expression. But while fluency is understood by reading researchers as a multidimensional process, the first two dimensions of reading fluency currently get a lot of attention in reading instruction (Allington, 2009; Rasinski, 2006). Often teachers think that if students can learn to decode words accurately and automatically, they will be successful in reading printed text. But while decoding is certainly important for fluency, it does not guarantee comprehension has occurred. Students might be able to read with great speed and accuracy but might not recall any of the ideas in the text (Buly & Valencia, 2002; Cunningham, 2006).

Rasinski (n.d.) stresses that it is the third dimension of fluency—prosody, or expression—that connects directly with students' ability to understand what they read:

> When readers embed appropriate volume, tone, emphasis, phrasing, and other elements in oral expression, they are giving evidence of actively interpreting or constructing meaning from the passage. Just as fluent musicians interpret or construct meaning from a musical score through phrasing, emphasis, and variations in tone and volume, fluent readers use cognitive resources to construct meaning through expressive interpretation of the text.

To encourage development of "cognitive resources" that aid fluency development in this third dimension with older, adolescent readers, reading researchers suggest teachers (including secondary ones) should model expressive reading through teacher *read-alouds* (Albright & Arial, 2005; Alvermann & Phelps, 1998; Richardson, 2000). In addition, teachers should create situations for *repeated reading* to develop fluency in reading comprehension (Hasbrouck, Ihnot, & Rogers, 1999; Rasinski, 2006; Samuels, 2002). Repeated reading can be a group or individual activity in which learners read a text with a fluent reader and then reread the text alone. Blau (2003) asserts that rereading is the "most powerful strategy available to all readers for helping themselves read more profitably, especially when they are reading difficult texts" (p. 143).

But high school English teachers may wonder, "How can we get older students to read a passage more than once?" Rasinski (2006) explains the best answer to this dilemma is to create situations in which students have real reasons for doing so. The verse novel lends itself to such situations. As Alexander (2005) explains:

The [verse novel] writer is able to craft the verse as though orchestrating for read-ing aloud. She can shape the rhythm, position the line-break so as to add empha-sis, vary the pace through the line-length, or borrow and exploit poetic devices such as repetition, caesura, and enjambment. Equally, readers are more likely to experience the words as sound as they read. The great majority of verse-novels … are a modern means of rendering soliloquy or dramatic monologue. (p. 271)

Tapping into the read-aloud potential of the verse novel is what this chap-ter's about. In what follows, after we share some prereading and foreground-ing strategies for teaching Ann Burg's verse novel (2009) *All the Broken Pieces*, we show how English teachers can create authentic situations for teacher read-alouds and repeated readings with the novel. In the strategies we describe here, we use read-alouds and repeated readings with the whole class before and dur-ing reading and then move into small-group differentiated fluency instruction once reading is completed. Working in small differentiated groups, students write and perform an original choral reading or poem based on their reading(s) and interpretation of the novel.

Teaching *All the Broken Pieces* to the Whole Class

Before Reading: Generating Background Knowledge

Because full appreciation of Burg's verse novel requires some understandings about the Vietnam War and the fall of Saigon prior to reading, teachers may first want to tap and then enhance students' background knowledge. Teachers could ask students to list everything they know about the Vietnam War, and ask if students know of family or community members who have personal history of the war. We also like Brassell and Rasinski's (2008) idea of the "jackdaw," or what they call a "mini-museum" of artifacts ranging from maps to food to music to jewelry to documents (e.g., photographs, letters) that relay information about the time period and culture under study. Teachers could include artifacts that help bring the historical time period of the 1960s and 1970s, and Vietnamese culture and history, alive for the students. Teachers might also want to share excerpts from popular movies depicting the Vietnamese War or the documen-tary *Hearts and Minds* (Davis, 1974), which weaves interviews with US soldiers and Vietnamese citizens with newsreel footage of the war and unexpected scenes of daily life in the United States.

Teachers could also design prereading knowledge assessment lists like those described by Barbara King-Shaver and Alyce Hunter (2003) in *Differentiated*

Instruction in the English Classroom: Content, Process, Product, and Assessment. As an example, King-Shaver and Hunter create a prereading list to use with a unit on the Harlem Renaissance. On the list are items such as "Zora Neale Hurston," "Langston Hughes," "jazz," and "author's voice" (p. 108). Students are asked to place a *T* beside any items they know enough about to teach others, an *H* beside items they have heard about, and a question mark beside items they're not sure about. Students who have marked *Ts* on their papers share their knowledge with the class, and teachers can plan whole-class and differentiated instruction based on what students already know and still need to know. A prereading assessment list to use with *All the Broken Pieces* might look like the one shown in Figure 4.2.

Teachers will want to give students background information on the fall of Saigon and Operation Babylift (teachers could make connections between orphan adoptions during the Vietnam War and after the more recent Haiti earthquake). Teachers also will want to foreground the book, asking students to journal about the cover and title and to make predictions based on these textual features. Teachers may then want to tell students that in the book they'll meet a boy named Matt, who was forced to leave his country and his family behind when he was very young. Teachers might ask students to journal about what that would feel like, and how they might continue to feel once in a new country, with a new family. Because the book centers on Matt's fragmented sense of self and struggle to move on from his painful past, teachers might also want to pose questions about identity for discussion or journal writing, such as the following:

Prereading Guide for *All the Broken Pieces* by Ann Burg

Place a *T* next to the terms you know well enough to teach to someone else.

Place an *H* next to the terms you have heard of.

Place a question mark (?) next to terms that are new to you.

_____fall of Saigon

_____Operation Frequent Wind

_____Operation Babylift

_____refugee

_____Black April

_____The Bee Gees

_____war veteran

_____Vietnam War

_____free verse poetry

FIGURE 4.2. Prereading guide for *All the Broken Pieces* by Ann Burg.

- Describe a memory from childhood. Why do you think you remember this event or person? Why is this memory important to you?

- What important memories of your family do you have? Why are these important to you?

- Do you think our memories and past experiences shape us or continue to define who we are years later?

- William Faulkner once wrote, "The past isn't dead. It isn't even past yet." What does that mean? Can we ever forget or get over our past experiences? Why do we sometimes want to?

- How do you think your parents/teachers/friends view or see you?

- Have you ever been wrongly judged by someone or negatively stereotyped? Explain.

Preparing Students to Read a Verse Novel

Before reading, teachers should define the term *verse novel* for students, explaining that the book is written in a nontraditional narrative format and employs nonrhyming free verse. Teachers can define *free verse* for students or ask students what they already know about free verse poetry (see prereading guide, Figure 4.2). Teachers can explain that one of the features of free verse is the breaking of the line and the use of white space on the page to highlight a key image or idea. In *Awakening the Heart*, the poet Georgia Heard (1998) writes, "The tension between sound and silence is what makes a poem. It is both the words—voices on the page—as well as the silence between words that poets work with when writing poetry." Teachers might want to emphasize this point by looking at some of the poems in Burg's book with students. For example, teachers could read pages 1–3 aloud to the students and then discuss with students why they think Burg made the line-break choices she did and why she uses white space between stanzas on page 3. Teachers could ask students to consider how the poems change if Burg had made different choices. Teachers could also teach students definitions of terms such as *caesura* (which plays an important role in Burg's book) and *enjambment*, which is a line-break technique that interrupts the natural rhythm or meaning of a line. Poets might use this technique to create tension and to disguise rhyme (Heard, 1998).

In addition, teachers could explain that because *All the Broken Pieces* is a verse novel, readers should expect to see characteristics they might expect to see in traditional fictional works. For example, talk to students about Burg's use of italics on pages 2–3 to represent Matt's mother's voice. Point out that Burg uses italics to indicate when characters are speaking, and show other examples, such as Matt's birth father speaking on page 5 and Matt's adopted father speaking on page 7. Note that Burg often cues the reader with "he said" or "she says" following the italics. At some point, teachers might want to ask students to consider what "hearing" all the different voices in the book does for the reader: Is it effective? Why does Burg tell the story from Matt's perspective, yet insert the voices of others? Does Matt continue to hear his mother's voice? Would it have been more effective if only certain voices were heard and not others?

Teachers will also want to explain that verse novelists tend to tell their stories in short fragments, or sections (like TV episodes), that are usually built around a single perspective, voice, or incident (Michaels, n.d.). These sections (like chapters) are usually one to two pages in length. Burg's novel is structured into thirty-one sections, with the first section acting as a frame for the book. In the first section, we meet most of Matt's family members (including his Vietnamese mother and brother) and get crucial information about Matt's history that helps us better understand the feelings he describes throughout the story. Other sections introduce other important characters in the book or describe Matt doing things in America (e.g., playing baseball, practicing piano) even as he is constantly reminded of Vietnam. During reading, teachers can ask students to pay attention to what goes on in each of the sections and how they differ.

Sections in verse novels typically have titles, which can sometimes be the first line of the poem. Titles in verse novels can also indicate the speaker, contextualize the content, or point to a core theme (Alexander, 2005). Teachers will want to point out that Burg doesn't title the separate sections or poems in her book but instead indicates new sections with the musical bass clef symbol. Burg also uses the five-line musical staff (or stave) throughout the book to denote the end of a poem. Ask students to predict why Burg made this choice as a writer. Is music going to be important to this story? During reading, teachers could ask students to come up with titles for each section as they read. As an example, the first section in Burg's book could be called "Family: Then and Now." Teachers can also use this time to explore reasons why an author might choose to write in a verse novel format. Once students have some thematic and textual background knowledge, it's time to start reading aloud and practicing repeated readings.

Reading Aloud and Repeated Reading

To model expressive reading and create authentic situations for rereading with *All the Broken Pieces*, the teacher should first read aloud the first three poems in Burg's book, on pages 1–6. Modeling plays a significant role in expressive reading, as readers learn how to interpret text orally by listening to an expert reader read to them in an expressive and meaningful way. Rasinski (2003) explains that hearing someone read aloud increases students' vocabulary, comprehension, and motivation for reading; provides students with insight into skilled readers' comprehension strategies; and helps students notice textual features, phrase/sentence boundaries, and learn new word meanings. The National Commission on Reading calls reading aloud "the single most important activity for building the knowledge required for eventual success in reading" (Anderson, Hiebert, Scott, & Wilkinson, 1985, p. 23), and urges teachers to continue reading to students through all grades. After modeling how the text should be read through read-alouds, teachers can employ any of the strategies listed next to engage readers in rereading the text.

Teacher and Volunteer Read-Alouds

Read a selection aloud and then ask for a volunteer to read it aloud. After this student reads aloud, wait about thirty seconds and call for another volunteer to read the same selection. After this student reads aloud, wait again and then call for a third volunteer to read the same selection. If no students volunteer, the teacher should read the selection aloud several times, changing tone, intonation, and so forth each time. The point of this exercise is to let students hear the text multiple times so they can begin to pair words and word sounds with meaning(s) and notice phrase boundaries.

An important part of reading fluency is the ability to read in syntactically and semantically appropriate phrases. Meaning is embedded in multiple word chunks of text or phrases, not in individual words themselves. Thus, one of the tasks of the fluent reader is to read in these phrases or chunks. Schreiber (1980) has theorized that many readers characterized as disfluent suffer from a poor ability to phrase text appropriately while reading. Hearing chunks of text and phrases read aloud helps the disfluent reader discover the text cues that mark phrase boundaries.

This read-aloud strategy is also helpful because when students hear the text read aloud multiple times, they notice words and phrases they didn't see on the first reading. As students hear the text read aloud again and again, they may also understand the text better each time (Elbow, 1973; Robertson, 1990).

Pointing

In conjunction with teacher and volunteer read-alouds of the selected text, teachers can ask students to point to and read aloud ("Quaker style," without raising hands, as the "spirit moves you") a line or phrase that strikes them as memorable or powerful or important. Students do not have to justify their line or phrase. Teachers should explain to students that no one has exclusive right to any one line, and there is no limit to how many times a line can be called out, even by the same person (Blau, 2003; Elbow, 1973). Students can call out a line they love as many times as they choose, or use the line as a kind of refrain during the activity. Blau (2003) suggests this activity helps to build confidence in reluctant readers:

> One of the differences between strong and weak readers is that strong readers trust that their responses to texts are worth paying attention to and talking about with other readers....
>
> Weak readers assume that their responses to texts are meaningless and not worth reporting. They would never presume to point to a line that they found interesting or important, because they would claim that they don't know what is supposed to make a line interesting or important. Yet, when these same weak readers hear students known to be strong readers calling out lines that they themselves might also have been struck by, they will start to recognize that they are not so unlike the strong readers as they may have imagined and that their responses may also be worthy of attention. (p. 144)

Blau also suggests that in addition to honoring every individual response, the repetition of lines helps to locate a "center of gravity" for a reading that can lead to interpretation of a text (p. 144).

Text Rendering

This is a variation on "pointing" that includes discussion about the lines students select. After reading the selected text aloud multiple times, ask students to say aloud any word, phrase, or sentence that they especially liked or noted, or that stuck with them for any reason, including confusion or lack of understanding. Once students have called out their lines, ask if there are any questions or comments (or pose some of your own about the lines students read aloud). If students volunteer questions and comments, collaboratively explore their ideas and use this opportunity to clarify the text as needed (Elbow, 1973).

Robertson (1990) describes this strategy as a way for students to "enter a piece of literature, as a way to begin to pay attention, to become involved in the world of the text" (p. 82). Further:

> [T]ext rendering—reading aloud and saying back—slows down the reading process, forces us to prolong our initial response to the text, and opens that initial response to the influence of other readers. Text rendering keeps our attention focused on the language, allowing us to live with the words for a few moments,

and allowing the text to disclose itself to us. In the same way our eyes become accustomed to a darkened room, our minds need to be allowed time to find our way around within the world created by the text. . . . Text rendering keeps the readers inside the text, reading and re-reading. (p. 83)

Linguistic Roulette

Similar to text rendering, this strategy incorporates writing. After hearing the selected text read aloud multiple times, students skim through the text looking for a single word or phrase that they find interesting, important, or puzzling. Teachers might prompt students to find what they think is "the most important line" (Blau, 2003). Students write the word or phrase on a piece of paper and explain why they picked this line. Students then pair up with group members, read the line, and their justification for why it's the most important (Rasinski & Padak, 1996).

Teachers can continue practicing these strategies as they read the book with the whole class. In conjunction with repeated readings and discussion, we suggest having students use the story map (see Figure 4.3) to keep track of changes in Matt's character over the course of the novel and his growing sense of self and identity. The chart will ultimately aid students in their end-of-unit consideration of such themes as belonging, reevaluation of the past, and individual and societal consequences of war, as well as poetic devices that will be helpful to students when they get ready to write and perform choral poems of their own.

Differentiated Small-Group Instruction

Students will work together in small differentiated groups at the end of the unit to write and perform a choral reading or poem based on *All the Broken Pieces*. Choral reading is another research-supported strategy for developing expressive reading, and thus fluency, especially with older readers. It is an interpretative reading strategy that involves the whole class or a group of students reading aloud in unison. Choral reading requires repeated readings of a particular passage and gives practice in oral reading.

To facilitate, teachers can divide students into groups and allocate to each group several sections of the novel about which they are responsible for writing. Or teachers may want to let students write a choral poem based on their understanding, interpretation, and exploration of one of the novel's themes (e.g., identity/belonging; reconciling the past) or the characterization of Matt. To group students, we recommend assessing students at this point, using the multidimensional fluency scale by T. V. Rasinski as shown on the website for Pacific Resources for Education and Learning, http://www.prel.org/products/re_/

Matt Pin at beginning of the story	Section	Words/images/poetic devices (e.g., use of figurative language, line breaks, spacing) that seem to support this idea (include page numbers)	Your thoughts/reflections
Matt doesn't have good memories of Vietnam.	1	"She pushes me forward, / through screaming madness / and choking dust, / through fear and fog, / through smoke and death, through whirring sounds/ of helicopter prayers, / and night falling like / rain-soaked stars." (pp. 4–5)	Matt seems haunted by the memory of his mom pushing him to go to America. Vietnam is a place of death. Matt is *bui doi*, "dust of life." I like the image of "night falling like / rain-soaked stars," although I'm not sure what that would look like. Stars are usually bright and shining, something you look up to and make wishes on. If a star is rain-soaked, it is going to be heavy, dim, and useless—like a light-bulb about to die out on you, so not a hopeful symbol. Night falls with a thud and a whimper—Matt's former life ending.
Matt can't say his brother's name.	1	"His name I will never say." (p. 1)	Why can't Matt speak his brother's name? What is he ashamed of?
Matt Pin at middle of the story			
Matt is bullied on the baseball field.		The school bully calls Matt "frog-face" and says, "My brother died / because of you."	Matt and the school bully both have brothers who were maimed or killed because of the Vietnam War. They have this pain and anger in common, yet they blame/misunderstand each other.
Matt starts going to veterans' meetings.	1		Matt hears American veterans' stories and begins to understand how they were treated when they returned to the US.
Matt Pin by end of the story			
Matt says his brother's name.	31	"His name is Huu Hein. He followed me everywhere. He follows me still, and one day, we're going to find him." (p. 219)	Matt is able to say his brother's name by the end of the story because he is beginning to come to terms with what has happened to him. He plans to go back to Vietnam and look for his brother.

FIGURE 4.3. Story map to use with *All the Broken Pieces* by Ann Burg.

assessing-fluency.htm. Teachers can use the scale to assess students' expressive reading abilities through informal, casual observations, or have students come up to the teacher one by one to read selected passages individually (or tape-record their reading at a reading station) while other students work on other anchor activities. Teachers might also want to keep this scale in mind when they are doing the whole-class read-alouds and repeated readings at the beginning of the unit.

The scale rates reader fluency on the dimensions of expression and volume, phrasing, smoothness, and pace. Scores range from 4 to 16. Generally, scores below 8 indicate that fluency may be a concern. Scores of 8 or above indicate that the student is making good progress in fluency. For the choral reading activity, we suggest using groups of three to four students, with the groups comprising a below, a mid-, and a high-range fluent reader. It will be important for both the students with scores at 8 or below to hear expressive reading modeled by the more fluent reader.

With that said, assign roles for each member of the group, such as:

1. *Reader/Literary Luminary:* This person reads the text that the choral poem is based on and works with director and writer to make interpretative decisions about the text that influence performance decisions.

2. *Director:* This person works in conjunction with reader and writer to make performance decisions and is responsible for securing any props or creating or locating special effects, art, music, and so forth that evoke the time period or mood of the novel.

3. *Writer:* This person works in conjunction with reader and director to create the script for the performance.

Explain to students that all group members will be expected to perform—whether through speaking or acting—in the final presentation.

Once you have assessed your students and made decisions about how to group them for the choral reading activity, it is time to introduce the activity. For this, we think it's important to show students what a choral poem looks like and provide opportunities to practice choral reading. In Figure 4.4 we share a choral poem Susan wrote based on the poems presented in the first four pages of Burg's book.

In preparation for sharing this with students, teachers might want to read the poems on pages 1–4 in Burg's book aloud first. Then teachers can explain that writing poems for choral readings involves writing for multiple voices, considering how words sound, and making interpretative decisions. Then teachers could put a transparency of Susan's poem on the overhead or make enough copies for all students. Teachers should read the choral poem aloud to the class to help set the pace, as well as model proper pronunciation. Teachers can then assign different parts to students to read. Teachers might also want to use this

Line #	Solo I (Matt)	Solo II (Matt's mother)	Chorus
1	My name is Matt Pin		
2	And her name		
3	I remember	I remember	Do you remember?
4	Phang My		
5		*You cannot stay here*	
6			Screaming madness Choking mist Crying children Burning flesh Whirring sounds Wailing dust Pushing forward Smoke and death
7		*You will be like dust*	
8	His name I will never say	Never	Never
9		*Who would want a little boy?*	
10			Mangled Deformed Missing fingers Stumps for legs
11	Though forever I carry his blood In my blood	Forever I carry his blood in my blood	Forever you carry his blood in your blood (all voices staggered) (all repeat three times)
12	Forever his bones Stretch in my bones	Forever his bones Stretch in my bones	Forever his bones Stretch in your bones (all voices staggered) (all repeat three times)
13	To me, he is nothing	Nothing	Nothing
14	If he stumbled on me now, I wonder, would he see himself in my eyes?		
15			What would he see?
16		*Survive.* *Remember not this shame.*	
17	And I?	I	I
18	Would I recognize the dragon?		
19	Who went beyond the mountain and never came back?	Go beyond the mountain	
			Come back Come back Come back

FIGURE 4.4. Sample choral poem by Susan for *All the Broken Pieces* by Ann Burg.

opportunity to explain to students that there are several ways to structure a choral reading, as seen next:

- *Refrain:* One person reads the narrative portion of the text while the rest of the class joins in the refrain. This is one of the most common forms of choral speaking.
- *In unison:* The teacher and the class read the poem together. Additional sound effects might be incorporated.
- *With an echo:* One person reads a line or phrase, and the group repeats (echoes) it.
- *In groups:* Two or more groups take turns reading different parts of the poem.
- *Solo lines:* Individuals read specific lines in appropriate places throughout the group activity.
- *Line around:* Each line is taken by a different person in the group.
- *Cumulative:* Groups of voices or individual voices are added to or subtracted from the choral reading, depending on the message or the meaning communicated by the selection.

Have students practice reading the model choral poem several times as a whole class, emphasizing different words in different ways. For example, have students try different ways of reading line 3, either simultaneously or staggered, in different tones (e.g., anguished, ashamed, nostalgic, courageous, hopeful, upbeat). Discuss which emphasis seems more appropriate and why. Point out to students that Burg sets the words "I remember" apart in her own poem (p. 1) with commas surrounding the phrase. Discuss with students what kinds of poetic pauses commas (brief stops) communicate, and explain to students they can use Burg's use of punctuation as a guide for interpreting what and how to emphasize important points in their own choral poems.

Also, have Chorus II pose the words *never* in line 8, and *nothing* in line 13 as questions, and then discuss why emphasizing these words as questions might be appropriate interpretations of Matt's feelings about his brother. Encourage students to consider their earlier predictions of the story—were they confirmed? Challenged?

Talk to students about Burg's dramatic use of the period midway through the poem, when Matt says, "To me, / he is nothing" (p. 1), and talk again about the importance of line breaks in free verse and the use of punctuation to create poetic pauses. Discuss with students how poets use punctuation devices to control the speed and pacing of a poem and to emphasize ideas. Explain to students that you'll expect to see their understandings of free verse poetry and poetic elements in the choral poems they write and perform (see rubric, Figure 4.5).

In addition, teachers might want to teach students such poetry performance tools as "punching," "pausing," and "painting" (O'Connor, 2004, p. 113). "Punching" tools include helping students play with stresses and look for words in poems that can be delivered with greater emphasis. "Pausing" tools include helping students understand occasions to pause in poems: at punctuation marks, individual words within poems (e.g., repeated lines; words that break patterns), and where line breaks fall (p. 115). "Painting" tools include helping students pay attention to vivid words that create images, word sounds and pronunciation, and word connotations.

As an example of a "painting" tool, teachers might explain to students that poets use words to paint images and pictures in the reader's mind (Noden, 1999). Explain that some of the "brushstrokes" poets use are called participles. Provide the definition of a present participle verb (-*ing* verb) and explain that participles often function as adjectives. Point out Burg's use of them in the poem on page 2 of her book ("choking mist," "wailing dust," "whirring helicopters") and on page 3, where Burg describes Matt's mother in one single line of participles: "pushing, praying, pleading" (p. 3). Noden explains writers use participles to add action and drama to their writing. Ask the students if Burg's use of participles achieves this goal. Who is the mist choking? How does mist choke someone? What does it mean to "wail"? Why would the dust be crying? Who would the dust be mourning? (Teachers could talk about personification here, as well). Ask: Why didn't Burg write, "My mother pushes, prays, and pleads?" or use the past participle form, "She pushed, prayed, pleaded"? Teachers could emphasize how poets condense and compress language for impact.

Another "brushstroke" poets use is the appositive (Noden, 1999). An appositive is a noun phrase used to provide additional information, explanation, or an alternate image to a noun or pronoun previously used in a sentence. On page 2, Burg uses appositives to describe how Matt remembers his mother's voice (appositives are underlined):

> I hear her voice,
> Thin, shrill staccato notes,
> her words short puffs of air
> that push me along,
> inch by inch, breath by breath. (p. 2)

Ask students why Burg didn't just write: "I hear her voice, her words." Ask what the additional information provides for the reader, and why it might be essential information. Encourage students to demonstrate understandings about how poets and authors "paint" images in readers' minds in their own choral poems. Remind students that they will track such images throughout the book as they read (see story map, Figure 4.3).

Students should have ample time to practice their choral poem performances. Teachers might want to provide them with a rubric such as that shown in Figure 4.5 to guide their in-class group work. Examples of poems that Susan's students have written in response to various young adult verse novels are shown for *Out of the Dust* by Karen Hesse (Figure 4.6), *Crank* by Ellen Hopkins (Figure 4.7), and *A Wreath for Emmett Till* by Marilyn Nelson (Figure 4.8).

Rubric for Choral Poem/Reading	

List group members' names in designated roles:
 	
   1. Reader/Literary Luminary (responsible for reading and reflection letter) _____
   _____
   2. Director (responsible for props, music, etc.) _____
   3. Writer (responsible for script) _____	

Demonstrates interpretation of theme or character in *All the Broken Pieces.* Be prepared to explain your interpretation in discussion following performance.	_____/20
Form fits function—how does your choral poem "fit" your interpretation of the text? For example, why did you design the performance the way you did? Be prepared to explain in discussion following performance.	_____/20
Demonstrates understandings of elements of poetry (e.g., free verse, enjambment, caesura, vivid word images, figurative language). Group members understand "painting" tools that poets use. Highlight at least one of each of these elements on the written script your group turns in.	_____/15
Performance: Demonstrates understanding of choral reading, in that all group members' voices are represented and used, and the poem sounds like it is meant to be "heard" (e.g., pay attention to word sounds, "punching" and "pausing" tools).	_____/30
Props, music, art, etc., are used well—they do not distract from interpretation but instead complement interpretation	_____/15
Total Points	_____/100

FIGURE 4.5. Rubric for evaluating students' choral reading presentations.

Narrator (Billy Jo)	Pa	Ma
After seventy days of wind and sun	Of wind and clouds	Of wind and sand
After seventy days	Of wind and dust	A little rain came.
But the dust came again	Tearing up the fields	Like prairie fire
And every day	With no rain	More wheat dies
Daddy, you can't stop the dust …	Right through the cracks it comes	Right through the gaps
Roaring dust Turning the day from sunlight to midnight (everyone reads together, repeat three times)	Roaring dust Turning the day from sunlight to midnight	Roaring dust Turning the day from sunlight to midnight
Now I slip under cover of darkness Inside a boxcar And let the train carry me west Out of the dust (Billy Jo and Pa read last line together)	Out of the dust	
Out of the dust (read together)	Out of the dust	

FIGURE 4.6. Choral poem for *Out of the Dust* by Karen Hesse.

Other Poem Options

If teachers want to provide other end-of-unit poem options or other poem-writing opportunities for students to do in conjunction with reading *All the Broken Pieces*, we suggest the following.

Name Poems

Burg's book opens with Matt saying his name and his mother's name. But Matt explains he "will never say" his brother's name, even though he carries the

Kristina (AKA Bree)	Crank	Adam	Chorus
	Fire! (scream)		
Your nose ignites Flameless kerosene (1)		That's my girl Let's forget and fly (2)	Forget and fly (whisper and repeat three times) (3)
	Powerful demons Bite through Cartilage and sinuses		
	Brain/brain/brain/brain (read all lines together with Adam, three times)	Take/take/take/take	
			It takes dead aim at your brain
You want to cry (sad) (1)	Cry/cry (sarcastic) (2)		You want to cry? (3)
	Jump inside! (evil voice) (1)	Jump inside! (seductive voice) (2)	
Want to scream Get urge to dance (repeat three times) (read at same time as chorus)			Louder, louder, louder (repeat three times)
Bree is who I choose to be / Kristina is who made me (1)		With you, I am Adam … let's run and find our garden and live happy (2)	Who Who Who Who are you? (3)
	You want to let me go? Ride the current? Let me sweep you away?		
Funny thing about the monster. The worse he treats you, the more you love him (1)	Love me Love me Love me Love me (whisper) (2)		

FIGURE 4.7. Choral poem for *Crank* by Ellen Hopkins.

memory of his brother with him. By the end of the novel, however, Matt is able to say his brother's name and vows to one day go back to Vietnam and find him. As Christensen (2000) explains, "To say the name is to begin the story" (p. 10). Matt's ability to heal, reconcile his past with his present and future, and reclaim his Vietnamese identity becomes apparent when he can finally say his brother's name. Both Christensen (2000) and O'Connor (2004) offer great ideas for getting students to research and write about their own or other family members' names. Christensen uses poems by Marge Piercy and Sandra Cisneros's *House on Mango Street* as models for students' name poems, and O'Connor features models by

Marilyn Nelson	News reporter	Community member	Chorus
What should my wreath for Emmett Till denote?			
	A running boy Five men in close pursuit		
			(Chorus should make screaming and slapping sounds, and jackal laughter)
For innocence, daisies and white lilacs			
		White folk Blind souls	
	A body left to bloat		
		Horror classic Axe at the front door	(Chorus should make sound of jiggling doorknob and screams)
		Heartless Heedless	
Spring wildflowers the bloodroot poppy bright as moonbeams			
	Accused found innocent by jury		
		Trees groan with the weight of black men slain for being black, their murderers acquitted every time	
			(Chorus sings) *My country 'tis of thee* *Sweet land of liberty,* *Of thee I sing…*
Rosemary for remembrance Forget me not			
		We must remember	
			(Chorus sings third verse of song) *Let music swell the breeze,* *And ring from all the trees,* *Sweet freedom's song;* *Let mortal tongues awake;* *Let all that breathe partake;* *Let rocks their silence break.* *Let freedom ring!*

FIGURE 4.8. Choral poem for *A Wreath for Emmett Till* by Marilyn Nelson.

Salman Rushdie and Nikki Giovanni. (We also like Christensen's [2000] use of poetry in a unit on the Vietnamese War. See Christensen's book for poems written by her students in response to watching the documentary film on the Vietnamese War, *Hearts and Minds* [Davis, 1974].)

Then and Now Poems

In their book *Inside Out: Strategies for Teaching Writing*, Kirby, Kirby, and Liner (2004) suggest that the best resource for student writers is often their own memories. Memory is certainly important to identity, as Matt's struggle to reconcile his past shows in *All the Broken Pieces*. One memory poem we have used with students is the "Then and Now" poem. In this poem, students "look back into their memories and compare a person or place they remember *then* with their perceptions of the same person or place *now*" (Kirby, Kirby, & Liner, 2004, p. 51). In Burg's book, Matt compares his "then" family to his "now" family, and the terrifying Vietnam he remembers to the Vietnam represented in fairy tales. Students could write their own "Then and Now" poems about their own memories, comparing such things as school, church, the family car, a relative, or a place when they were younger to those things now. Or students could take on Matt's voice and perspective at the beginning of the book (the "then" of the poem) and compare it to Matt's perspective at the end of the book (the "now" of the poem). When we have used this activity with our own students, we have provided a template for those who might need more support:

Then, I was_____.
Then, I was_____.
Then, I was_____.
Now, I am_____.
Now, I am_____.
Now, I am_____.

Seasonal Poems

Teachers could also use Burg's seasonal poems about Matt and his "now" family members as models for students' own poems about themselves and their family members. One of Burg's poems can be found at http://nicolepoliti.wordpress.com/2009/12/03/all-the-broken-pieces-by-ann-e-burg/. Read this poem with students and ask: How does Matt see himself if he describes himself as "too much fall"? As "wet brown leaves under a darkening sky"? What are happier fall images? Why doesn't Matt describe himself as winter? Is fall a "hopeful" season? What seasons would students describe themselves as? Teachers might want to use O'Connor's (2004) prewriting activity idea to get students started. He asks students to assign a corresponding season to a list of words. He gives students words like *icicle*, *suntan*, and *fallen leaves* but then pushes them toward more sophisticated associations with words like *moon*, *shovel*, and *kiss*. O'Connor explains, "Asking students to justify the seasonal association they ascribe to each word leads to interesting debates, and students begin to imbue words with personal experience" (p. 21). Another prewriting activity teachers could use is O'Connor's "image pool" (p. 24), in which teachers provide the first line (e.g., "a wintry night") and students call out images and words they associate with the line.

After the End

Once students have read *All the Broken Pieces* and written (and possibly performed) original poems, teachers could move students into smaller literature circles where students could continue exploring verse novels in their various formats, or teachers could have students continue to explore war-related themes in small-group literature circles. See our list of other kinds of verse novels and war-themed companion titles to use in the resource guide that follows.

As we've shown, verse novels provide rich opportunities for wordplay, sophisticated interpretation, and fluency development in the high school English classroom.

Resource Guide for Chapter 4

Next, we list some of our favorite verse novel titles and the varying types of verse novels available. An asterisk (*) denotes a novel appropriate for middle school.

Verse Novels That Explore Poetic Forms

Dizzy in Your Eyes: Poems about Love (Mora, 2010)—sonnet, cinquain, blank verse
The Realm of Possibility (Levithan, 2006)—haiku, ballad, and other contemporary forms
Crank (Hopkins, 2004)—concrete poetry and other contemporary forms
Keesha's House (Frost, 2003/2007)—multiple sonnet forms, sestina

A Wreath for Emmett Till (M. Nelson, 2005/2009)—Italian sonnet, sonnet corona

Sister Slam and the Poetic Motormouth Road Trip (High, 2004)— rhythm and rhyme of rap

Your Own, Sylvia (Hemphill, 2007)—explores poetry and life of Sylvia Plath

Here in Harlem: Poems in Many Voices (Myers, 2008)—modeled after Edgar Lee Masters's *Spoon River Anthology*; highlights multiple poetic forms

Shakespeare Bats Cleanup (Koertge, 2003) and *Shakespeare Makes the Playoffs* (Koertge, 2010)—haiku, sonnets, free verse, sestina, ballad

*Love That Dog (Creech, 2001)—multiple forms; highlights poems by William Carlos Williams, Robert Frost, William Blake, and others (see also *Hate That Cat*)

*Miss Crandall's School for Young Ladies and Little Misses of Color (Alexander & Nelson, 2007)—sonnet

*God Went to Beauty School (Rylant, 2006)—personification

*Diamond Willow (Frost, 2008)—concrete poems, diamante poetry

*Blue Lipstick (Grandits, 2007); **Technically It's Not My Fault* (Grandits, 2004)—concrete poems

Verse Novel Narratives with Single, First-Person Narrators

The Sky Is Everywhere (M. Nelson, 2010)

Glimpse (Williams, 2010)

The Best and Hardest Thing (Brisson, 2010)

Everything Is Fine (A. D. Ellis, 2010)

Jinx (Wild, 2004)

True Believer (Wolff, 2002)—sequel to *Make Lemonade*; National Book Award winner

Sold (McCormick, 2006)

Planet Pregnancy (High, 2008)

Crank (Hopkins, 2004) (also see others by Hopkins, including *Tricks* and *Identical*)

*What My Mother Doesn't Know (Sones, 2003)

*All the Broken Pieces (Burg, 2009)

Girl Coming in for a Landing: A Novel in Poems (Wayland, 2004)

Geography of Girlhood (K. Smith, 2006)

Because I Am Furniture (Chaltas, 2009)

*Home of the Brave (Applegate, 2008)

*Reaching for Sun (Zimmer, 2007)

*Locomotion (Woodson, 2003) and sequel, *Peace, Locomotion*

Verse Novel Narratives with Multiple Narrators

Think Again (Lawson & Morstad, 2010)
*Witness (Hesse, 2003)
Bronx Masquerade (Grimes, 2003)
*Bat 6 (Wolff, 2000)
What My Girlfriend Doesn't Know (Sones, 2008)
The Realm of Possibility (Levithan, 2006)
Keesha's House (Frost, 2003/2007)
Dark Sons (Grimes, 2005)
The Brimstone Journals (Koertge, 2001)
One Night (Wild, 2006)
Your Own, Sylvia (Hemphill, 2007)
Carver: A Life in Poems (M. Nelson, 2001)

Verse Novel Historical Fiction

Wicked Girls: A Novel of the Salem Witch Trials (Hemphill, 2010)
The Firefly Letters: A Suffragette's Journey to Cuba (Engle, 2010)—based on the diaries and letters of Swedish suffragist Fredrika Bremer
*We Troubled the Waters (Shange, 2009)—civil rights leaders
The Surrender Tree: Poems of Cuba's Struggle for Freedom (Engle, 2008)—details years of Cuba's wars for independence, 1850–1899
The Poet Slave of Cuba (Engle, 2006)
*Crossing Stones (Frost, 2009)—WWI
All the Broken Pieces (Burg, 2009)—Vietnam War
*Kaleidoscope Eyes (Bryant, 2009)—Vietnam War
*Almost Forever (Testa, 2003)—Vietnam War
*New Found Land: Lewis and Clark's Voyage of Discovery (Wolf, 2004)
*Witness (Hesse, 2003)
*Out of the Dust (Hesse, 2005)—Great Depression/Oklahoma Dust Bowl
*Aleutian Sparrow (Hesse, 2005)—Japanese invasion of the Aleutian Islands
*Birmingham, 1963 (Weatherford, 2007)—1963 bombing of Sixteenth Street Baptist Church in Birmingham, Alabama
*Miss Crandall's School for Young Ladies and Little Misses of Color (Alexander & Nelson, 2007)—Prudence Crandall struggles to open and run a school for African American girls in Connecticut in the early 1800s
Song of the Sparrow (Sandell, 2008)—a feminist retelling of the "Lady of Shallott"

Sweetgrass Basket (Carvell, 2005)—two sisters from the Mohawk tribe are sent to the Carlisle Indian School in the early 1900s
Good Masters! Sweet Ladies! Voices from a Medieval Village (Schlitz, 2007)

Verse Novel Biographical Portraits

Clemente! (Perdomo & Collier, 2010)
Emma's Poem: The Voice of the Statue of Liberty (Glaser & Nivola, 2010)
Black Jack: The Ballad of Jack Johnson (Smith & Evans, 2010)
A River of Words: The Story of William Carlos Williams (Bryant & Sweet, 2008)
Borrowed Names: Poems about Laura Ingalls Wilder, Madam C. J. Walker, Marie Curie, and Their Daughters (Atkins, 2010)
The Dreamer (Ryan & Sis, 2010)
Your Own, Sylvia (Hemphill, 2007)
Becoming Billie Holliday (Weatherford, 2008)
Twelve Rounds to Glory: The Story of Muhammad Ali (C. Smith, 2007)
Carver: A Life in Poems (M. Nelson, 2001)
I Heard God Talking to Me: William Edmondson and His Stone Carvings (Spires, 2009)
Diego: Bigger Than Life (Bernier-Grand & Diaz, 2009)
Frida: Viva La Vida! Long Live Life! (Bernier-Grand, 2007)
Fortune's Bones: The Manumission Requiem (M. Nelson, 2004)

Companion Titles for War-Themed Unit

Vietnam War
Fallen Angels (Myers, 1988/2008)
Patrol: An American Soldier in Vietnam (Myers, 2002)—picture book for older readers
Kaleidoscope Eyes (Bryant, 2009)—verse novel
Almost Forever (Testa, 2003)—verse novel
Shooting the Moon (Dowell, 2008)

War with Afghanistan/Iraq
Sunrise over Fallujah (Myers, 2009)
Baghdad Burning: Girl Blog from Iraq (Riverbend, 2005)
Purple Heart (McCormick, 2009)
The Breadwinner (D. Ellis, 2001)—also see the sequels, *Parvana's Journey* and *Mud City*

The Kite Runner (Hosseini, 2007); *A Thousand Splendid Suns* (Hosseini, 2008)
Pride of Baghdad (Vaughan & Henrichon, 2006)—graphic novel

Living under Occupation or Oppression
Persepolis: Story of a Childhood (Satrapi, 2004)—graphic novel
Real Time (Kass, 2006)
A Little Piece of Ground (Laird & Nimr, 2006)—see also *Habibi,* by Naomi Shihab
    Nye (1999)
**Samir and Yonatan* (Carmi, 2002)
How I Live Now (Rosoff, 2006)
When My Name Was Keoko (Park, 2002)
Before We Were Free (Alvarez, 2002)

World War II
**I Had Seen Castles* (Rylant, 1993/2004)
**A Boy at War: A Novel of Pearl Harbor* (Mazer, 2002)
Postcards from No Man's Land (Chambers, 2004)
The Book Thief (Zusak, 2006)
What I Saw and How I Lied (Blundell, 2009)
Flygirl (S. Smith, 2009)
Ten Cents a Dance (Fletcher, 2008)
Tamar: A Novel of Espionage, Passion, and Betrayal (Peet, 2008)
Maus: A Survivor's Tale; Vol. 1: My Father Bleeds History (Spiegelman, 1973/1986)
    —graphic novel

War Refugees
**Home of the Brave* (Applegate, 2008)—verse novel
Over a Thousand Hills I Walk with You (Jansen, 2006)
Children of War: Voices of Iraqi Refugees (Ellis, 2009)
Refugees (Stine, 2006)
**Mud City* (D. Ellis, 2004)—third book in the Breadwinner trilogy
**Making It Home: Real-Life Stories from Children Forced to Flee* (Naidoo, 2005)

Boy Soldiers
Deogratias: A Tale of Rwanda (Stassen, 2006)—graphic novel
A Long Way Gone: Memoirs of a Boy Soldier (Beah, 2008)—memoir
Notes for a War Story (Gipi, 2007)—graphic novel
Refresh, Refresh (Novgorodoff, Ponsoldt, & Percy, 2009)—graphic novel
Blindspot (Pyle, 2007)—graphic novel

Short Story/Nonfiction Collections

Shattered: Stories of Children and War (Armstrong, 2003)
Zlata's Diary: A Child's Life in Wartime Sarajevo (Filipović, 1994)—memoir
*My Father's Summers: A Daughter's Memoir (Appelt, 2004)
Stolen Voices: Young Peoples' War Diaries, from World War I to Iraq (Filipović & Challenger, 2006)

Teaching the Memoir: Responding to Others through Reader Response

5

A lthough students in high school primarily write expository, argumentative, and analytic essays, they most often read fiction, and as one teacher-researcher has pointed out, "Shouldn't they be reading more of what they're writing?" (Pederson, 2002, p. 59). We agree and would like to see more full-length nonfiction titles integrated into the English language arts curriculum.

Today's nonfiction texts are much different from those we grew up with—black-and-white informational books and pictureless biographies—and are often targeted toward adolescent readers and adults alike as evidenced by literary honors such as the American Library Association's ALEX Award (adult books that would appeal to teenagers), the Robert F. Sibert Award (informational books), and ALA Outstanding Books for the College Bound. The fact that a nonfiction book—Phillip Hoose's powerful *Claudette Colvin: Twice toward Justice*—won the 2009 National Book Award for Young People's Literature shows the interest in and importance of quality nonfiction texts.

Research shows that students' interest in nonfiction begins at around fourth grade and increases during adolescence, and that struggling readers actually prefer nonfiction texts (Carter & Abrahamson, 1990). Nonfiction titles provide students with factual-based accounts of events that they can compare not only to the other texts they are reading in class but also to their own lives.

In this chapter, we focus on one form of nonfiction—the memoir, because it is another genre of young adult literature that we find to be very sophisticated and suitable for skilled and nonskilled readers alike. After describing the memoir and comparing two that we especially like, we define reader-response theory and suggest strategies for its use in differentiated reading instruction with the memoir.

Teaching Memoirs

When we were high school teachers, we often found that disengaged readers connected with memoirs, especially those stories that presented someone overcoming hard times or bad luck. We noticed that the hard-luck-to-success stories like that of "The Three Doctors" (in *We Beat the Street*) resonated more with adolescents than Pip's in *Great Expectations* or Jay Gatsby's in *The Great Gatsby*. It is because of this connection that students turn to memoirs.

Milner and Milner (2003) suggest that autobiographical writing can "take us into the lives of others but at a closer, more intimate range," making us "eyewitnesses to actual events" (p. 252). Milner and Milner further assert that works like memoirs often catch adolescents' natural interest about the lives of others. Memoirs differ from autobiographies in that "unlike autobiography, which moves in a dutiful line from birth to fame, omitting nothing significant, memoir assumes the life and ignores most of it. The writer of a memoir takes us back to a corner of his or her life that was unusually vivid or intense" (Zinsser, 1987, p. 13, cited in Milner & Milner, 2003). Both of the memoirs we feature in this chapter indeed take us back to some vivid, intense corners in the writers' lives.

In addition, as Dawn and Dan Kirby (2010) explain in a recent *English Journal* article, well-crafted memoir

> [derives its] power not from narcissistic recounting or triviality, nor from a text version of reality television, but rather from the honest unfolding of human struggles and triumphs from which important lessons are learned, significant family events are preserved, and generations of family members braid the cord of their lived experiences. (p. 23)

Both of the memoirs we describe in this chapter present "honest unfoldings of human struggles and triumphs" and depict authors learning important lessons.

While both books would appeal to male and female students, we purposely selected one from each perspective. Because there are many thematic ties between the two titles, this gives teachers the option to read one or both as whole-class titles; assign titles according to gender; or have students read the book(s) in literature circles (either along with another title as a whole-class read or in stand-alone literature circles in a memoir or autobiographical writing unit). In *Jesus Land*, Julia Scheeres (2005) takes readers on a present-tense journey through her turbulent teenage years, a time that still profoundly affects her; in *Hole in My Life*, Jack Gantos (2002), author of the popular Joey Pizga series, recounts how he went from being accepted to the University of Florida to serving time in a federal penitentiary. In Figure 5.1, we present side-by-side glimpses of both titles and show how they match up with Jago's criteria for whole-class teaching.

In what follows we define reader-response theory and suggest strategies for its use in differentiated reading instruction of *Jesus Land* and *Hole in My Life*.

Defining Reader-Response Theory

Louise Rosenblatt advanced reader-response theory as a challenge to New Critical approaches to reading instruction. New Criticism emphasizes the text-as-sole-authority and a curricular style that can position students and their views as unimportant to the meaning-making process (Probst, 2004). (See Figure 6.2 in Chapter 6 for an overview of New Critical, reader-response, and critical literacy reading theories.) In New Criticism, the text is the authority on meaning, and if readers are diligent enough in their textual analysis, the text will unlock its secrets and "right answers." Unnecessary to this process are the readers—their prior knowledge, their past experiences, how they view the world and others. These things don't matter to the reading process in the New Critical classroom, where teachers focus on helping students locate such literary elements as plot, setting, and character to better understand themes.

Faust (2000) uses the "courtroom metaphor" to describe New Critical classrooms, where "literary texts bear witness to hidden meanings" and students and their academic knowledge are "put on the stand" (p. 19). Faust goes on to say that New Criticism approaches to literature instruction more often than not teach students to devalue and distrust their responses to literature.

In contrast, Rosenblatt viewed reading as an interaction, or transaction—a "two-way process" (1982, p. 268), between the reader and the text through which meaning occurs. Rosenblatt wrote in her landmark book, *The Reader, the Text, the Poem*, that "built into the literary process itself is the particular world of the reader" (1978/1994, p. 11). According to Rosenblatt, any response or reaction to literature comes from the unique, individual connection between the reader and the text: "Meaning is the product of a transaction between active minds and the words on the page—it does not reside in the ink, to be ferreted out, unearthed, uncovered. Rather, it is created, formed, shaped, by readers in the act of reading, and thus it is *their* meaning" (Probst, 1988, p. 34).

These personal meanings and connections to texts are important for all readers: reading researchers have shown that when students can generate personal responses to texts, their memory and comprehension of literary works improve. These effects in turn lead to higher intrinsic motivation to read and higher reading comprehension performance (Guthrie & Humenick, 2004).

	Jesus Land by Julia Scheeres 2006 ALA Alex Award winner	*Hole in My Life* by Jack Gantos 2003 ALA Printz Award winner 2003 Sibert Informational Book Award
Summary	In the mid 1980s, Julia and her family, including two adopted black brothers (David and Jerome), are living in rural Indiana. The children are raised by aloof and unkind parents—a nurse mother and doctor father—and Julia's troubles, including being molested by Jerome, go unnoticed. When Julia and David can't "fit in" the family, they are sent to a religious reform school in the Dominican Republic, where they endure "Christian" abuse.	In the early 1970s, Jack Gantos was a teenager living on his own; while his family was in Puerto Rico, he was in south Florida going to high school, working, and hanging out. Instead of going to college after being admitted, Jack took a different road and got caught up in transporting and selling drugs. He was eventually arrested and spent time in federal prison for drug dealing. The memoir recounts these troubled years.
Criterion 1: *Written in language perfectly suited to the author's purpose*	Scheeres has an amazing ability with language. Writing about topics that are painful and disturbing, she never glosses over the events that took place in her life. Instead, she describes them in such a way that readers are aware of how she tried to remove herself emotionally from the situations she faced. Julia disturbs us, makes us see the significance of her experiences without asking for pity. Describing being raped by her brother Jerome, she writes: "I hear him lock the door and creep toward my bed. The mattress tilts under his weight. By the time he touches me, I'm far away. I breathe deeply, pretending to be asleep, falling through layers of numbness, sensation draining from my body like dirty bath water. My mind flits through a collage of images and thoughts—a horse galloping across a field of clover, the conjugation of *to be* in French, the marigolds on Deb's table" (p. 78).	Gantos writes in a way that readers, especially teenage male readers, will understand and appreciate. His language is clear, yet lyrical with abundant use of descriptive similes—and his descriptions of his life in prison have the power to "scare straight" anyone who thinks that the criminal life is anything but demoralizing and dangerous. "'Are you funny?' I wasn't feeling funny. 'What do you mean?' 'You know, like funny. Like do you do it with guys?' Now I knew I wasn't funny. 'No,' I said. 'No.' 'But you're young,' he said. 'You can still learn. I can be your master.' 'I don't need a master,' I said. 'Believe me, you do,' he said. 'You can either be my booty-boy and I'll protect you, or all these other dudes will take turns making you a mama.' 'Go away,' I said. My fear was so great I couldn't endure another moment of the conversation. 'You'll see,' he said. 'You got a tax on your ass and you'll have to pay up'" (p. 151).
Criterion 2: *Exposes readers to complex human dilemmas*	This book does nothing if not expose the reader to complex human dilemmas: religion, racism, incest, rape, sexuality, and human relationships. Julia is the sister of two black brothers and the "favored" white daughter. Her brothers are treated unfairly by their peers and by their own parents. Julia craves a loving relationship with her parents, but she also hates them for their neglect and physical abuse. She also hates their hypocrisy: she loves David but resents how he negatively impacts her popularity at school.	From the first line, where Gantos talks about the prison picture that makes the cover of the book, to the very end, where he debates digging up the drugs, the entire memoir is a series of choices and dilemmas over a two-year period. If you were living on your own, how would you live? If you were accepted into college, would you give it all up to "hang out"? How tempting is it to make quick money by selling drugs? How would you keep yourself safe and alive in prison? These are all dilemmas readers can explore.
Criterion 3: *Includes compelling, disconcerting characters*	The character development in *Jesus Land* is so skillful that a few pages into the book you feel you could recognize the characters if you met them on the street. "She's in one of her moods. . . . She was in the kitchen, ripping coupons from the newspaper, her lips smashed into a hard little line. She didn't say hello and neither did we. We took one look at her and went downstairs; it's best to fall under the radar when she gets like this" (p. 16). Even the minor characters are compelling and disturbing. Scott, Julia's boyfriend, begins as an attempted gang rapist, then becomes someone who dates her just for sex, but later professes his love and wants to marry her. These changes and contradictions make the characters very real.	Jack is a compelling character, and the reality of his story should interest readers. The people he meets over the duration of the memoir are also disconcerting in their own ways. Rik is an enticing and romantic ideal (even if he is a criminal) to the lost Gantos. Hamilton is part pirate, part cranky old man, part lunatic, and he keeps Gantos on edge throughout the journey on the boat. And these are just two characters the reader meets *before* Gantos goes to prison! We don't get the full character development of his fellow prisoners, but this vagueness actually characterizes them more because readers are left to imagine what they look like and the horrible acts they commit against each other. *continued on next page*

FIGURE 5.1. Reviews of *Jesus Land* by Julia Scheeres (in Scherff et al., 2008) and *Hole in My Life* by Jack Gantos, based on Carol Jago's criteria for selecting a whole-class novel. The review of Scheeres appears in "Teaching the Memoir in English Class: Taking Students to *Jesus Land*," by L. Scherff et al., 2008, *ALAN Review, 35*(3).

FIGURE 5.1. Continued

Criterion 4: Explores universal themes that combine different periods and cultures	Jesus Land presents a different time period for readers, and for some the religious culture will be different, too. Its themes are ageless and universal. Cultural differences, religious struggles, bigotry, and hypocrisy are all as current as they were when Julia lived through them.	The themes in Hole in My Life are universal. Temptation, right versus wrong, justice versus injustice, self-doubt, blaming others—all of these thread their way throughout the memoir.
Criterion 5: Challenges readers to reexamine their beliefs	Throughout the book, readers are challenged to reexamine their beliefs, values, and morals. Scheeres does not hold back her feelings on her church, "religious" parents, and the leaders of the religious reform school; organized religion is portrayed in a negative and hypocritical light. Julia's parents give the appearance of sanctity, yet they emotionally and physically abuse their children. Escuela Caribe more closely resembles a prison camp than a Christian reform school. Students who break the rules don't get to eat. Punishments include hauling rocks up and down hills. Shortly after her arrival, Julia witnesses a forced boxing match between the dean of students and a small boy. "This can't be real. I glance at Susan, but her sorrowful eyes are pinched shut.…Ted jogs a half step back, then swings his glove, hitting Boy 0 squarely in the jaw.…I don't bend my head or close my eyes while Ted prays. I stare at him in shock" (pp. 204–205).	Readers will have their beliefs challenged. Teens will see how Jack's wandering—in his eyes it was more significant than going to high school, college, or working—ended up causing him problems. Students will also understand the consequences of bad decisions and that bad things happen to good people. Some mistakes can't be undone, and some students might see themselves in Gantos. "Lucas was curled up like a shrimp with a blanket.…[H]e was naked…he had been raped, and when he finished telling me what happened…I didn't know what to say.…I was eager to get away from him. I was beginning to fill up with fear and wanted to put some distance between us. It was the fear of being next in line. I had that terror people must have had during the war, when they denied they were Jews or Gypsies or homosexuals as the Nazis dragged off their families and friends. At that moment I hated myself" (p. 153).
Criterion 6: Tells a good story with places for laughing and crying	This last criterion is met, despite the book's bleakness. One of Lisa's students wrote in her review of the book: "This last criteria is my favorite.…[I]n Jesus Land, the moment when brother and sister leave the camp for the first time is the funniest because they both started spouting more profanity than they had ever used in their lives—words like 'papaya ass' made me laugh." Julia's wit and sarcasm are what save her. Referring to one student who left the school because she had an affair with a preacher and got pregnant, Julia writes, "Secretly, I admire Rhonda's craftiness. Not only did she manage to get laid, she also escaped The Program" (p. 282). Another one of Lisa's students, however, didn't outright laugh, but rather found poignant moments and places for crying—Julia's rapes, the mistreatment at Escuela Caribe, David and Jerome's physical abuse, and David's death. To quote her directly, "Even the beautiful moments, though, were clouded by a feeling that this cannot last.…[T]he whole tone of the book was such that doom seemed imminent at all times. That being said, there were moments that were humorous.…The most memorable was when the Sunday School teacher tells their class that they can't 'jack off with Jesus.' Moments like this are plentiful, and make you shake your head."	To be honest, there are not many places for laughing, but plenty for crying—at least on the inside. Mostly, there is the feeling of fear that Gantos faces, and that feeling is felt by readers, too. There are some light moments, though, because Gantos has an ability to paint a vivid, amusing picture. For example, there is his initial description of checking in to the King's Court motel, where he lives for a brief period. "I rang the buzzer, and an old woman with brown wrinkled skin like a well-used pirate map opened the door and flicked a cigarette butt over my head. 'Does the name Davy Crockett mean anything to you?' she asked. 'Yeah, he was king of the wild frontier,' I said, quoting the theme song from the TV show. 'Well he was the king of the frontier,' she said, then, pointing at her chest, added, 'and I'm the queen of King's Court. I'm Davy Crockett the fourth, his great-great-granddaughter.' 'Great,' I said, thinking she looked old enough to be his daughter, but I liked her right off because she was the opposite of what I had just left" (pp. 16–17).

Students' personal responses, and thus multiple meanings and interpretations, are possible in the reader-response classroom, but this does not mean that students can engage in interpretative free-for-all, with any and every response accepted. Reader response begins with students' personal associations with a text—which are evoked as students read and consider the text. These associations in turn serve as points of entry into the text—and not as the last word. Readers are still responsible, not for "proving" their interpretation as correct or incorrect based on textual evidence, but instead to account for the associations the text evokes for them, consider the reasons why such associations are evoked, and reflect upon differences based on their own and others' ways of reading the same texts (Athanases, 1998).

Teachers sometimes misinterpret Rosenblatt, however, and fail to get students beyond their personal associations with texts. Teachers might ask students vague questions such as, "How did you like this book?" and "What character was your favorite?" but they might not help students go beyond these questions to consider why some texts resonate with our experiences while others don't, and how authors encourage us to have certain kinds of responses toward characters and events. As Deborah Appleman claims, "Meaning is a result of a kind of negotiation between authorial intent and the readers' response. It is not simply the question, 'What does this mean to me?'" (2000, pp. 28–29). In what follows, we share a strategy that can help teachers get students beyond too-simple "likes" and "dislikes" of texts.

Reader-Response Activities with Memoir

There are many ways that teachers could incorporate *Jesus Land* and *Hole in My Life* into classroom instruction through reader response. While we advocate both novels as worthy of whole-class reading, by letting students choose which title to read or by assigning a particular book according to students' readiness, teachers can vary the *content*. The activities we present next provide options for varying the instructional *process* and *products* that students generate.

Dialogue with a Text

In a 1988 *English Journal* article, Robert Probst presented the strategy "dialogue with a text" as a way for students to transact with a text the way Rosenblatt originally intended and to avoid classroom discussions that remained at the surface level (e.g., Did you like the book? Who is your favorite character?). This strategy was meant to help students move from personal associations with a text to consideration of one's own and others' associations with the text. Rosenblatt has suggested several guidelines that support reader-response-based activities like "dialogue with a text:"

- Students must have opportunities to consider and share their personal reactions to texts. Students can do this through journal writing as they read or small-group discussions.

- Students need time to consider the personal implications of stories on their own lives. In other words, with what concrete events and experiences in students' lives do the stories resonate? Teachers must provide opportunities for students to articulate these.

- Teachers should find points of contact among the opinions of students. Who believes one thing, and who another? And why?

- Teachers should capitalize on students' points of interest and engagement with stories to make connections between literature and lived experience. (Probst, 1988, p. 34).

When teachers are operating by such guidelines, then "dialogue with a text" can occur. To facilitate the dialogue, teachers can pose questions that range from the generation of first reactions, feelings, and perceptions to questions that encourage students to consider others' reactions and perceptions. These questions include, but are not limited to, those presented in Figure 5.2 (see Probst [1988] for all questions).

Teachers can differentiate this process for students by limiting the number of questions they ask or by encouraging less-skilled or less-confident readers to articulate personal responses to the text while encouraging more sophisticated readers to consider their patterns of response, how they responded to the text (e.g., emotionally, intellectually), or authorial intent or purpose. We recommend

First reaction	What is your first reaction or response to the text?
Feelings/emotions	What feelings did the text awaken in you? What emotions did you feel as you read the text?
Perceptions	What did you see happening in the book?
Associations	What memories does the text call to mind?
Thoughts, ideas	What idea or thought is suggested by the text?
Judgments of importance	What is the most important word in the text?
Author	What sort of person do you imagine the author of this text to be?
Patterns of response	How did you respond to the text?
Other readings	How did your reading differ from that of your discussion partner?
Evolution of your reading	How did your understanding of the text or your feelings about it change as you talked?

FIGURE 5.2. Questions that encourage students to "dialogue with a text." Adapted from "Dialogue with a Text," R. E. Probst, 1988, *English Journal, 77*(1), pp. 35–36.

having students answer these questions individually and then share responses in small groups of two or three members. Then the teacher can facilitate whole-class discussion about students' responses. Next we share how one of Lisa's students, Tracy Windle, responded to some of these questions based on pages 115–165 in *Jesus Land*:

1. What is your first reaction or response to the text? Describe it briefly.

As I read this section, I wondered how Julia's parents could ever justify themselves as parents. Her mother obviously ruled the household and her father, who had an explosive temper, did whatever punishment the mother deemed fit. Her parents considered themselves to be religious but never practiced what they preached. They were not very in tuned to their family but were always worried about what people at their church thought.

The way in which Julia describes her parent's house is just as dismal as she felt. To me, she truly hated her home, parents, and her environment. She describes the physical aspects of the house as being cold and stark, and how she froze at night waiting for Scott to come to her room because her mother would not turn the thermostat to a warmer temperature. As I was reading, I felt like Julia was always looking to be loved or emotionally connecting with someone such as Scott. Her only ally growing up was her brother David, who took the brunt of her parents' abuse. I wondered why teachers or people from her church did not investigate the situation more closely, or did her parents do such a good job to cover up the darkness in the house such as the abuse? I also thought that Julia is so scarred by her older brother Jerome raping her, that she is looking for other means as consolation. She uses her sexual encounters with Scott as a means of pushing out the memories and the disgust of Jerome. I felt that her parents are total jackasses who should never have become parents. But the sickest part of it all is that they use the name of "religion" as the justification for emotionally and physically abusing their children.

2. What did you see happening in the book? Retell the major events briefly.

To me, as the chapters progressed, her parents, especially the mother, became more agitated. It was like something dramatic was going to happen, especially to David. And, I feel that her parents were looking for something, anything minor to send him away. Her parents wanted the attention and the glory that they were these good Christian people who took the poor black boy in and gave him a home. But, little did everyone know, what really went on behind closed doors. After David was sent away, it almost seemed to me, that Julia got sloppy about not being caught with Scott in her room. It seemed as if the life was sucked out of her, even more so after she was raped by her brother. Her parents wanted to be rid of their children and obviously so; the older ones fled as soon as they were old enough to hold down a job and take care of themselves.

A major event in the book was when Julia decided to have sex with Scott. Even though she knew that Jerome had already taken her virginity from her, it was her choice to let Scott become her sexual partner. In this event, it saddened me because she was searching to belong and be loved by someone and Scott basically just laughed at her. I don't think that it mentioned this, but I got the picture that Julia just gave up on emotional support by people in her life that were supposed to love her. So, she just decided to get any love that she could in any way that she could.

3. What is the most important phrase in the text?

"If my father wanted to choke me over a forgotten milkshake, what would he do to me for losing my virginity?"

This to me is the most important phrase in the text because it tells you a lot about Julia and the relationship with her father. I think that Julia's father is a religious fanatic jackass. I think, though, that the statement is meant to be sarcastic, but not really. I think that her father would have really abused her or killed her; ultimately, he sent her away, but it tells readers that he exploded over stupid stuff that he considered to be materialistic, like blaming Julia's behavior before she was sent to the Dominican Republic on the *Glamour* magazine her sister, Debra, gave her.

4. How did your reading of the text differ from that of your group members? In what ways were they similar?

The main way that I differed from my group was that when I read a book, I imagine myself as the character in the book. And, I have to say that imagining myself as Julia Scheeres has been one of the most difficult characters I have ever tried to be. I tried to put myself into her shoes to experience her life that was so completely different from my own.

5. How did your understanding of the chapters or your feelings about it change after your small-group discussion?

The discussions of my group justified the feelings that I already had about the book. One of the things that we discussed is the irony of the title. "Jesus Land" is a positive connotation and just seeing and hearing "Jesus" brings about a sense of calm and serenity for people. But, as Julia Scheeres quickly brings to light, it is a negative connotation for her. Another aspect of these pages that our group discussed was the idea that her mother loved her stupid dog, Lecke, more than she loved her children and is probably the reason why Julia was arrested, sent to juvenile hall, and then sent to the Dominican Republic. How ironic is that?

By moving from overall personal reactions to a retelling to selecting a particular aspect (the quote), and then moving to comparing her responses with her group members, Tracy was required to transact with the text at several levels. Tracy realized something about herself as a reader—that she imagines herself as the characters she reads about, even when that character is a real-life person like Julia Scheeres. It also seems that with more time to develop their thoughts and ideas, this group might have some interesting things to say about the author's use of irony in the story. We think this proves our point: when students are given support to consider personal associations with text and then move beyond those associations, they will get to sophisticated understandings of text, sometimes without us. Isn't that our goal as English teachers?

Learning Contracts

In her book *The Differentiated Classroom* (1999), Carol Tomlinson writes about the opportunities that learning contracts provide: students work independently on material that is essentially teacher-centered. A learning contract is a negotiated agreement between teachers and their students. Teachers predetermine the skills, tasks, and understandings they would like students to reach, and students are given choices in how to accomplish them. Tomlinson points out at least three beneficial aspects of learning contracts: (1) they assume students can take on some of the responsibility for learning themselves; (2) they set positive consequences; and (3) they establish criteria for successful completion and quality of work. So, even when the whole class reads the same text, students are given options for completing activities individually, based on interest and ability. We offer two examples of learning contracts next: Tic-Tac-Toe and the Bloom's Taxonomy Project.

Tic-Tac-Toe

One option with reader-response questions is to include them as part of a student's learning contract. Our next example, Figure 5.3, pulls reader-response questions (Myers, 1988) and places them in a standard tic-tac-toe (3×3) grid. Students could be directed to answer questions vertically, horizontally, or diago-

Learning Contract

Directions: Your task is to answer three questions of your choice. Like the game tic-tac-toe, you can answer vertically (up and down), horizontally (side to side), or diagonally (slanted). Read over all of the choices first before deciding which direction you want to go.

How are you like a person in this memoir? Explain with specific examples.	Who are your favorite person and least favorite person in the book? Why?	If you could interview any person in this book, who would it be? Why? List 5 questions you would ask him or her.
Do you think the title of the book fits the story? Why or why not?	Why do you think the author chose to title the book this way? Explain what you think the meaning of the title is.	What do you think the overall message of the book is? In other words, why do you think the author wrote it?
On a scale of 1–10, rate this book. Provide at least three reasons why you gave it the score you did.	What do you feel is the most important word, phrase, passage, or paragraph in this book? Explain why it is important.	If you were an English teacher, would you teach this book to your class? Why or why not?

FIGURE 5.3. Learning contract with reader-response questions. Adapted from "Twenty (Better) Questions," K. L. Myers, 1988, *English Journal, 77*(1), p. 65.

nally according to their readiness and interest in the questions. The questions in the top row are based on people in the memoir; the middle row focuses on the memoir as a whole; the bottom row is more evaluative. The questions could be revised and adapted as students progress through the memoir and at the end as a summative response.

Using the learning contract in Figure 5.3, a student who is not as comfortable with inferential/thematic questions (middle horizontal row) could choose to answer questions from the top or bottom row. Or a teacher working with this student to scaffold and challenge his or her thinking could assign the questions in the left column to provide some level of inferential thinking while not making the task too difficult.

Bloom's Taxonomy Project

In his research, Benjamin Bloom (1956) found that very few questions teachers ask in their instruction call for higher-order thinking (synthesis, evaluation) but instead focus more on simple recall (knowledge, comprehension). Bloom's levels and their accompanying tasks (verbs) can be used by teachers as a guide to plan differentiated reading instruction. Over the years we have adapted a project, shared by a former colleague, that is based on literary works or time periods using Bloom's taxonomy. More recently, Lisa adapted the project guidelines based on a revision of Bloom's original taxonomy by Anderson and Krathwohl (2001). The following charts show some of the terms associated with Bloom's 1956 taxonomy (Figure 5.4) versus the new taxonomy (Figure 5.5).

The key for teachers in creating a learning contract based on the revised Bloom's taxonomy is to (1) use the taxonomy's verbs correctly, (2) create tasks that fall under each level appropriately, and (3) provide students with enough equal choices so that all can succeed. Students, alone or in small groups, contract with the teacher to complete one task at each level. The project works well because it involves student choice and takes students from lower to higher levels of thinking. Moreover, the project follows Rosenblatt's (in Probst, 1988) four reader-response guidelines. An example of a revised Bloom's learning contract to use with Gantos's *Hole in My Life* is presented in Figure 5.6.

Extension Project

The reader-response assignment shown in Figure 5.7 is one that Lisa's former students created for *Jesus Land* in her young adult literature class (see Scherff, et al., 2008). Lisa's former students now assign the project in their AP literature classes, either for individual or group work. We include it here because it shows another way that reader response can be meaningfully employed in the high school English classroom with the memoir.

Knowledge	define, label, list, memorize, name, order, recognize, state, recall, repeat
Comprehension	classify, describe, discuss, explain, identify, locate, restate, summarize
Application	apply, demonstrate, dramatize, employ, illustrate, interpret, sketch, solve
Analysis	analyze, categorize, compare, contrast, differentiate, distinguish, question
Synthesis	arrange, collect, compose, create, design, develop, formulate, organize
Evaluation	appraise, argue, choose, defend, judge, predict, rate, select, support, evaluate

FIGURE 5.4. Bloom's taxonomy.

Remembering	Retrieving, recognizing, and recalling relevant knowledge from long-term memory
Understanding	Constructing meaning from oral, written, and graphic messages through interpreting, exemplifying, classifying, summarizing, inferring, comparing, and explaining
Applying	Carrying out or using a procedure through executing or implementing
Analyzing	Breaking material into constituent parts, determining how the parts relate to one another and to an overall structure or purpose through differentiating, organizing, and attributing
Evaluating	Marking judgments based on criteria and standards through checking and critiquing
Creating	Putting elements together to form a coherent or functional whole; reorganizing elements into a new pattern or structure through generating, planning, or producing

FIGURE 5.5. Revised Bloom's taxonomy. L. W. Anderson and D. R. Krathwohl (Eds.), 2001. *A Taxonomy for Learning, Teaching, and Assessing: A Revision of Bloom's Taxonomy of Educational Objectives*, New York: Longman.

Name: _____   Due Date:_____

Working alone or with one, two, or three other people, create a study unit on the novel *Hole in My Life*.

1. Following is a set of six categories with choices within each (the "applying" category does not offer choices). Your group must agree to complete one item in each category, including the "applying" category.
2. Once you have decided on the activity within each section, submit your list to the teacher.
3. Some class time will be used to work on this project; however, if you need additional time, that is your individual responsibility.
4. Primary resource: Novel. The school library or home library may also be used. All references must be documented in a bibliography (MLA format).

Complete one activity of your choice from each category, as well as the entire "applying" category.

Remembering

1. On a timeline, plot out the events in *Hole in My Life* from beginning to end. (*Note:* There might be flashbacks or events out of order in the novel.)
2. List the major characters and provide a short description of them and their role in Jack's story (life).
3. Rename each chapter according to what you think is the most important element (plot, mood, theme, etc.) of the section. Include at least two sentences explaining your choice of title.

Understanding

1. Explain and discuss the relationship between each chapter title and the action in that chapter.
2. Why do you think Gantos chooses to use curse words in the book? Explain their impact and how they influence your reading of the book.
3. Gantos opens the book with a quote from Oscar Wilde: "I have learned this: it is not what one does that is wrong, but what one becomes as a consequence of it." How does this quote relate to the memoir? Use examples from the book in your response.

Applying

Choose a person, symbol, or theme from the memoir and explain the who, what, where, when, and why about this item in a classroom exhibit. Each exhibit should prominently display a sign to identify which person, symbol, or theme is represented in the display. Each exhibit must contain a written explanation to introduce the importance of your person, symbol, or theme. Each explanation should be one or two typed paragraphs arranged attractively on a display board or somehow attached to the display. These explanations should contain at least one of the following devices to showcase your investigations: books, dioramas, mobiles, papier-mâché, scrolls, patchwork quilt squares, pop-up books, matchbooks, pyramids, music, charts and tables, collages, annotated maps, replicas of art and artifacts, or computer-generated displays.

continued on next page

FIGURE 5.6. An example of a revised version of Bloom's learning contract to use with *Hole in My Life* by Jack Gantos.

FIGURE 5.6. Continued

Analyzing

1. Gantos refers multiple times to novels (such as *On the Road*) and characters in novels throughout his book. Choose three such references and analyze the action or the character's thoughts, feelings, and behaviors against *Hole in My Life* or a character in this literary work.

2. What evidence and examples can you find that depict the culture of this 1970s memoir as mirroring our present-day cultural beliefs and practices? Create a Venn diagram illustrating your results.

3. Gantos divides his memoir into three parts; your task is to figure out why. Compare and contrast the three parts using whatever method you choose. You can use a triple Venn diagram to present your findings.

Evaluating

1. Do you think Jack's two-year (and 150-day) prison sentence was fair? Imagine you are a judge in court, and Jack's case is brought to you. How do you rule and why?

2. A major theme in the novel is communication—letters, Jack's journals, reading, the graffiti on the walls. Why do you think communication is so important to Jack? Be sure to provide evidence from the book.

3. Write a book review of *Hole in My Life*, imagining that your audience is a group of teenagers. You might want to look at examples of book reviews in the newspaper or magazines like *People*.

Creating

1. Imagine that you find Jack's prison journal/novel. Create three diary entries writing from his perspective.

2. Write a three-paragraph newspaper article as if you were a reporter writing about Jack and his fellow drug smugglers getting caught.

3. Write, perform, and videotape a piece of performance poetry imagining you are Jack Gantos, making a social commentary on today's youth and the pressures and effects of society on him.

Suggestions:

1. Keep plans and other work in the folder so others can use your research if you are absent.

2. Use all resources and materials creatively.

3. Remember this is a group project. You will be evaluated on the final product no matter who does "the most work."

Reader Response: Option 1

Read the following information taken from the Escuela Caribe promotional materials. After reading the chapters in *Jesus Land* that detail the students' experiences at the school, create a brochure (or promotional guide, poster, etc.) of your own, using an ironic tone, advertising the school's negative aspects.

Do you have an adolescent who ...
Rejects your family's Christian values?
Is out of control?
Has a low self-image?
Is irresponsible, showing lack of character?
Runs with a negative crowd or has no friends?
Is unmotivated and failing in school?
Is disrespectful, rejecting your love and others?
New Horizons Youth Ministries can help.

Concept
Why in the Dominican Republic? Three reasons: atmosphere, culture shock, and distance.

Atmosphere
Escuela Caribe is set far away from the pervasive influences of American society; the materialism, the social ills, the negative peers, and the struggles in one's family.

Culture Shock
A change in climate, racial differences, geographic surroundings, friends, daily routine, and language all make adolescents remarkably more dependent upon others for direction. This also renders them more malleable....

Distance
Living in a structured environment, teens start to appreciate Mom and Dad and begin to share their parents' dream of a united family again.

Reader Response: Option 2

Each member of the family lives in his or her own special world. In Chapter 6, Julia is sleeping with Scott, her mother is alone in the kitchen, her father is relaxing in his Porsche, and David is languishing in the basement. Write a monologue for each of the characters to describe their thoughts at this point in the narrative. Compare your monologues with other students' responses. Choose your best monologue and combine it with those from classmates to perform a readers theater presentation of the Scheeres's household.

Reader Response: Option 3

What is most damaging to the family is what they do not say to each other rather than what they do talk about. Find a scene in the novel that you feel is the most important missed opportunity for communication between the characters. Rewrite the dialogue to include what the characters should have said to each other. Write in Julia's style and stay true to the characters.

Reader-Response Extra Credit Option

Identify specific scenes in the novel and comment upon how the author's style shapes the reader's perception about the events. Email the author with particular questions that will serve to clarify the narrative, especially pertaining to her writing style.

FIGURE 5.7. Sample reader-response project for *Jesus Land* by Julia Scheeres.

Differentiating for Cultural Difference: Moving from Reader Response to Critical Literacy with Multicultural YA Literature

6

We talk a lot about difference in this book. Indeed, differentiated reading instruction is based on the idea that acknowledging students' learning differences and their varied interests is an important element motivating student engagement and academic achievement. But thus far, while we have written about addressing differences in reading ability, we have not taken into account the fact that students' reading abilities are intimately tied to the diverse social and cultural worlds in which they and their families live. Reading researchers suggest these worlds—and the diverse cultural, linguistic, and economic experiences and practices that constitute them—affect how students understand and respond to literary works, as well as how they participate in the high school English classroom (Au & Kaomea, 2008; Beach, Thein, & Parks, 2007; Compton-Lilly, 2009; Dressel, 2003; McNair, 2003). These researchers suggest teachers find ways to bridge students' diverse home and community worlds with school tasks so students see such tasks as relevant, meaningful, and connected to their out-of-school identities.

One thing that seems to bridge students' diverse sociocultural practices with reading achievement is *reading engagement*, which includes a student's motivation to read and beliefs about reading (Guthrie, Rueda, Gambrell, & Morrison, 2009). A known principle of classroom instruction for reading engagement is using texts that students find relevant to their lives, experiences, and interests. When students read texts that call on their background knowledge and connect to concrete experiences, they can generate a personal response to the text (Lee, 2001; Rosenblatt, 1995). Extensive research reviews and surveys on motivation to read (see Ivey & Broaddus, 2001) also affirm the importance of a wide range of interesting texts to students' motivation to read.

Connecting high school readers to relevant, interesting texts requires teachers learn about the multiple cultures of students in their classrooms; students' diverse linguistic, economic, and academic needs, and the larger community in which their school is positioned. In the differentiated-for-diversity high school

English classroom, this knowledge should inform teachers' selection of texts and literary works for classroom study, and thus multiple cultural and literary traditions should be represented. Lee (2001) suggests students need exposure to multiple story worlds if they are to develop awareness and tolerance of—as well as strategies for engaging with—unfamiliar story worlds. Other reading researchers suggest high school students need to see themselves in the literary works they read to see school as relevant and important (Mason & Schumm, 2003). Romero and Zancanella (1990) explain that nonwhite students need "to know that authors . . . of substance and value come from their culture" (p. 29).

But too often high school students are asked to identify with characters and life events (as well as authors) that they perceive as unconnected to the worlds they know. High school English teachers continue to teach such works as *The Scarlet Letter, Beowulf,* and Shakespeare plays that students struggle to read because they often lack the background knowledge (and reading skills) needed to navigate the social codes, historical contexts, and esoteric language of such works. Therefore, the results of reading classic texts for many students are difficulty, disengagement, and an inability or refusal to appreciate the works. Many students read classic works only to say they hope they will never have to read them again (Lee, 2001; Spangler, 2009).

As Stallworth, Gibbons, and Fauber (2006) and Applebee (1993) suggest, even the multicultural literature that is predominantly taught in high schools—*To Kill a Mockingbird, Invisible Man, Black Boy, Things Fall Apart*—describes people and events that occurred in the past. Therefore, students reading such works may get the sense that racism and oppression are things of the past as well, or that the racism and oppression some students experience on a daily basis out of school (and in school) are not important or relevant to their teachers or school officials. Stallworth, Gibbons, and Fauber (2006) also explain, "It is troubling that [*Black Boy* and *Invisible Man*] may be the only representative literature about black experiences that students in most high schools will read. It would be similar to having Huck Finn as the single spokesperson for the white experience" (p. 487). Ultimately, a high-quality and balanced literature curriculum is necessary in today's diverse high school English classroom "so that no single story speaks for everyone in a particular group" (p. 487).

Multicultural young adult literature can certainly help add quality, balance, multiple voices, and diverse story worlds to the secondary literature curriculum. But which books? Which authors? In this chapter, we provide some tips for selecting good multicultural YA novels to teach in the high school English classroom. Then we feature Walter Dean Myers's (2000) *Monster*, a Coretta Scott King Award and Michael L. Printz Award winner, as an exemplary multicultural young adult novel and share a strategy for scaffolding students' responses to

Monster from personal response to more critical response, as students consider issues of identity and societal racism.

Selecting Quality Multicultural Young Adult Literature for the High School English Classroom

We turn to several sources when choosing quality young adult literature to feature in our teacher education courses and in our instructional work out in schools. First, Rudine Sims Bishop (1992) makes a distinction among three different types of books that deal with diversity:

1. *Culturally neutral,* or those literary works in which diversity plays a minor, or casual role—it is not the focus of the works, and usually they are "fundamentally about something else" (Bishop, 1992, p. 46).

2. *Culturally generic,* or those literary works that feature multicultural characters but depict white/European American themes, activities, and values. Stover (2000) describes books in this category as "generically American in theme and plot" (p. 103).

3. *Culturally specific,* or those works that "illuminate the experience of growing up a member of a particular nonwhite cultural group" (Bishop, 1992, p. 44). Bishop explains these books are typically written by people of the culture they are depicting.

Bishop (1992) goes on to say that the books in this third category are not "exclusionary," but they have the potential to increase the understanding and appreciation for those not of the culture. Teachers should understand that books in this category also have the potential to increase nonwhite students' affinities to these texts (Willis & Parker, 2009). For this reason, and because we think such *culturally specific* texts also afford much-needed opportunities to interrogate privilege, racism, and issues of power in society with adolescents, we encourage high school English teachers to locate, read, and use culturally specific young adult literature in the classroom. As Willis & Parker (2009) explain, "If students consistently read texts that fail to depict people of color in authentic ways, there is no potential to challenge their own thinking or move toward understanding and appreciating difference" (p. 40). See the resource guide at the end of this chapter for some of our favorite young adult titles that fit into this *culturally specific* category.

A second resource we use in selecting high-quality multicultural young adult literature for use in the high school English classroom is Slapin and Seale's (1992/1998) *Through Indian Eyes: The Native Experience in Books for Children*, which advocates consideration of the following aspects of books when selecting multicultural titles:

- Look for stereotypes—are members of other cultures portrayed as complex individual human beings? Are the cultural details included oversimplified?
- Look for distortions of history—are historical events accurately portrayed from the perspective of individuals who may have different conceptions of the causes and reasons for those events? Are the contributions of members of other cultural groups to the history and culture of this country recognized and valued?
- Look at the representation of the lifestyle—is it treated condescendingly or in a paternalistic fashion, or is it treated with respect?
- Look at the dialogue—are multicultural characters allowed to speak with skill and to be articulate, or do they use stereotypical speech patterns?
- Look at the standards of success—do members of the dominant white/European-American culture appear to know "what is best" for individuals from other cultural backgrounds, or are these individuals portrayed as mature and able to make their own decisions? Are such characters judged against the "norm" of white, middle-class suburban culture?
- Look for any content that might embarrass a young adult from the cultural group being portrayed—are there positive role models provided?
- Look for some indication that the author is qualified to write about the people in the work in an authentic, artful, and truthful way. (pp. 242–265)

Third, we consult the annual Pura Belpré and Coretta Scott King Award lists to stay abreast of high-quality multicultural young adult literature. The Pura Belpré Award, established in 1996, is given by the American Library Association to a Latino/Latina writer whose work best portrays and celebrates the Latino cultural experience in an outstanding work of literature for children and youth. The award is named after Pura Belpré, the first Latina librarian at the New York Public Library. Pura Belpré young adult winners include Julia Alvarez's (2009) *Return to Sender*, Margarita Engle's (2006) *The Poet Slave of Cuba: A Biography of Juan Francisco Manzano*, and Viola Canales's (2005) *The Tequila Worm*.

Founded in 1969, the Coretta Scott King Award is given by the American Library Association to African American authors and illustrators for outstanding inspirational and educational contributions. The award was designed to commemorate the life and works of Dr. Martin Luther King Jr. and to honor Mrs. Coretta Scott King. The purpose of the award is to encourage understanding and appreciation of the culture of all peoples and their contribution to the realization of the American dream. Winning works must be written by an African American in the United States and portray some aspect of the African American experience, past, present, or future. Coretta Scott King young adult award winners include Sharon Draper's (2008) *November Blues*; Julius Lester's (2005) *Day of Tears,* and Angela Johnson's (2003) *The First Part Last.*

In this chapter we feature a former Coretta Scott King Honor Book and Michael L. Printz Award winner, *Monster,* by Walter Dean Myers (2000). We consider this text *culturally specific,* as Myers is an African American man who grew up in Harlem. Myers has explained that writing books that feature people of color and places where people of color live is important to him because he wants these people and places to be valued. He states:

> When you're looking at a book and your home and you are being depicted, you want that home and depiction to be at least friendly, at least, you don't want everything connected with your home and family shown in a bad way. So I think about Harlem and I write my books, I have photographs of Harlem on my wall, and I try to show Black life in a way that is going to be friendly to all children, Black and White. (www.walterdeanmyers.net)

Finally, we look for multicultural young adult literature of high literary quality. In what follows, we show how *Monster* stacks up against Jago's criteria for selecting a literary work to use in whole-class instruction (see Figure 6.1). We then share a strategy for using *Monster* in an identity-themed unit.

Teaching *Monster* in an Identity-Themed Unit

As Stover (2000) explains, there are school districts in the United States serving students from more than thirty different cultural and ethnic groups. To provide novels reflective of and relevant to each student's background and personal experience would require that many different titles be available. It might be easier, and perhaps smarter, to organize instructional units by themes representative of issues that cross cultural boundaries and are relevant to the adolescent experience. As Stover explains, "If the focus of the unit is on an issue, individuals from diverse cultural backgrounds can respond to that issue, sharing their own experiences as shaped by culture, as they respond to the text and its presentation

	Monster by Walter Dean Myers Coretta Scott King Honor Book, 2000 Michael L. Printz Award Winner, 2000 ALA Best Book for Young Adults, 2000 ALA Quick Pick for Reluctant Young Adult Readers, 2000
Summary	Steve Harmon is a young black man on trial for being an accomplice to murder. He's also a film student at a prestigious high school and a devoted brother, with parents who love him. Steve says he's innocent, but he's already guilty in the eyes of the judge and attorneys. As one lawyer says, Steve is a "monster": just another black violent criminal. Throughout the story, Steve struggles to humanize himself against the violent backdrop of institutional racism.
Criterion 1: Written in language perfectly suited to the author's purpose	Myers based this book on interviews with prisoners he conducted for a college class project. Myers also has sat in courtrooms and visited juvenile detention centers. He grew up in Harlem and was himself a high school dropout. No wonder the language of the street, of Steve's inner turmoil, and descriptions of "juvie" and the trial ring true. Also, Myers strives to tell two stories in Monster: the story of Steve as viewed through the lens of racism, and a "counterstory" of Steve's attempt to stay human and speak truth to power. These stories are powerfully handled through Myers's use of multiple text types (e.g., journal entry, screenplay, black-and-white photos).
Criterion 2: Exposes readers to complex human dilemmas	What is racial identity? Or, as this book seems to ask, are multiple racial identities possible? Why do certain groups of people get "lumped" together in terms of identity? How do we come to believe things about certain groups of people? How does racism work through society's institutions, such as judicial and economic systems? These questions are at the heart of Myers's novel and point to the complex human dilemma that race and racism continue to be in the United States.
Criterion 3: Includes compelling, disconcerting characters	Steve is certainly complex—no one-dimensional, culturally neutral or culturally generic character here. Steve experiences an identity crisis in the novel, struggling to understand what "type" of black man he wants to be and can be if society will let him. Readers will cheer for Steve, and mistrust him, and ultimately judge him, and Steve knows it. Therefore Steve presents multiple sides of himself to the reader, making it hard to pin him down.
Criterion 4: Explores universal themes that combine different periods and cultures	From Frederick Douglass's self-described experiences in Narrative of the Life of Frederick Douglass: An American Slave to Tom Robinson in Harper Lee's To Kill a Mockingbird to Steve Harmon in Monster, racial identity in a racialized America has been a universal theme sure to provoke, incite, and call forth the uglier sides of human nature. This is a timeless, but no less volatile, theme that Myers takes up in the postmodern age.
Criterion 5: Challenges readers to reexamine their beliefs	The book certainly challenges readers to reexamine the beliefs about people of color they bring to the text. Steve struggles throughout the book to understand who he is as a young black man. Readers, too, will struggle to "pin him down," and thus must negotiate their own prior assumptions and beliefs about racial identity.
Criterion 6: Tells a good story with places for laughing and crying	The book doesn't call for extremes of crying and laughing, but it packs an emotional punch—perhaps more poignant because racism's continued presence and negative effect on people of color isn't funny, and crying hasn't seemed to have gotten us anywhere.

FIGURE 6.1. Review of Monster by Walter Dean Myers, based on Carol Jago's criteria for selecting a whole-class novel.

of the issue as shaped by the cultural background of the author" (p. 104). Using multicultural literature in this way can cut down on the number of books classroom teachers need to locate and buy, and can also help teachers avoid tokenism, or using one text to represent or speak for a cultural group or subculture.

An issue or theme we think crosses cultural boundaries and relates to adolescents' lived experiences is that of identity. Questions of character identity and values are common in many young adult novels. As Niday and Allender (2000) explain, "During adolescence, young adults often question, 'Who am I? How do I see myself? How do I fit into the world?' While an identity struggle may be prevalent throughout life, adolescence seems to accentuate self-probing questions. When teens have a bicultural or multicultural heritage, self-identity questions can become even more complex" (para. 1).

Add to this complexity the postmodern forces of globalization, rapid technological change, fast capitalism, and the inundation of media and new Internet technologies in teens' daily lives. As Bean and Moni (2003) suggest, adolescent identities in the postmodern age are in flux and can no longer be defined as stable or unchanging. Instead, Bean and Moni suggest that today's adolescent identities are fluid processes or "problems to be undertaken by actors" (p. 487). In other words, adolescent identity can be likened to performances teenagers enact, where they use such props as consumable objects (e.g., cell phones, clothes) or other actions and practices to symbolize certain identity affiliations (e.g., gang colors, graffiti, language use, joining online chat groups, eating disorders, etc.) (p. 487).

Lewis and del Valle (2009) emphasize the "hybrid, improvisatory" nature of such postmodern identities, explaining that adolescents embody several identities at once and also move from one identity position to another as they reposition themselves in relation to others. Niday and Allender (2000) call on Root's (1996) four definitions of *border crossings* to describe some ways adolescents may position and reposition themselves in relation to others: (1) by having both feet in two or more camps, or groups—"straddling" groups; (2) by foregrounding and highlighting, or hiding and de-emphasizing, certain identities; (3) by "camping" in one cultural group "for an extended period of time and [making] forays into other camps from time to time" (para. 4); and (4) by resisting, inventing new, or revising old identity categories. This last instance of *border crossing*, especially, resonates with Lewis and del Valle's point that adolescents are well aware of the ways in which they are positioned in relation to others in their various social worlds and to societal discourses of economics, race, and gender, and adolescents will "embrace, resist, and critique" such positionings as they see fit (p. 317).

As Susan and others have described elsewhere (see Groenke & Grothaus, forthcoming; Groenke & Grothaus, in press; Groenke & Maples, 2008, 2009; Ward, 2008; Willis & Parker, 2009), Walter Dean Myers's *Monster* certainly encourages adolescents to consider their own identities, how people are positioned in relation to race and ethnicity, and how adolescents might *border cross* in their daily lives. In *Monster*, Steve Harmon is a sixteen-year-old African American man who is a successful high school student and loving son and brother. But he is also on trial for being an accomplice to murder, and thus he gets deemed a *monster*, a person "who [is] willing to steal and to kill . . . [and disregard] the rights of others" (p. 21). Jury members in the novel are asked not to "prejudge" Steve, to "consider him innocent until proven guilty" (pp. 26–27), but Steve's race is a strike against him. His attorney must try to make Steve look "human" in front of the jury, and she worries that jury members won't see a "difference between [Steve] and all the other bad guys" (p. 116). Court proceedings are a mere formality, as one guard explains: "It's a motion case. They go through the motions; then we lock them up" (p. 14).

To complicate matters, Steve reveals information throughout the story that makes readers question his innocence and, perhaps more important, wonder what might have caused Steve to get involved in the crime to begin with (if indeed he did). Does he choose to "perform" the identity of a criminal or thug (Bean & Moni, 2003), and if so, why? Steve certainly questions his own identity—is it something he decides, or has it already been decided for him?—and struggles to resist and reinvent a new identity for himself that transcends the limited, negative, and stereotypical options he finds available to him. A theme running through many of Myers's books is the protagonist's search for identity and self-worth in an environment of poverty, drugs, gangs, and racism. Myers explains he tries to portray well-rounded black male characters who can live in the inner city, play basketball, *and* be "voracious readers." He says, "These 'different' identities are too often considered mutually exclusive" (Author profile: Walter Dean Myers, 2001).

For these reasons, we see *Monster* as a good choice to use as a whole-class text to introduce an identity-themed unit. But teachers can't assume that adolescents will be able to grapple with such complex and sophisticated issues without guidance from teachers. We can't assume that simply asking students to read such a work as *Monster* will ensure that they will understand and be ready to talk about (racial) identity in the postmodern era, especially if those students are predominantly white/European American. Susan learned this the hard way when she worked with a beginning high school English teacher, Michelle, to teach *Monster* to predominantly white, affluent ninth-grade students (see Groenke & Grothaus, forthcoming).

Susan and Michelle hoped the students would be able to make connections between their lives and Steve's life and identity struggles, but the students complained about not understanding the book. They ultimately could not make personal connections to Steve or his life experience. Thus, Susan and Michelle couldn't get to the more critical questions about race and racial identity they wanted to pose for discussion.

However, when Susan taught the book later at a more diverse high school, many students could relate to Steve, disclosing that they had family members who had done time in jail, or felt that they had been victims of racial profiling. Students in the more diverse context seemed to understand Steve's identity struggle, and students of color in particular were less quick to judge Steve as guilty. Other classroom researchers describe similar experiences teaching *Monster* to preservice teachers (Willis & Parker, 2009) and urban high school students (Howard-Bender & Mulcahy, 2007).

We view students' different, culturally situated responses to works like *Monster*, as well as the need for students to be able to develop a personal response to the literary work, as reasons to use reader response as a first step toward more critical analysis of the larger themes of race and identity at work in the novel. Ultimately, we see moving between reader response and critical literacy as a way to differentiate students' responses to multicultural literature in the high school English classroom, no matter who the students are or what diverse worlds they represent. We encourage high school English teachers to inform students of these two reading theories and discuss them as alternatives to the New Critical approaches with which they're probably already very familiar (Koukis, 2008).

Reader Response: A First Step

As we stated in Chapter 5, Louise Rosenblatt (1978/1994) is probably best known for introducing reader-response theory to the field of reading instruction. Reader-response theory emerged as a challenge to New Critical approaches to reading instruction (see Figure 6.2).

In Figure 6.3, we have used Probst's "dialogue with a text" questions (see Chapter 5) as a frame for eliciting reader response to *Monster* that takes into account the following important tenets of Rosenblatt's theory, namely that:

	New Criticism	Reader-Response (Transactional) Theory	Critical Literacy
Where textual meaning is located	Solely in the text; usually one "correct" meaning.	In transaction between reader and text; "each reader comes to the text with a unique history, a unique set of circumstances and abilities and inclinations, and has to take that into account as he or she shapes an understanding of the text and his or her reading of it" (Probst, 2004). Multiple meanings possible.	Meanings are socially constructed by author and reader; because readers bring different experiences and beliefs to reading, meanings of texts will be multiple and varied—readers don't solely ask, "What does text mean?" but also "What different interpretations are possible?"
How meaning is constructed	Readers search for meaning in text; external factors (e.g., author's biography, sociocultural context) not important to understanding text.	Meaning occurs as readers bring their personal experiences to bear on the story, and the story acts on readers' understandings of experience; meaning occurs in the *process* of reading.	Active construction between author, reader, and text; readers fill in gaps provided by authors; authors have "implied readers" in mind.
Role of text	Holds authority in meaning making; if it's not in the text, it doesn't matter; texts are neutral.	An experience shaping and affecting readers' emotions, perceptions, and beliefs; encourages connection making.	Texts are not neutral; they represent particular views, silence other points of view, and influence people's ideas. Texts try to represent reality and define what is necessary and socially acceptable. Texts distribute discourses (messages) about people and ideas, but these messages can be challenged or interrogated by readers.
Role of reader	Uncovers meaning in text; focuses on literary elements such as plot, character, setting—usually in isolated ways.	Juxtaposes personal experiences with story; reshapes and revises perceptions and beliefs through juxtaposition.	Questioning and challenging the ways in which texts have been constructed and the messages they distribute. Readers should ask: Why is the text written this way? Readers also consider the author, time, and culture in which the text was created.
Act of reading	A search for "the right" meaning.	An "event" that unfolds in time; a process of exploration and creation.	An act of questioning and interrogating the text and author's purpose.
Texts typically used	Classic, canonical works; scripted, federally funded reading programs; textbooks.	Young adult literature; students' self-selected texts.	All texts, including popular culture (e.g., commercials, TV, film, posters) and other "everyday texts" (e.g., cereal boxes, junk mail, fliers).
Instructional strategies typically used	Lecture; teacher-centered discussion (e.g., recitation; I-R-E); teaching close textual analysis; teaching and locating literary elements (e.g., POV; irony).	Whole-class and small-group student-centered discussion; journals. Idea is that interpretation and textual analysis begin with personal response.	Discussion; questioning activities; activities involving popular media (e.g., commercials, TV, film).

FIGURE 6.2. Reading instruction theories. Adapted from *Response and Analysis: Teaching Literature in Secondary School*, by R. E. Probst, 2004, 2nd ed., Portsmouth, NH: Heinemann; and "Taking on Critical Literacy: The Journey of Newcomers and Novices," by M. Lewison, A. S. Flint, and K. Van Sluys, 2002, *Language Arts, 48*(7).

First reaction	What is your first reaction or response to the text?	• Does Steve seem like a real person to you? Why or why not? Do you feel like you can relate to Steve? Explain. • Have you ever gotten in trouble for something you didn't do? Have you ever been wrongly accused of something? Why did you get blamed? How was this experience similar or different from Steve's? • Do you identify with any characters or events in the story? Explain. • How do you react to Steve? To his situation? Do you approve or disapprove of Steve's behavior/attitudes and social situation in the story? • What in your own experience might be influencing how you identify with and react (or don't) to Steve? • Do you think Steve is innocent or guilty? What in the text influences your opinion? What in your own personal experience/background might be influencing your opinion?
Feelings/ emotions	What feelings did the text awaken in you? What emotions did you feel as you read the text?	• How do you feel about Steve and his situation? • What must it feel like to be Steve? His parents? Is it easy or hard for you to consider how Steve feels? • What emotions does Steve experience in the story? How do you know? What are your beliefs about why Steve may be experiencing such emotions? • Do you feel you understand how Steve feels? Do you sympathize with him? Why or why not? • Do you feel the author wants you to sympathize with Steve? To judge Steve? Point to places in the text where you think the author is trying to influence you either way.
Perceptions	What did you see happening in the book?	• Do you think Steve's experience is realistically portrayed? Explain. • Could the events described in *Monster* really happen? What is your personal experience with such events? Have you personally experienced such events, or had a family member experience such events? Or have you only experienced such events through the media or other stories you've heard or seen? Explain. • Do you think African Americans might be offended by *Monster*? Explain.
Asso- ciations (including literary associa- tions)	What memories does the text call to mind?	•What other texts (e.g., books, stories, etc.), movies, music, etc. does *Monster* remind you of? What other texts or genres have you read or seen that depict African American men? How are they portrayed? •Have you seen African American men portrayed as criminals in another book or the media? •How does *Monster* compare to this other work? What are the similarities? What do you make of these similarities—are they a coincidence? Or do you think there's a pattern at work? Where do you think this pattern comes from? •How did you react to this other work? •How does this other work make you think or feel about *Monster*? How does this other work affect your understandings of *Monster*? •What do you make of the different kinds of text types (journal, screenplay, black-and-white photographs) that Myers uses in the novel? Why does he use these? Why not just tell the story in a traditional format? How would the story change if Myers did so? *continued on next page*

FIGURE 6.3. Framing reader response to *Monster* by Walter Dean Myers. Adapted from "Dialogue with a Text," by R. E. Probst, 1988, *English Journal*, *77*(1), pp. 35–36.

FIGURE 6.3. Continued

Thoughts, ideas	What idea or thought is suggested by the text?	• Steve seems to have multiple sides or identities in the story. What are they? How does Myers show these different sides? • Do you have multiple sides or identities? Explain. • How do you think your parents view or see you? As what kind of person? What about your teachers? Your friends? How do these views differ? • Do you ever wish you could be someone else or a different type of person? Explain. • Are you someone different at home than at school/community/church, or in private? Explain. • Have you ever been wrongly judged by someone or negatively stereotyped? Explain. • Have you ever felt someone just doesn't understand or "get" you? Explain. • How are the different cultural groups you belong to (e.g., age, race/ethnicity, gender) portrayed in the media? Other places (e.g., school, community)? • How are African American men typically portrayed in the media? • How do you define race? Racism? Do you believe racism exists in America? • What implications for your own life do you derive from reading *Monster*? In other words, has reading *Monster* caused you to rethink or reconsider your own behavior? Beliefs? Explain.
Author	What sort of person do you imagine the author of this text to be?	• What do you know about the author, Walter Dean Myers? • Why do you think Myers wrote this story?

• Reader response is a process that begins with evocation of the story world and the reader's spontaneous reactions to the text (including doubts, questions, and agreements) as the reader transacts with the text.

• Reader response encourages readers to examine the personal associations and reactions that are evoked during the reader's transaction with literary works and to critically scrutinize responses to literary works for social and cultural influences.

While reader response is helpful in getting adolescents personally engaged with texts and attuned to how they are reading a text, adolescent readers might need help considering the social and cultural influences at work upon their responses, including the role texts (and authors) play in influencing their responses. Students might also need help in learning to notice the systems of power and oppression at work in the literature they read. This is where critical literacy, another theory of reading, can be helpful—but only *after* students have developed personal responses and reactions to the literary work. Indeed, Rosenblatt suggested critical readings of texts should be anchored in the reader's personal response. Cai (2008) suggests teachers can use readers' personal responses to texts to better understand the assumptions, expectations, and attitudes adolescent readers bring to texts. Teachers will need to address these assumptions and expectations in their instruction if readers are to learn to read texts critically (Cai, 2008). Critical literacy can help teachers in this process.

From Reader Response to Critical Literacy

Critical Reading

Shor (1987) explains that a critical reader "does not stay at the empirical level of memorizing data, or at the impressionistic level of opinion, or at the level of dominant myths in society, but goes beneath the surface to understand the origin, structure, and consequences of any body of knowledge, technical structure, or object under study" (p. 24). "Going beneath the surface" of facts and personal opinion to a deeper understanding of our own reading processes and the sociopolitical systems we belong to requires that readers adopt a questioning stance toward texts (McDaniel, 2004). Lewison, Flint, and Van Sluys's (2002) "Four Dimensions of Critical Literacy" can help teachers better understand what critical literacy and critical questioning entail.

The "Four Dimensions" represent a synthesis of critical literacy definitions as they have appeared in the literature over the last thirty years. The dimensional perspective emphasizes critical literacy as a "process of becoming conscious of one's experience as historically constructed within specific power relations" (Anderson & Irvine, 1993, p. 82). This process is demonstrated in the integration of four interrelated dimensions:

1. Disrupting the commonplace
2. Interrogating multiple viewpoints
3. Focusing on sociopolitical issues
4. Taking action and working for social justice

According to Lewison, Flint, and Van Sluys (2002), the first dimension encourages people to question "everyday" ways of seeing and problematize all subjects of study. Emphasis in this dimension is given to how language shapes identity, constructs cultural discourses, and supports or disrupts the status quo. In the second dimension, emphasis is given to multiple viewpoints and contradictory perspectives on an issue. In this dimension, readers seek out silenced or marginalized voices and make differences visible to one another. In the third dimension, emphasis is given to going beyond personal responses to texts to consideration of the sociopolitical systems to which we belong. And finally, Lewison, Flint, and Van Sluys (2002) explain that the last dimension—taking action—is "*the goal of critical literacy,*" but it cannot be attained without "expanded understandings and perspectives gained from the other three dimensions" (p. 384, emphasis in original).

In Figure 6.4 we have considered these four dimensions as they might apply to Myers's *Monster* and have posed questions we think help adolescent readers begin to see the larger sociopolitical contexts shaping not only Steve Harmon's life and experiences in *Monster* but theirs as well.

It is our hope that adding the critical to reader-response repertoires enhances readers' understandings of how they come to have the reactions and associations to texts that they do, and deepens (and complicates) their understandings of others.

Dimension 1: Disrupting the Commonplace	Dimensional topics and questions as they apply to *Monster* by Walter Dean Myers
Studying language to analyze how it shapes identity, constructs cultural discourses, and supports or disrupts the status quo Including popular culture and media as a regular part of the curriculum	• The white female prosecutor calls Steve "monster" during her opening comments (p. 5), and Steve describes James King as a "thug" (p. 10). What larger unvoiced fears of young black men do these labels represent? • Osvaldo calls Steve's school a "faggot school" (p. 80), and calls Steve a "lame looking for a name" (p. 81). For what purpose is Osvaldo using these words? What might he hope the words do? How is language power in Osvaldo's case? • How are African American men predominantly represented in the media? What language (e.g., words, pictures, graphics) does the media use in such representations? Consider the black-and-white photos within Steve's screenplay of a young black man sitting in a prison cell and in a police car, as well as the young man's mug shot. Why include these photos? • How has the media helped to create and/or appropriate the image of black man = violent criminal? • What are dominant beliefs about people of color? • How do these beliefs affect the lives of people of color?

continued on next page

FIGURE 6.4. Framing critical literacy response to *Monster* by Walter Dean Myers. Adapted from "Small Openings in Cyberspace: Preparing Preservice Teachers to Facilitate Critical Race Talk," by S. L. Groenke and J. Maples, 2009, in *Critical Pedagogy and Teacher Education in the Neoliberal Era: Small Openings,* edited by S. L. Groenke and J. A. Hatch, Dordrecht, Netherlands: Springer; "Taking on Critical Literacy: The Journey of Newcomers and Novices," by M. Lewison, A. S. Flint, and K. Van Sluys, 2002, *Language Arts, 79*(5); "'O Say, Do You See?' Using Critical Race Theory to Inform English Language Arts Instruction," by A. I. Willis and K. N. Parker, 2009, in *Breaking the Silence: Recognizing the Social and Cultural Resources Students Bring to the Classroom,* edited by C. Compton-Lilly, Newark, DE: International Reading Association.

FIGURE 6.4. Continued

Problematizing all subjects of study and understanding existing knowledge as a historical product	• Why do the judges, attorneys, and some jury members already judge Steve as guilty? • Why might readers already judge Steve as guilty? • What is race? Ethnicity? Racism? • Is racial identity influenced by broad historical social and economic context, or by local situations and individual histories? • Is racial identity a personal decision or a social label, or both? • Myers has said he tries to portray well-rounded black male characters in his novels who can live in the inner city, play basketball, *and* be "voracious readers." He says, "These 'different' identities are too often considered mutually exclusive." Why? • Does a life of crime seem attractive or unavoidable to Steve?
Interrogating texts: "How is this text trying to position me?"	• Do you believe Steve is innocent or guilty? Why? • What beliefs about and experiences with people of color do you bring to your reading of this text? • What systems of power, privilege, and racism exist that allow readers to automatically doubt Steve's innocence and denounce the judicial system for not finding him guilty? • Would we be as quick to judge Steve if he were white?
Dimension 2: Interrogating Multiple Viewpoints	**Dimensional topics/questions as they apply to Myers's *Monster***
Reflecting on multiple and contradictory perspectives Paying attention to and seeking out the voices of those who have been silenced or marginalized Analyzing how nondominant groups can gain access to dominant forms of language and culture, how diverse forms of language can be used as cultural resources, and how social action can change existing discourses	• How does the author, Myers, construct a "counternarrative" or "counterstory" in the text that rejects dominant, negative perceptions of young black men? • How does the reader "hear" Steve's voice in the novel? How does Steve attempt to humanize himself? • How does Steve use literacy to "talk back" to dominant, negative representations of himself? Why the screenplay? Why not another genre?
Making difference visible	• Steve's detention center echoes with "voices [that] are clearly black or Hispanic" men (p. 7). If research shows that white men commit as many, if not more, crimes as black and Latino men, why are more black and Latino men incarcerated?
Dimension 3: Focusing on Sociopolitical Issues	**Dimensional topics/questions as they apply to Myers's *Monster***
Going beyond the personal and attempting to understand the sociopolitical systems to which we belong Challenging unquestioned legitimacy of unequal power relationships	• What are the multiple intersecting oppressions in Steve's world? • What is institutional racism? • How is institutional racism illustrated within the judicial system? The current economic system? • The regulation of poor blacks to urban areas, and the deliberate impoverishment of urban areas populated by poor blacks—and thus the lives of the urban youth who live there—is not a "natural" occurrence, but one that can be tied to racist economic decisions made by those who hold legal and political power. • Why is there a lack of jobs and law enforcement in neighborhoods of people of color?

continued on next page

FIGURE 6.4. Continued

Dimension 4: Taking Action and Promoting Social Justice	Dimensional topics/questions as they apply to Myers's *Monster*
Engaging in praxis—reflection and action upon the world in order to transform it (Freire, 1972) Using language to exercise power to enhance everyday life and to question practices of privilege and injustice	• Create a media clip (e.g., video, commercial) that "talks back" to dominant, negative representations of African American men and upload to YouTube (transformative storytelling) • Research incarceration rates by gender and race/ethnicity in your city or town. Write a letter to a local judge or local police enforcement inquiring about what you find.

After *Monster*

After whole-class reading and discussion of *Monster* around the reader-response and critical questions we share, teachers can place students in small literature circle groups based on their preference of other young adult novels to read (see the resource guide that begins on this page for some suggested titles that make good identity-themed choices), and students continue considering how identity and border crossing is addressed in other works. Teachers might also want to bridge to more canonical works such as *To Kill a Mockingbird* and compare Steve's plight with that of Tom Robinson, who must also prove his innocence to a jury that already believes him guilty. Ultimately, pairing such works would emphasize that racism and racial identity continue to be pressing issues in the twenty-first century.

Resource Guide for Chapter 6

Next, we list other identity-themed young adult novels for classroom use. An asterisk (*) denotes a novel appropriate for middle school.

African American Cultural Groups

Tyrell (Booth, 2007)
Upstate (Buckhanon, 2006)
Imani All Mine (Porter, 2000)
Copper Sun (Draper, 2008)
November Blues (Draper, 2009)
Money Hungry (Flake, 2007)
Miracle's Boys (Woodson, 2001)

47 (Mosley, 2006)
Jumped (Williams-Garcia, 2009)
Like Sisters on the Homefront (Williams-Garcia, 1998)
Chill Wind (McDonald, 2006)
Project Girl (McDonald, 2000)
Dope Sick (Myers, 2009)
The Rock and the River (Magoon, 2009)
After Tupac and D Foster (Woodson, 2008)
Elijah of Buxton (Curtis, 2009)

Latino/a Cultural Groups

Return to Sender (Alvarez, 2009)
The Circuit (Jimenez, 1997/2000) (also see *Breaking Through*)
Buried Onions (Soto, 2006)
Mexican Whiteboy (de la Peña, 2008)
Muchaco (L. Johnson, 2009)
Cuba 15 (Osa, 2005)
Parrot in the Oven: Mi Vida (Martinez, 1996/2004)
La Linea (Jaramillo, 2008)
First Crossing: Stories about Teen Immigrants (Gallo, 2007)
Once upon a Quinceañera: Coming of Age in the USA (Alvarez, 2008)
Red Hot Salsa (Carlson, 2005)

American Indian Cultural Groups

The Absolutely True Diary of a Part-Time Indian (Alexie, 2007)
Rain Is Not My Indian Name (Smith, 2001)
Moccasin Thunder: American Indian Stories for Today (Carlson, 2005)
No Parole Today (Tohe, 1999)

Asian American Cultural Groups

American Born Chinese (Yang, 2008)
Kira-Kira (Kadohata, 2006)
Red Scarf Girl: A Memoir of the Cultural Revolution (Jiang, 1997)
A Step from Heaven (Na, 2002)
Same Difference and Other Stories (Kim, 2004)

Indian American/Middle Eastern American Cultural Groups

Shine, Coconut Moon (Meminger, 2009)
Born Confused (Desai Hidier, 2003)
Does My Head Look Big in This? (Abdel-Fattah, 2008)

White Cultural Groups

Looking for Alibrandi (Marchetta, 1992/2006)
Jellicoe Road (Marchetta, 2007)
Saving Francesca (Marchetta, 2004)
Will Grayson, Will Grayson (Green & Levithan, 2010)
Looking for JJ (Cassidy, 2007) (also see the movie, *Boy A)*
Fighting Reuben Wolfe (Zusak, 2002)
What I Saw and How I Lied (Blundell, 2009)
Alabama Moon (Key, 2008)
Funny How Things Change (Wyatt, 2009)
Wintergirls (L. H. Anderson, 2009)
Feed (L. H. Anderson, 2004)
Black and White (Volponi, 2006)
The Disreputable History of Frankie Landau-Banks (Lockhart, 2009)

An Exciting Story and Some Soil: Exploring Biography Graphic-Novel Style

7

Graphic novels, like young adult literature, have often been treated as a means to an end in the English classroom, more as a *bridge* or *companion to* traditional literary works rather than literary works in their own right, deserving of careful and critical literary study. As an example, Art Spiegelman's Pulitzer Prize–winning *Maus*—a graphic novel about Spiegelman's father's life in pre–World War II Poland and survival at Auschwitz—is rarely the central text used in a Holocaust unit and instead often complements more canonical works like *Anne Frank: The Diary of a Young Girl* (1953) and Elie Wiesel's (1982) *Night*.

It's time high school English teachers take graphic novels more seriously. The genre is hugely popular with adolescents if teen book sales are any indication (Goodnow, 2007), and there are lots of resources available now for teachers that describe the multiple ways graphic novels can be used in the English classroom (Carter, 2007; Cary, 2004; Finkle & Lilly, 2009; Frey & Fisher, 2004).

Graphic novels are especially suited for differentiated reading instruction because they appeal to both reluctant and advanced readers. Reading researchers have long encouraged the use of graphic novels and comics as a "first step" for reluctant readers who might find it easier to make inferences, gain contextual information, and thus better comprehend the story from visual images (Koenke, 1981). Yang (2008) suggests reluctant readers might appreciate the "visual permanence" graphic novels afford. Yang explains this permanence allows readers to "rewind and revisit information" (or keep going) at will. Botzakis (2009) explains: "The words and pictures contained in graphic novels do not move and are fixed on a page, allowing readers to choose how fast or slow they wish to read and also the degree to which they should attend to the words and pictures. Graphic novels give the illusion of time passing, but they leave the rate of change up to the reader" (p. 16).

Similarly, Norton (2003) suggests readers like graphic novels because they "feel a certain amount of control in the reading process" (p. 143):

> The student can construct meaning, make hypotheses, and predict future developments. In contrast, when a student [reads] a [more traditional] literary text, there is little room for invention and creativity[;] … the meaning of a text is not co-constructed, but needs to be ferreted out. (p. 143)

The sense of ownership and active reading that graphic novels afford may give readers confidence to engage enthusiastically with graphic novels. Versaci (2001) suggests it is the "in between" spaces between panels (the typically empty, white spaces between panels are called "gutters" [see McCloud, 1994]) that readers must fill in on their own that fosters an intimacy between the author and reader. Versaci explains this intimacy might encourage readers to sympathize and empathize with graphic novel characters in unique ways.

Other graphic novel enthusiasts say the blending of the visual and textual is what makes the graphic novel a complex and sophisticated form, and is thus aptly suited for advanced readers as well. Versaci (2001) explains that not only do graphic novels make use of traditional literary devices (e.g., point of view, conflict, tone, theme), but their blending of image and text "[forces] students, rather directly, to reconcile these two means of expression" (p. 64).

Jacobs (2007) might call such "reconciliation" *multimodal literacy,* in which multiple systems of meaning making work in conjunction to inform interpretative processes. Jacobs describes five multimodal design elements that are present in graphic novels—*linguistic, audio, visual, gestural,* and *spatial. Linguistic* elements refer to text boxes and dialogue balloons that can help to "place the reader temporally and generically" and can work as audio and "narrative voice" to aid in indicating tone, voice inflection, cadence, and emotional tenor" (Jacobs, 2007, p. 22). *Visual* elements refer to line and white space, shading, perspective, distance, and composition, while *gestural* elements can refer to facial expressions and body postures of characters. *Spatial* elements refer to the layout of panels on the page and relation between panels and gutters (McCloud, 1994). Jacobs says interpretative meaning making of graphic novels requires consideration of *all* these elements, and not just the linguistic element (which tends to be the focus in the English classroom). Jacobs explains that depending on the level of the class, teachers can stress different elements at varying levels of complexity (p. 22).

Obviously, the sophistication and broad appeal of the graphic novel makes it a worthy choice for whole-class instruction, and resources abound with suggestions for young adult graphic novel titles that teachers should consider using in their classrooms (Miller, 2005; Weiner, 2006; Yang, 2008). For this reason, we want to focus on a growing trend or subgenre in the graphic novel publishing industry: the biographical graphic novel, or BioGraphic novel.

Whether this trend results from the explosion of memoir and nonfiction that started in the 1970s, we don't know, but we do know that the graphic novel seems especially suited for biography, a genre that aims to bring long-gone famous individuals to life for readers. The graphic novel can provide a "you-are-there" intimacy that engages readers with an individual's life story and can also capture details (e.g., gestures) that allow readers to make inferences about the individual's life. Perhaps most important, the format can depict a broader context in which to understand the social forces shaping the individual's life journey. Not all biographical graphic novels do this, or do it well, but some do it masterfully, such as those published by the Center for Comic Studies (CCS). Currently, these include James Sturm and Rich Tommaso's (2007) *Satchel Paige: Striking Out Jim Crow*, Jason Lutes and Nick Bertozzi's (2007) *Houdini: The Handcuff King*, John Porcellino's (2008) *Thoreau at Walden*, and Sarah Stewart Taylor and Ben Towle's (2010) *Amelia Earhart: This Broad Ocean* (2010). A graphic biography about Helen Keller is forthcoming.

In this chapter, we briefly describe these works, drawing on information gleaned from our interview with James Sturm, director of the CCS and coauthor of *Satchel Paige: Striking Out Jim Crow*. We end with a reading guide to use with *Satchel Paige* that focuses readers' attention on both the elements of good biographical writing and the graphic elements that make this blended genre a unique medium in which to describe an individual's life. Ultimately, we want to introduce these important biographical graphic novels to high school English teachers and encourage teachers to consider the graphic novel genre as an alternative to the traditional research paper.

We like all of the works produced thus far by the CCS for their unconventional biographical treatment of the individuals they portray. Sturm says what the writers and illustrators of the biographies try to do is stay away from the "clichéd you're-born-into-the-world, you-have-a-defining-moment, and then-you-change-the world formula." Sturm states further: "You can go online and get the basics, and some graphic novels just dress up a Wikipedia entry. We didn't want to do that, cram in exposition and get in the way of the story. We want to tell an exciting story because that inspires people to want to know more" (personal communication, October 29, 2009).

An exciting story is certainly what you get in *Houdini: The Handcuff King*. Rather than provide a broad overview of Houdini's life with matter-of-fact dates and figures, the narrative lens zooms in on one of the myths surrounding Houdini's ability to escape many different locks—that his wife concealed picks in her mouths and passed them to Houdini by way of a good-luck kiss! But just as the narrative zooms in on details like this, the graphic novel format also affords the ability to zoom out to show larger, contextual details about the time period in which Houdini lived. Readers see the Boston and Cambridge of 1908, early forms of self-promotion and marketing, and the anti-Semitism that Jews faced in Europe in the late 1800s (and in America).

Similarly, in Porcellino's minimalist-inspired *Thoreau at Walden*, readers see simplicity in the two-toned line drawings depicting whip-poor-wills and owls, floating ripples on spring lakes, and the rows of vegetables that made up Thoreau's two-year experiment at Walden Pond and inspired his writings. Thoreau felt "befriended" and "sustained" by the natural world, so it seems fitting that this natural world figures so prominently in the graphic novel. The pictorial representation afforded by the graphic novel can certainly enhance readers' understandings of and appreciation for Thoreau's classic works, but the graphic novel is an important book in its own right.

In the most recent publication, *Amelia Earhart: This Broad Ocean*, the novelist Sarah Stewart Taylor—former journalist and distant relative of Amelia Earhart—teams up with cartoonist Ben Towle to describe Earhart's triumphant crossing of the Atlantic Ocean in 1928. Taylor and Towle show readers Earhart's "moxie" but also depict the sexist and discriminatory attitudes Earhart and other women faced in the 1920s and 1930s when they wanted to do "men's jobs." As Eileen Collins, the first female pilot of a space shuttle, writes in the introduction to the book: "What Earhart achieved in her short lifetime is astounding enough on its own, but to do it in a time when women were expected to be something else . . . . well, I think that is the biggest accomplishment! Amelia opened doors for so many women, including me, in the field of aviation (and beyond)" (p. vii).

James Sturm says the presentation of the broader historical context in which great people have lived is what the authors and illustrators of the CCS graphic novels strive for. Sturm says, "The great names are less important than the other social forces at work on their lives. These people do shape history, but sometimes the context is not taken into account. The soil they grew up in is just as important as the individual" (personal communication, October 23, 2009).

The "soil" of racism, segregation, and violence are what Satchel Paige and people of color had to "grow up in" in the Jim Crow South. In *Satchel Paige: Striking Out Jim Crow*, the reader comes to learn that while Satchel Paige was probably one of the greatest pitchers to ever play the game, he was not allowed to join a major league team until 1948, when he was forty-two years old, because he was black. As Paige said, "All the nice statements in the world ain't gonna knock down Jim Crow" (Sturm & Tommaso, p. 30). To make a living in his early days, Paige pitched on all-black baseball teams that were part of the National Negro League, but he eventually became so wealthy he flew from game to game on his own private airplane.

To many people of color who lived during the Jim Crow era, Satchel Paige was more than a sports hero. He was someone who could talk back to white power through his dominance on the field and get away with it. Many people of color lived vicariously through Paige and got the occasional spiritual uplift from watching him strike out white man after white man. This relationship between the common, everyday black sharecropper who suffered under Jim Crow and as a symbol of resistance to white authority, Paige is the narrative focus of Sturm and Tommaso's graphic novel. The story is told through the lens of Emmet Wilson, a sharecropper who shares not only a brief baseball history with Satchel Paige but also a larger legacy of hope in the struggle for equality and justice. The story has a resonating, recursive force—the reader sees the impact of social and cultural mores on individual lives, and the impact individuals can have on changing those social and cultural mores, and thus other peoples' lives and the course of history. Don't let the simplicity of the graphics fool you—*Satchel Paige: Striking Out Jim Crow* packs a punch.

Rethinking Traditional Research

The unconventional biographical focus on telling a good story that makes readers want to know more, and the careful attention to sociocultural forces at work during the time the individuals lived, are reasons why we think the biographical graphic novels we describe in this chapter lend themselves to students' own research projects in the high school English classroom.

Traditional high school research papers have received much criticism over the years. In the 1980s, Macrorie called research papers "the most unoriginal writings the world has ever seen" (1988, p. 54). Zemelman and Daniels (1988) stated that "teachers dread term papers as much as students do" (p. 256). Other teachers have called traditional research papers "cut and paste" exercises that lack creativity and engagement, and thus result in poor writing (Dickson, DeGraff, & Foard, 2002). We agree with Shafer (1999) that the research paper should "be about creating new truths, provocative theories, modern stories. While we must respect the traditional practices of doing research, we must allow for voices and personalities to make their presence felt" (Shafer, 1999, p. 46).

The graphic novel format affords possibilities for "modern stories" in which student voices and personalities are present. Teachers could guide whole-class reading of one of the graphic novels described earlier or let students read them all in small literature circles. The focus of reading and discussion should be on how the graphic novel format communicates facts and ideas about both the individual lives portrayed and the times in which the individuals lived. Teachers could use (or modify) the reading guide we provide here (see Figure 7.1) to facilitate discussion about the works and then let students research famous people or events of interest to them and graphically represent their findings (see Figure 7.2 for a research planning guide). Students could be encouraged to consider controversial myths surrounding their topics in their representations (as in *Houdini*) or who should narrate their biographical stories (as in *Satchel Paige*). If students were researching authors, they could be asked to include excerpts from the selected author's works and to use pictures, graphics, or other visuals to represent the context in which the author's most well-known works were written (as in *Thoreau at Walden*). Teachers could also identify students in the class who like to draw and illustrate and have them work with student writers to decide how best to tell the stories they want to tell.

Satchel Paige: Striking Out Jim Crow by James Sturm and Rich Tommaso Reading Guide	
Elements of Biography	**Questions to Consider**
Point of View	• Who is telling the story? • Why do you think the author and illustrator chose to tell the story this way? • How do the author and illustrator weave the story of Emmet Wilson, a sharecropper, with the story of Satchel Paige? • Who is another "Emmet" in our country's history? How might this person's story be connected to that of Emmet Wilson and Satchel Paige? • What do you know about the author and illustrator? Are they reliable biographers?
Details about Individual(s)	• You first "see" Satchel Paige on pp. 4–5. How would you describe him? • It takes twelve panels, across two pages, to show Paige pitch a ball (pp. 6–7). Why is this? What does this tell you about Paige? • How would you describe Paige's pitching style? How do the visual images in the novel support this? • What were some of Paige's pitches called? • What does the game on pp. 9–23 reveal about both Paige and Wilson? • What else do you learn about Paige throughout the story? • Why was he so important to Emmet Wilson?
Contextual Factors	• The novel begins in 1929 and ends in 1944. What do you know about what was going on in America around this time? What was it like to live during this time if you were black? • What was Jim Crow? Segregation? What was life like for black sharecroppers? Black baseball players? • What is barnstorming? Lynching? • What can you find out about the National Negro League? • What do you make of Emmet's words on pp. 82–83? What effect does Paige have on Emmet and his son? Why do you think this is? <div align="right">*continued on next page*</div>

FIGURE 7.1. Reading guide for *Satchel Paige: Striking Out Jim Crow* by James Sturm and Rich Tommaso. Adapted from "Teacher's Guide for *Satchel Paige: Striking Out Jim Crow*," by T. V. Zimmer, 2009, retrieved November 5, 2009, from http://www.cartoonstudies.org/books/paige/guide.html; and "Palestine: In Graphic Detail," by S. L. Finkle and T. J. Lilly, 2009, *Classroom Notes Plus, 26*(3).

FIGURE 7.1. Continued

Elements of Graphic Design	Questions to Consider
Linguistic/audio (text boxes, words, dialogue balloons). Can also include such rhetorical techniques as tone/mood, irony/satire.	• Where/how does the narration occur in the story? • How do you know on p. 1 that the person walking is telling the story? • What dialect does the narrator use? How do you know? • What other linguistic/audio cues are provided throughout the novel that help you know what is going on?
Visual (line, white space, shading, color; characters—who or what is depicted on the page?)	• Based on the visual details and language provided on p. 2, what do sharecroppers do? How do they live? Do they live well? • On pp. 24 and 30, the color changes. Why do you think this is? What purpose(s) do these pages serve? • How would you describe the tone of p. 31? Why? Can you make predictions about what might happen later in the story? • Pages 38–39 are yet another color—a different shade of the muted browns used throughout the story. Why the change in color here? • What do you make of the juxtaposition between the bigger panels on pp. 74–75 and 78, which have a lot of white space between Paige and Mr. Wallace, and the smaller panels on the same pages? • What seems to be the mood and tone on pp. 82–83? How do you know? • Both shades of brown are used in the final two pages of the novel (pp. 84–85). Why do you think this is? • The graphics or pictures in *Satchel Paige* have been described as "simple, yet powerful." What do you think this means? Do you agree? How are the pictures "simple"? Why might the illustrator have chosen to use "simple" pictures?
Gestural (facial expressions, body gestures) and *Spatial* (layout of panels on page, gutters, angles, and frames [e.g., close-ups, long shots, head shots])	• How would you describe the Jennings twins on p. 26? • What do you make of the full two-page spread on pp. 42–43? How are we supposed to see Emmet Wilson and his son? What emotions does this spread evoke? • How does Emmet Wilson feel after the incident with his son and the Jennings twins? How do you know? • What about the full one-page spread on pp. 66 and 80 of Paige? Why are these spreads effective? Why might the author and illustrator have chosen to portray these scenes in this way? • How do the author and illustrator portray the fast-paced nature of the baseball game? What kinds of shots do they use (e.g., close-ups, long shots)? What is included in the shots?

We think the possibilities are endless, but teachers must be willing to consider alternatives to the traditional research paper or report for these possibilities to come to light. Teachers must also be willing to let go of any preconceived notions or biases they may hold against graphic novels. As we've tried to show in this chapter, graphic novels are sophisticated, complex works worthy of our attention and whole-class instruction. When we asked James Sturm what he'd say to high school English teachers who pooh-poohed graphic novels, he said, "I'd tell them to just read the books!" Indeed, the biographical graphic novels published by the Center for Comic Studies speak for themselves. English teachers! Read the books!

Research Planning Guide

Directions: Fill out one of these sheets for every source you use in the biographical research project. Fill out the columns to help you plan how to use this information in your graphical representation of the topic you are researching. I have filled out the sheet as an example of how to use it.

Topic: <u>Sylvia Plath</u>

MLA Entry for Source: Hemphill, Stephanie. *Your Own, Sylvia*. New York: Knopf, 2007.

Interesting Fact about Individual	Questions	Interpretative Ideas	Scene or Action(s) That Communicates Your Interpretation	Landscape/ Background Ideas	Colors/Lines/Other Graphic Elements
Sylvia suffered from manic depression and attempted suicide several times.	What is manic depression?	Manic depression is a brain disorder that causes unusual changes in the person's mood, energy, and ability to function. Maybe Sylvia Plath was depressed because she wanted to be a famous poet but became a wife and mother. Her husband, the poet Ted Hughes, became the famous poet instead.	Could show a series of "happy" moments when Sylvia is feeling good about her life, followed by scenes of "low" moments when Sylvia contemplates suicide. "Happy" moments—when Sylvia gets a poem published, or gets a scholarship. "Low" moments?? When she finds out her husband has an affair.	England—where Sylvia and Ted lived for a while. Backdrop of husband/babies and foreground of a desk where Sylvia wants to be writing but can't because she is cooking or doing a domestic chore.	Black, dark colors for "low" scenes. Bright, vivid colors for "happy" scenes. Go back and forth between these scenes/colors.

FIGURE 7.2. Research planning guide. Adapted from *A Teacher's Guide to the Multigenre Research Project: Everything You Need to Know to Get Started*, by M. Putz, 2006, Portsmouth, NH: Heinemann.

Adventure and Mystery Novels: Scaffolding Comprehension to Improve Inference and Prediction Skills

8

Adventures and mysteries. Classroom reading researchers continue to tell us these are adolescents' preferred genres of young adult literature (Hopper, 2005; Ivey & Broaddus, 2001). Perhaps it is the action in adventures—the conflicts, tensions, frustrated heroes, and surprises—that entice adolescents (Donelson & Nilsen, 2004). With mysteries, perhaps it is the invitation to suspend disbelief, the not knowing, or a desire to beat the detectives at their own game that hooks readers. While adventure stories may call to mind Gary Paulsen's *Hatchet* (1987) or Louis Sachar's *Holes* (2000), in which young men struggle for survival out in the wild, the genre also includes tales such as Geraldine McCaughrean's (2007) *The White Darkness* and Alane Ferguson's (2006) *Christopher Killer* (Forensic Mystery) series, in which female protagonists contend with mystery, and physical and psychological struggles. When adults think of mysteries, authors such as Agatha Christie, Sir Arthur Conan Doyle, and Sue Grafton come to mind. For today's teens, though, popular mysteries include Patrick Carman's (2009) *Skeleton Creek*, Gail Giles's (2007) *What Happened to Cass McBride?*, and Carl Hiassen's eco-thrillers *Hoot* (2002) and *Scat* (2010), just to name a few.

Elements of Adventure and Mystery Novels

Donelson and Nilsen (2004) note that adventure tales usually focus on themes of either person-versus-person or person-versus-nature, with a person-versus-self element becoming significant only as the story develops and the protagonist faces frustration and potential failure. They further claim that good adventure stories should possess the following elements:

- a likeable protagonist with whom readers can identify;
- an adventure that readers can imagine happening to them themselves;

- effective characterization;
- an interesting setting that adds to the story without getting in the way of the plot; and
- action that draws readers into the plot within the first page or so of the story.

As with variations in the adventure novel, there are several types of young adult mystery novels: fantasy, forensic/crime, historical, humorous, puzzles, and time travel (Cole, 2009). Regardless of the type of mystery, critics usually agree that quality mystery novels meet several criteria:

- Clues must be carefully placed and available to the reader.
- Teasers must be introduced early on.
- The outcome should not be predictable.
- The setting should be integral.

It is the previous criteria and elements that make adventure and mystery tales the ideal support for teaching inference and prediction skills. Solving a mystery and then overcoming the psychological struggle in an adventure both require inferential thinking and predicting.

English teachers may worry that these mystery and adventure genres are good for entertainment value only, but in this chapter we focus on two titles, one with a male protagonist and the other with a female hero, that should disprove such worries and show how these two genres of young adult literature are naturals for teaching and reinforcing inference and prediction skills. Marcus Zusak's (2006) *I Am the Messenger* and E. Lockheart's (2008) *The Disreputable History of Frankie Landau-Banks* integrate elements of the adventure and mystery novel: the protagonists in both novels are on quests that involve mystery and intrigue but are faced with confronting their own personal issues as the story develops. We summarize both next and provide information on how they stack up against Jago's criteria (see Figure 8.1). Then we provide background on the importance of inference and prediction skills for adolescent readers and some instructional ideas teachers can use in their classrooms for both whole-class and small-group instruction.

	I Am the Messenger by Marcus Zusak **2006 ALA Top Ten Best Books for Young Adults** **2006 ALA Michael L. Printz Honor Book**	*The Disreputable History of Frankie Landau-Banks* by E. Lockhart **2008 Michael L. Printz Honor Book** **2008 National Book Award Finalist**
Summary	Nineteen-year-old Ed is a simple, average Australian cab driver until he begins receiving mysterious messages on playing cards. As he figures out what he is supposed to do for each one, he meets a range of characters to comfort, protect, and befriend. As readers follow Ed throughout his missions, they are left questioning who—or what—is behind the cards. What is their ultimate purpose? What is Ed's ultimate purpose?	"Though not, in hindsight, so startling as the misdeeds she would perpetrate when she returned to boarding school as a sophomore, what happened to Frankie Landau-Banks the summer after her freshman year was a shock." So begins Lockhart's witty, yet serious, novel about a fifteen-year-old girl who wreaks havoc on her boarding school by infiltrating and pranking the school's all-male secret society.
Criterion 1: *Written in language perfectly suited to the author's purpose*	Aside from the Australian terms/dialect/slang (*bloke, Norsca spray*, etc.), which might trip up some readers, the language works well. Ed's conversations with his friends and his mother are particularly realistic, and although there is a required suspension of disbelief in his dialogue with the people he is sent to help, that seems to work as well. Ed's narration comes across as just a guy telling a story, which may be the point. Ed is an average guy, with an average job—until he is given missions to complete. The witty humor of the dialogue is complemented by short, one-liner sentences—most are a sole word or a short fragment breaking up the text. The style fits the book beautifully.	Frankie is smart, very smart, but she is also a "real" girl. Told in third-person point of view, Lockhart manages to effectively capture all the nuances and contradictions of a teenager—and the reader forgets the story isn't coming from Frankie herself. The descriptions and the dialogue (including Frankie's inner speech) are real and vivid: "Matthew called her harmless. Harmless. And being with him made Frankie feel squashed into a box—a box where she was expected to be sweet and sensitive (but not oversensitive); a box for young and pretty girls who were not as bright or powerful as their boyfriends" (p. 214).
Criterion 2: *Exposes readers to complex human dilemmas*	The entire novel is centered on a complex dilemma: deciding between right and wrong, getting involved, or minding one's own business, while exploring one's own moral integrity. Each of Ed's messages and ensuing missions exposes readers to real situations and decisions. Ed encounters spousal abuse, rape, family problems, loneliness, fear of loving, poverty, failed hopes, and discouragement. Beyond these, Ed faces a dysfunctional relationship with his mother, who clearly does not like him, and his feelings for Audrey, who seems forever out of his grasp.	Admittedly, very few readers will attend a private boarding school. However, most readers will face some of the issues Frankie does: divorced parents, an overprotective mother, bucking the system, dating, conforming (or not), etc. Yet the main dilemma Frankie faces is one that all teens encounter: discovering who you are and what you believe in and stand for. "It is better to be alone, she figures, than to be with someone who can't see who you are. It is better to lead than to follow. It is better to speak up than stay silent" (p. 342).
Criterion 3: *Includes compelling, disconcerting characters*	Though the novel does require a suspension of disbelief, the characters are very compelling, especially Ed. For all his flaws, Ed is a likeable protagonist set out on a journey, and his loyal band of friends—although they're abrasive, lazy, or emotionally damaged—have characteristics that make them compelling. Ed's mother is very disconcerting, nearly hate-able, but redeems herself. The people Ed meets through the anonymous messages—a rapist and wife beater, a lonely old woman pining for her lost love, a young runner who never seems to come in first—are all compelling or disconcerting in their own way. Then there is the deliverer of the messages himself or herself. As one student in Lisa's course reflected, "The unknown identity of this complex scheme is the most disconcerting character in the book [and] compelled me to continue to read. It also kept me guessing throughout the story as to who could have concocted this elaborate game."	"I, Frankie Landau-Banks, hereby confess that I was the sole mastermind behind the mal-doings of the Loyal Order of the Basset Hounds. I take full responsibility for the disruptions cause by the Order" (p. 1). With this opening, readers will be compelled to read further. What mal-doings? What disruptions? Frankie will captivate readers, both male and female, and along with her are numerous others. Particularly intriguing is "Alpha," Frankie's nemesis. Beyond these characters themselves, what pulls the reader in are the complex relationships between them. Despite the animosity between them, do Frankie and Alpha secretly like each other? The story between them is ripe for analysis and psychoanalysis. Students can play armchair Dr. Phils or Oprahs and discuss what Frankie and Alpha do and say, as well as say and don't say. *continued on next page*

FIGURE 8.1. Reviews of *I Am the Messenger* by Marcus Zusak and *The Disreputable History of Frankie Landau-Banks* by E. Lockhart, based on Carol Jago's criteria for selecting a whole-class novel.

FIGURE 8.1. Continued

Criterion 4: Explores universal themes that combine different periods and cultures	Set in the present, in Australia, the novel explores the universal themes of hope and achieving one's purpose in life. Hope will always be a theme in life and literature. Ed brings hope, compassion, and tenderness to himself and the other characters through his actions. The idea of finding one's place or becoming something better is something that teens can appreciate.	Alabaster Prep, an exclusive boarding school in Massachusetts, will be millions of miles and experiences away from most readers. Yet high school for teenagers is nearly the same, no matter what type of school one attends. Themes like loss, sorrow, guilt, love, hate, envy, confusion, difference, revenge, and regret are timeless and universal.
Criterion 5: Challenges readers to reexamine their beliefs	This novel could definitely challenge teens to reexamine their beliefs. Even older students are impacted by the book, as the following quote shows: "I think the message isn't enough to simply skate through life. What are you doing to help humanity? What could buying someone an ice cream cone really do? I definitely reexamined my beliefs. It made me think about what could happen by just helping one person." This is a natural book to pair with the popular movie *Pay It Forward* (2000) or, better yet, the book of the same title by Catherine Ryan Hyde (2000) who also has a foundation with teacher resources, http://www.payitforwardfoundation.org.	Revenge is an action that is quick to happen, often without thought for many people, but especially children and teenagers. Readers will sympathize and support Frankie in her quest to infiltrate the "boys' club" and bring them down. However, readers will also see the negative aspects of payback, including losing friends, credibility, and respect. A life lesson will also be learned about how juvenile actions can have serious consequences. Readers will be challenged to rethink rash and seemingly harmless pranks and activities.
Criterion 6: Tells a good story with places for laughing and crying	This story has both humor and despair. The Doorman, Ed's dog, is a source of sadness and comic relief. His physical description alone is quite humorous: "he stinks a kind of stink that's impossible to rid him of" (p. 18). His faithful companionship is significant to Ed and very touching. Ed's messages lead him to pain and horror, and those are places for crying. Yet Zusak is able to balance this tension with moments of wit and humor to keep the reader going.	There are plenty of places for laughing in Lockhart's novel. The witty language only adds to the humor. The email exchanges between Frankie and Alpha, in particular, are entertaining. Yet despite the laughter, the book is rather serious. Readers who have experienced similar events in their life will be sad for Frankie. In her quest to challenge the boys at her school, she loses a boyfriend and countless friends. In the end, she is left alone. And, with the last line, "She doesn't feel like crying anymore," readers will have to discern whether that is due to contentment or resignation.

The Importance of Inference and Prediction Skills

Blank stares when you ask a question about the text. No hands raised, everyone looking busy. Sound familiar? Your first thought: they didn't read last night's assignment. Then you move on: Could it be the question you asked? Could it be their level of understanding? Could it be both?

The data are shocking: very few eighth-grade students read at the advanced level, and approximately one-third of high school ninth graders are two or more years below grade level in reading (Balfanz, McPartland, & Shaw, 2002; Perie, Grigg, & Donahue, 2005). The problem often lies in students' inability to comprehend what they read. What does it mean to comprehend? And where do students have difficulty?

As Kylene Beers (2003) states, "Comprehension is both a product and a process, something that requires purposeful, strategic effort on the reader's part—anticipating the direction of the text (predicting) . . . connecting what's in the text to what's in our mind to make an educated guess about what's going on (inferencing)" (pp. 45–46). However, what complicates this effort is that making inferences and predicting are complex interrelated processes; making inferences involves six mental processes in order to arrive at a conclusion (Block, 2004; see also Britton & Graesser, 1996). Also, when teachers tell students to *"read between the lines, make an inference, draw a conclusion, think harder,* they are not showing students *how* to infer, they are merely *telling* them how to infer" (Tovani, 2000, p. 99).

It is a mistake to assume that students understand what they read simply because they can: (1) answer questions, (2) restate, retell, or summarize text, and (3) learn vocabulary (Keene, 2007). Many students can comprehend at the literal level. However, in order to reach higher levels of comprehension—and interpret, evaluate, predict, and make inferences—students need scaffolding experiences that encourage them to question and discuss texts and to make them active meaning makers (Fisher, 2008; cited in Scherff, in press).

In this chapter we focus on ideas to assist students who might have problems with comprehension and need scaffolding—especially when it comes to answering the types of questions that are posed on standardized tests. We present two strategies that can be varied for whole-class, small-group, and individual use: the Seven Cs of Comprehension and Reading Level Inventories (see also Scherff [in press] for a discussion of how both of these strategies can be combined with literary theory and for use with middle school readers).

The Seven Cs of Comprehension

Farmer and Soden's (2005) "Seven Cs of Comprehension," although originally designed to be used with the teaching of a new concept or part of an inquiry project, is perfect for novel study. This strategy is very similar to the KWL (Know–Want to Know–Learned; Ogle, 1986), except that it includes more opportunities for students to speak, listen, and write.

In Figure 8.2, we outline one way a modified version of the Seven Cs could be used with the first few chapters of *I Am the Messenger*. We provide information about how teachers could complete the first four steps; the final three steps need little explanation. At the *connect* stage, teachers stimulate background knowledge and prediction through questions or other prereading strategies. In the *clarify* stage, teachers have students confirm or challenge their initial assumptions from the *connect* stage through discussion. The *consider* stage requires that students pose their own questions about what they will read. These questions are used to guide their reading of the novel and then are answered in the *collect*

Seven Stages	Examples from *I Am the Messenger* by Marcus Zusak
Connect—In this prereading stage, teachers introduce the novel to students; a number of reading strategies could be used (brainstorming, anticipation guide, etc.).	Possible questions to pose: —"Look at the front cover. What do you think a playing card might have to do with the title?" —"Read the back cover; who do you think is behind Ed's mission?" Prereading strategies to "connect" students—use probable passage (see Figure 8.3).
Clarify—Teachers work to confirm or challenge students' prior knowledge.	
Consider—Students write three questions that they will consider throughout their reading; these should be relevant and detailed.	If probable passage is used, then students can use the questions generated.
Collect—Students try to find answers to their questions (from the novel).	If probable passage is used, then students can use the questions generated.
Converse—In pairs, one student shares knowledge learned with his or her partner while that person writes a summary of what is said; then the writer reads the summary back to the speaker.	In these stages, students continue to build upon their initial predictions by reading, writing, summarizing, speaking, and listening. This cyclical pattern serves to clarify and reinforce knowledge and comprehension.
Conclude—Students use the written summary in the Converse step to write a more lengthy summary in their own words.	
Calculate—Students add to their summaries by predicting what will happen in the next stage of reading.	

FIGURE 8.2. Seven Cs of Comprehension. Adapted from "The Seven Cs of Comprehension," by M. Farmer and J. A. Soden, 2005, *Voices from the Middle, 13*(2), pp. 20–23.

phase. The final three steps are cyclical in nature—students revisit their questions as they discuss, summarize, and predict. This Seven Cs process can be repeated throughout the course of the novel study. In what follows, we present steps we would follow based on the first three chapters of *I Am the Messenger*.

First, we would complete the probable passage worksheet with students (see Figure 8.3). Probable passage (Wood, 1984) is a prereading strategy designed to build background knowledge and aid in building predicting and inference-making skills. To complete the worksheet, teachers would follow the following steps:

1. Choose eight to fourteen important words or phrases from the story that reflect important story grammar elements, such as *characters, setting,* and *plot* (beginning, rising action, ending, etc.) and write them on an overhead or the chalkboard (you can also include some unknown words that are critical to the story).

Probable Passage

Title of Selection: I Am the Messenger

Characters	Setting	Problem
Marv Ed Audrey Ritchie gunman	bank 45 Edgar St.	robbery cops car envelope

Gist Statement

I think I'm going to read about.... a gunman who robs a bank located at 45 Edgar Street. People in the bank are named Marv, Ed, Audrey, and Ritchie. The cops catch the robber while he is driving his car.

Outcomes

The robber goes to jail.

Questions I have

1. What does the Ace of Diamonds mean?
2. Did anyone get shot?
3. How much money was stolen?

FIGURE 8.3. Sample probable passage worksheet for *I Am the Messenger* by Marcus Zusak. Adapted from *When Kids Can't Read, What Teachers Can Do: A Guide for Teachers, 6–12* by K. Beers, 2003, Portsmouth, NH: Heinemann.

2. Present students with a probable passage worksheet that includes boxes that are labeled according to the elements selected in step 1 (characters, setting, problem, outcomes, etc.) In addition to the boxes, create lines or spaces designated for writing a prediction statement (gist).

3. Read the words and phrases to the students, directing them to place the words in the appropriate boxes (based on where they think they go). Point out that some words may fit in more than one box.

4. Working alone, in pairs, or in small groups, students discuss the words and phrases and decide into which boxes to place them.

5. Using the boxes, students create a gist statement and pose three questions.

6. When the worksheets are finished, each student (or group) reads his or her gist statement out loud and shares three questions.

7. Next, read the text aloud or have students read it themselves, depending on their ability level.

8. After reading, students compare their probable passages to the story and discuss where the author would have placed the words.

9. As a follow-up, students can revise their gist statements. (For more on "probable passage," see Beers, 2003.)

While the probable passage can be used for the book as a whole, because the story is complex and involves a series of missions, each with its own set of characters and problems, we would recommend using it with the first few chapters and then repeating it again. Figure 8.3 shows a completed probable passage sheet based on the first three chapters of *I Am the Messenger*. This sheet could then be used to address the *connect*, *clarify*, *consider*, and *collect* stages in the Seven Cs of Comprehension (see Figure 8.2).

Reading Level Inventories

While reading *English Journal* last year, we came across an article by Declan Fitz-Patrick. FitzPatrick found that his students had problems discussing complex texts because they needed support at "lower levels of comprehension" (2008, p. 57). He turned to George Hillocks's (1980) Reading Level Inventories, which were designed to determine "students' ability to make increasingly complex inferences about fiction" (p. 57). Because the questions increase in sophistication, teachers can use the inventory to better gauge their students' comprehension levels.

If students struggle with higher levels of questioning, then teachers can better plan and scaffold literature instruction and discussion. The levels start with the most basic information—the stated (characters, setting)—and increase in complexity, moving on to a simple inference (level 4) and ending with questions that ask readers to pull everything together (level 7). Next we show

FitzPatrick's reading levels and example questions from *The Disreputable History of Frankie Landau-Banks* that students in Lisa's young adult literature class created. As you can see, the questions build in task demand and complexity. Teachers have several options: (1) they can assign all questions to the class, for individual or group work; (2) they can differentiate according to student ability and assign certain questions to individual students or groups; or (3) they can pose these as oral discussion questions, starting at a midpoint to gauge students' understanding and ability to make inferences and then proceed from there.

Level 1: People, Location, and Action. Basics of who is in the story, what people are doing, where they are; restating important information; identifying major revelations.

- Who are Frankie, Alpha, Matthew, Porter, Zada, Trish, and Dean? Describe them and their relationships to one another.
- Summarize what has happened in the story so far.

Level 2: Turning Points, Key Details. Determining which events change the course of the story; distinguishing between important and irrelevant information; identifying facts that have the greatest impact on the plot.

- Refer to the list of six things on pages 23–25 of the novel; what details do you think are important? Which ones are unimportant? Why?
- On page 236, Frankie changes the Halloween plans by way of email. How does this affect the course of the novel?

Level 3: Reasons and Explanations, Cause and Effect. Reexplaining a connection stated in the text.

- Compare and contrast how Frankie's mom and dad treat her.
- How does Frankie's impression of Alpha change from when she encounters him on the boardwalk to when she meets him at Alabaster?

Level 4: Inference. Explaining the implication of a particular statement in the text.

- Go back and read Chapter 1 again. From what Frankie writes, do you think she is really sorry? Explain.
- Referring to page 333, in Alpha's last email to Frankie, when he writes, "That was the guy I'd like to be. The guy I'm not, really," what does this say about him? What especially in regard to his status as "Alpha dog"?

Level 5: Generalization and Evaluation. Demonstrating the implied connection between several details from various places; generalizing about a major change in a character; generalizing about implied comparisons or contrasts.

- So far, throughout the first ten chapters, we have come across multiple references to dogs (alpha dog, pack, runt, etc.). Go back through all the chapters and note the dog references. Once you have your list, make some guesses as to what this means in general to the story.
- On page 329, Porter asks Frankie, "Why did you do all that?" Why do you think she did "all that" (the pranks, impersonating, etc.)?

Level 6: Application of Generalization. Supporting a generalization about the world using evidence from the text; applying the generalizations suggested in the text to the world; demonstrating the implications of the author's representation of the world.

- In Chapter 10 ("The Panopticon"), we learn about the panopticon and how it influenced behavior. Frankie says, "so you follow the rules whether someone's watching you or not" (p. 54). Is this true? Do we operate differently if we think we are being watched? Explain/justify your response.
- Do you think the Bassets were wrong to exclude women from their society? Do you think it would have made the society strong to include women? Explain.

Level 7: Structural Generalization. Supporting a generalization about the purpose of literary elements used in the story; explaining how the author's generalization is supported by the structure of the story; connecting literary techniques to a generalization about human experience.

- Why does the author write in the third person (he, she, they) instead of the first person (I, me) point of view? Is this point of view effective? Why or why not?
- Considering the heavy pro-feminist/equality point of view in the story, how would the novel be different if told from Matthew or Alpha's perspective?

When asked to reflect on this exercise, Lisa's students all agreed that knowing how to craft different levels of questions was extremely important. Kevin wrote, "It helps develop the critical thinking skills of students. It challenges them to think about what they read and take their thoughts a little deeper by analyzing them." Mollie added, "Novels have more value than just what can be found simply on the shallow surface. Students need to be guided through the different levels of reading comprehension in order to develop their own reading skills." Other students thought of ways to extend this exercise. Capri plans on using this for essays. She suggests that teachers could "provide varying levels of questions for students to choose from, each having their own individual point value. Set a certain number of points that the student must have, and they must answer the number of questions that will help them get full credit. For example, a level four question may be worth four points, while a harder question would be worth more." We think the activities we describe in this chapter will help you and your students be on your way toward improved comprehension skills.

9 Fantasy, the Supernatural, and Science Fiction: Reading Ladders and Ethical Discussions

Harry Potter. The Twilight series. *Feed*. Why are some teachers hesitant to incorporate science fiction and fantasy titles like these into literature instruction? Common hindrances include curricular limitations, censorship fears, a lack of books, and questions about how to introduce these texts as whole-class reading rather than as individual recommendations (Bucher & Hinton, 2010; Zigo & Moore, 2004). Yet "science fiction and fantasy themes are the driving force behind much of popular culture, from movies, comics, and graphic novels to video and computer games" (Arnold & Kunzel, 2007, p. 118). Arnold and Kunzel (2007) explain that science fiction and fantasy genres ask "What if?" and involve strong underlying themes (e.g., good versus evil, being different, taking responsibility for one's actions, hope in a cruel and menacing world, self-reliance) (pp. 118, 121).

Donelson and Nilsen (2004) claim that the boundaries between fantasy/ supernatural fiction and science fiction are "fuzzy" (p. 199), but we think there are some unique differences between the two that make their consideration for whole-class instruction worthwhile. As an example, the predominant characteristics and themes in fantasy/supernatural young adult literature genres—namely, the macabre manipulation of human-hood; the portrayal of, attraction to, and sympathy for the grotesque, the unusual, the transfigured, and the outcast; the identity making that goes on at the margins of "civilized" life; the necessary ability to shape-shift, to adapt and change to one's evolving environment; the blurring of good versus evil—have much in common with characteristics found in more traditional Romantic and Gothic literature (think *Frankenstein*, *Dracula*, and *Dr. Jekyll and Mr. Hyde*).

According to Bucher and Hinton (2010), a well-written fantasy should have the following characteristics:

- The impossible should seem possible.

- Characters should behave in reasonable and expected ways.

- Magic must work consistently.

- Rules must be followed.

- The fantasy world must bear a relationship to our own.

- The fantasy should not be unfairly taken away at the book's end under the pretext that everything that happened was just a dream.

- Once the reader is committed to the fantasy world, the author should never trick or deceive the reader. (p. 197)

Science fiction, unlike fantasy/supernatural literature, tends to be based on current science as well as trends and technology in an effort to envisage or describe the future (Arnold & Kunzel, 2007; Ochoa & Osier, 1993). And unlike fantasy's typical restoration of order, science fiction usually "establishes a new order" (Arnold & Kunzel, p. 118). Bucher and Hinton (2010) describe several types of young adult science fiction: (1) earth's future tales, such as nuclear war and alien invasions; (2) tales that contradict known laws of nature (time travel, anti-aging, etc.); (3) other worlds; (4) utopias, dystopias, and anti-utopias (utopias that have become flawed); and (5) alternative histories. While the genre often sets its stories in futures we can only imagine, it affords teachers and students opportunities to question and critique contemporary society and man's ability to use technology wisely. As Bucher and Manning (2001) explain:

> Its appeal comes from its imagination and vision of the past, present, and future. Imagination comes into play as science fiction challenges readers to first imagine and then to realize the future of not only the novel they are reading but, in juxtaposition, the world in which they live. Well-written science fiction both warns and teaches readers to build the future they want, based upon logic and knowledge, and does so in a pleasing and entertaining manner. (p. 4)

When selecting science fiction titles, teachers should look for the following characteristics:

- Strong themes that are basic to human existence and that do not rely on time or place

- Nonstereotypical characters who believe in the science and who rise to meet and overcome challenges

- Well-developed and plausible plots

- Believable details and accurate and well-researched science and/or technology
- Reliance on science, not coincidence
- Escapist aspects with an interesting story that does not talk down to the reader. (Bucher & Hinton, 2010, p. 190)

In this chapter, we have attempted to include the best well-written young adult literature we could find to aid teachers' decision making as they consider the genres' use in whole-class instruction. Rather than present titles by specific genre (i.e., science fiction, fantasy), we offer related titles organized by "reading ladders," which we explain in the next section.

Reading Ladders

Reading ladders are sets of related books (by genre, by theme, etc.) that can be grouped by age level or by increasing level of difficulty to serve students' needs and interests. The concept of reading ladders emerged in 1947 as part of an effort to "find materials and techniques for improving human relations" (Tway, 1981, p. 3). In selecting books for reading ladders, Tway noted that several factors must be taken into account; most notably the titles must be of superior literary quality.

More recently, Teri Lesesne (2010) has authored a book entitled *Reading Ladders: Leading Students from Where They Are to Where We'd Like Them to Be*. In this book, Lesesne describes the need for "diagonal" reading. Unlike horizontal or serial reading that some teens like to do, or the vertical reading typically seen in secondary schools (e.g., moving from a YA novel to a difficult classic), Lesesne explains that *diagonal* reading takes students from one level of reading to the "next logical level" (p. 47): "If students like certain types of books, certain genres, or certain qualities in a book, we can help them stretch as readers by showing them books that mirror what they already like but that perhaps are a little longer, are a bit more abstract, or will challenge them more" (p. 48).

Lesesne describes criteria for selecting books for reading ladders: (1) the books should be related in some way (e.g., thematically) and (2) should demonstrate a slow, gradual development from simple to complex. Ideally, the first rung of the reading ladder is a book that already has found a connection to a student and should be one that students will read without much prodding. The second book should be almost identical to the first, thereby making it likely that the student will read it. At each successive rung, the books are still reminiscent of the ones that preceded them but are increasingly complex. The books may or may not remain in one genre.

Borrowing from Lesesne's work, the reading ladders we feature in this chapter (see Figures 9.1 and 9.2) group a mix of fantasy, supernatural, and science fiction according to two general themes: *government regulation and control* and *humans playing God/man manipulating man*. (Note that some titles could fit under either theme and are marked with #.) Given the rapid changes in technology and medicine, the growth in globalization, and the multiple social and political conflicts (both here and abroad), most students will have enough background knowledge—and, we would argue, concern—to be interested in and think about these two broad themes. Both these themes, moreover, naturally lead to ethical discussions, the instructional emphasis of this chapter, which we address later in "The Need for Ethical Discussions."

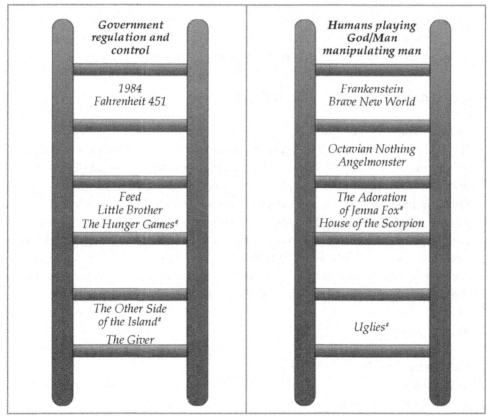

FIGURE 9.1. Reading ladder on the theme of government regulation and control.

FIGURE 9.2. Reading ladder on the theme of humans playing God/man manipulating man.

Our reading ladders are ranked according to increasing level of sophistication and reading ability. Thus, students who are interested in the theme of government control, but whose reading ability makes reading *1984* or *Fahrenheit 451* difficult, can read a related title, such as Suzanne Collins's (2008) *The Hunger Games*.

Also, we know Lois Lowry's (1993) *The Giver* is popular with students, as is Scott Westerfeld's (2005) *Uglies*. We don't imagine teachers would have trouble getting students to read these works, and thus we placed them on the bottom rungs. We think books like M. T. Anderson's (2004) *Feed* and Nancy Farmer's (2004) *The House of the Scorpion* propose logical, diagonal movement toward more difficult texts by preparing students to grapple with the sophisticated themes at play in *Frankenstein* and *1984*, without requiring an immediate jump to these novels from *The Giver* or *Uglies*.

Reading ladders grouped by theme also provide teachers with a ready-made set of titles for differentiating instruction. Through the reading ladders, all students experience the same content (by theme) but through a different process (specific novels). Moreover, these thematic groupings offer teachers titles they can use with different-ability literature circle groups. (Brief summaries of the books listed on the two thematic reading ladders follow.)

Government Regulation and Control

1984 by George Orwell

It is 1984 in London, the largest population center of Airstrip One, which is part of the immense entity of Oceania. In a terrifying country, where Big Brother is always watching and the thought police can virtually read your mind, Winston Smith is in serious danger because his memory still functions. He knows the Party's official image of the world is a fabrication and that the Party controls everyone by telling lies and narrowing their thoughts, isolating people from one another. Pulled into an illicit love affair, Winston finds the courage to join a secret revolutionary organization called The Brotherhood, which is dedicated to the destruction of the Party. This dystopian novel will resonate with those who read *The Other Side of the Island* or *Little Brother* first. (Adapted from a review at amazon.com)

Fahrenheit 451 by Ray Bradbury

In *Fahrenheit 451*, firemen don't put out fires; they start them in order to burn books. The appearance of happiness is the highest goal; trivial information is good and knowledge is bad. The protagonist, Guy Montag, is a book-burning fireman undergoing a crisis of faith. His wife spends all day with her television "family," begging Montag to work harder so that they can afford a fourth TV wall. Their empty lives sharply contrast with that of his next-door neighbor Clarisse, a young girl thrilled by the ideas in books. When Clarisse disappears, Montag is motivated to change and starts hiding books in his home. In time, his wife turns him in. After running away to avoid arrest, he joins a fugitive group of scholars who keep the contents of books in their heads, waiting for the time society will again turn to the wisdom of literature. (Adapted from a review at amazon.com)

Feed by M. T. Anderson

In this multiple award winner (e.g., National Book Award for Young People's Literature Finalist, 2002; Winner of the *Los Angeles Times* Book Prize, 2002), it is the future, and computers are no longer outside our bodies but wired directly into our brains when we're born. There is no quieting the Internet feed and its constant barrage of infomercials, news, and fashion advice. Want new jeans? The feed reads your mind and sends you images of all the latest brands. Fifteen-year-old Titus has it all—so he thinks—until a trip to the moon disrupts his feed, and he meets Violet, who teaches him about the importance of human connection.

Little Brother by Cory Doctorow

This 2008 ALA Best Books for Young Adults (which the author lets readers download for free from his website) is a fast-paced story of government control gone overboard and how technologically savvy teens can work together to stand up to it. Marcus (aka w1n5t0n) and his friends are skipping school when their city is attacked by terrorists. Thought to be attackers, the teens are held against their will and interrogated, even through extreme measures. Once out, they decide to take down the Department of Homeland Security and bring reason back to their city. Readers will cheer for this modern *1984* homage.

The Hunger Games by Suzanne Collins

A 2009 ALA Teens Top 10 book, this disturbingly fantastic futuristic novel tells the tale of a North America (now called Panem) divided into twelve districts. Each year the districts select, by a lottery system, one boy and one girl between the ages of twelve and eighteen to compete in "The Hunger Games," a televised fight to the death in which only one victor emerges. In order to save her younger sister, sixteen-year-old Katniss takes her place in the games. Not planning to win, Katniss soon decides that she must and can win. Blending fantasy, the supernatural, and science fiction, this novel will captivate male and female readers with its action, suspense, horror, romance, and readability. In 2009 the sequel, *Catching Fire* (which is just as good, if not better), was released, and the third installment, *Mockingjay*, was published in 2010. (Two years in a row, a majority of Lisa's students have voted *The Hunger Games* as their favorite book in the young adult literature course.)

The Other Side of the Island by Allegra Goodman

Ten-year-old Honor is the protagonist in this futuristic dystopian novel. It is sometime after Earth is ruined by global warming and pollution, and Honor and her parents move to Island 365 in the Tranquil Sea. Tranquil is an apt name because that is how Earth Mother (some "corporation" that controls everything) wants it. All citizens are shut in, enclosed by clear walls to keep things safe and calm. Gone is anything negative: books, songs, weather, feelings, and knowledge. As Honor and her parents learn, severe consequences await anyone who wants reality back in their lives. Will the Forecaster and his or her Partisans take down the Corporation and bring back truth and all that comes with it? At the end of the book, Goodman will leave readers hanging . . . and eagerly waiting the sequel that is sure to follow.

The Giver by Lois Lowry

In the first title of the ladder, *The Giver*, Lowry creates a utopian community where there are no choices; everyone has his or her place in the world assigned according to "gifts" and "interests." It is time for twelve-year-old Jonas to become the new Receiver of Memory. He will be the one to assume the collective memories of a society that lives only in the present, where "sameness" is the rule. However, Jonas quickly realizes the losses and uncovers the lie that supports his community. He decides he will change his world, but he can't foresee how that change will occur or what that change will mean for himself and the "newchild" Gabriel, whom he has resolved to protect. (Adapted from the publisher's website, randomhouse.com)

Humans Playing God/Man Manipulating Man

Frankenstein by Mary Shelley

Frankenstein, first published in 1818, opened the door for the new genre of science fiction. Shelley's novel also introduced a theme that is very important today: moral responsibility in light of scientific invention. The story centers on young Dr. Frankenstein and his obsession with giving an inanimate object life.

Upon seeing the grotesqueness of his creation, Dr. Frankenstein flees from it. The creature, however, pursues Frankenstein in order to be accepted. When he is rejected, both the creator and the creature are destroyed. Students who read *The Adoration of Jenna Fox* or *The House of the Scorpion* will be able to make connections between the novels. (Adapted from glencoe.com)

Brave New World by Aldous Huxley

In *Brave New World*, first published in 1931, "Community, Identity, Stability" is the motto of Huxley's utopian state. Everyone consumes daily grams of soma (to fight depression), babies are born in laboratories, and the most popular form of entertainment is a "feelie," a movie that stimulates sight, hearing, and touch. There is no violence, and everyone is provided for. Bernard Marx, the novel's protagonist, feels something is missing. He thinks that his relationship with a young woman has the promise to be more than the boundaries of their existence allow. In his classic, Huxley foreshadowed much of what we take for granted today. Those students who read several titles from this ladder will be able to make many connections between them. (Adapted from a review at amazon.com)

The Astonishing Life of Octavian Nothing, Traitor to the Nation; Volume 1: *The Pox Party* by M. T. Anderson

It is the late eighteenth century in the American colonies in this 2007 Printz Honor Book. Octavian grows up in a strange house full of men who appear to be almost magicians; he is loved by a beautiful mother, a royal queen whom everyone adores. Octavian seems the pampered prince in this setting: he is taught classical languages, science, and the violin. Slowly we learn, as he does too, that he and his mother (Cassiopeia) are black and slaves. The magician-like men are actually scientists, seeking to "scientifically" discover whether blacks really are inferior to whites. Octavian begins to understand the lies that his mother tells about herself and her world in order to survive; at the same time he grapples with their situation and his feelings for her. As Octavian matures into manhood and recognizes the harm done, his anger grows. He eventually escapes to fight in the Revolutionary War, only to learn that this is just another lie—freedom is not meant for him. In the end, he is forced to create a new future for himself.

Angelmonster by Veronica Bennett

Angelmonster is a part-true, part-fictional tale based on the life of Mary Shelley, the author of *Frankenstein*. Readers are presented with the background and ideas that influenced Mary's writing. In the spring of 1814, the sixteen-year-old girl meets the poet Percy Shelley and immediately falls for him. Despite the fact that he is married with children, they have an affair. They end up fleeing from England to Europe, taking her sister Jane with them (Jane later is involved with Lord Byron). Their families and society look down on them, and they become the object of merciless gossip. Their relationship is beset by jealousy, substance abuse, tragedy—as well as a deep love. As one reviewer wrote, Percy was both angel and monster to Mary, hence Bennett's title.

The Adoration of Jenna Fox by Mary E. Pearson

It is sometime in the (near?) future, and the Federal Science Ethics Board controls all research and medical procedures. Ever since illegal cloning "at the turn of the century," the FSEB now allows everyone 100 points—with all major procedures worth a certain amount. Jenna Fox has just awoken from a coma—and something isn't right. Does she trust the bits and pieces she is remembering or the home movies of her life that her parents show? As she puts the pieces together, she begins to understand the enormity of the reality of her life and the danger that she and her parents are in if the truth regarding her life gets exposed. This novel blending science fiction, ethics, and mystery will provide readers with much to discuss and debate. As a bonus, the publisher's website offers a discussion guide and biomedical ethics links.

The House of the Scorpion by Nancy Farmer

The first line of the back cover of this Newbery (2003) and National Book Award (2002) winner provides an ominous foretelling of the action, "Matteo Alacrán was not born; he was harvested." Early on in Farmer's book we learn that a clone, a child named Matt, in a country called Opium, is kept hidden from the outside world with no human contact. Celia, his caretaker, protects him from those who would seek to use and destroy him, not simply because he is a clone, but because he is clone of El Patrón, the 142-year-old ruler of Opium. Matt is El Patron's ticket to longevity. Once Matt's secret is out, El Patrón's ruthless, greedy family members begin to fight to protect what they think is theirs. The only way out is for the teenaged Matt to escape and attempt to live a life of his own. (One of Susan's students, Jessica, sees *House of the Scorpion* as encompassing *Frankenstein*, *Brave New World*, and *1984* all in one book. Jessica shared in class, "I couldn't teach *Frankenstein* and *Brave New World* and *1984* because I just don't have time, but I could teach *House of the Scorpion* and get at all the themes present in those three other works.")

Uglies by Scott Westerfeld

In the futuristic society portrayed by Westerfeld in his 2006 ALA Best Books for Young Adults title, *everyone* turns pretty on their sixteenth birthday. Gone are the days when people are judged by their appearances and people kill one another over skin color. In three months, Tally Youngblood will be sixteen, and she can't wait to join her best friend, Peris, in New Pretty Town, where everyone is equal, everyone looks beautifully similar, and everyone lives by the same motto: Act Stupid, Have Fun, and Make Noise. But then Tally meets Shay, who doesn't like imagining herself as a pretty and has traveled to the remote and mysterious Rusty Ruins. Slowly but surely, with Shay's encouragement, Tally begins to wonder why no one ever leaves New Pretty Town. Ultimately, Tally will have to make a choice that will change her life forever.

The Need for Ethical Discussions

In thinking about the importance of students taking part in ethical discussions, we are reminded of Postman and Weingartner's (1969) classic text, *Teaching as a Subversive Activity*. In it, they argue:

> The student must be central in any curriculum development . . . in that our curricula begin with what he feels, cares about, fears and yearns for. . . . If we can say that all human discovery, regardless of discipline, starts with an answerable question, then we ought to look at the curriculum as a series of questions from students that the school helps them to explore—regardless of how indelicate those questions might be. Any curriculum, after all, ought to recognize the existence of the real world. (p. 152)

Although written forty years ago, Postman and Weingartner's call for the pressing need for inquiry-driven instruction is very relevant today:

> The new education has as its purpose the development of a new kind of person, one who—as a result of internalizing a different series of concepts—is an actively inquiring, flexible, creative, innovative, tolerant, liberal personality who can face uncertainty and ambiguity without disorientation, who can formulate viable new meanings to meet changes in the environment which threaten individual and mutual survival. The new education, in sum, is new because it consists of having students use the concepts most appropriate to the world in which we all must live . . . [the] question-questioning, meaning-making process that is to be called "learning how to learn." This comprises a posture of stability from which to deal fruitfully with change. The purpose is to help all students develop built-in, shock-proof crap detectors as basic equipment in their survival kits. (pp. 184–185)

Science fiction/fantasy/supernatural texts, beyond their appeal to teens, offer not only a natural starting point for ethical discussions but also curricular connections to the fields of science and technology. The National Science Teachers Association's (NSTA) standards advocate for inquiry in the classroom and for such inquiry to be explicitly taught. Inquiry will, in turn, lead to "the development and use of higher-order thinking to address open-ended problems" (NSTA). The NSTA adds that because the objective of inquiry is to guide students to create their own knowledge, questioning is an essential skill. But how do teachers know when (and that) students are ready for complex discussions? Wolsey and Lapp (2009) pose several questions that help teachers consider and establish curricular conditions that might be necessary for meaningful discussion about sophisticated themes and issues to take place:

1. What background knowledge do students have about the topic?
2. What knowledge might students need to be exposed to before they can engage in meaningful discussion about the topic?
3. What discussion skills might students need to develop to participate in effective discussion?
4. Are multiple constructions of knowledge possible? (p. 373).

Depending on the answers to these reflective questions, students may need to spend a bit of time acquiring some background knowledge in order to better understand their own perspectives and the ideas of others before taking part in whole-class ethical discussions. One tool that can be especially helpful in assisting with this is Donna Alvermann's (1991) discussion web.

The Discussion Web

The discussion web (see Figure 9.3) is a tool (graphic organizer) to help scaffold and structure classroom discussions. It helps students think about the main elements of an issue and identify opposing points of view. This graphic organizer guides discussion by helping students to find ideas of disagreement, to consider opposite viewpoints, to critically assess the arguments, and to draw conclusions. This strategy provides a comprehensible "point–counterpoint" visual scaffold for analyzing texts (Just Read Now, n.d.). While discussion webs are useful tools for readers, they also aid in building background and challenging assumptions, and they can even serve as a prewriting tool for persuasive essays. Although originally developed by Duthie (1986), their use became more well known from Alvermann's (1991) article in *The Reading Teacher*.

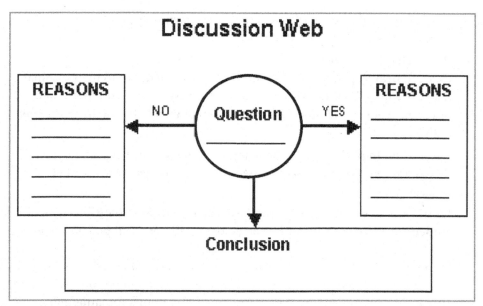

FIGURE 9.3. Discussion web.

We like how Billmeyer and Barton (1998) use the discussion web with students; it is modeled after a think-pair-share. Rather than immediately grouping students, have students first work individually, then move to pairs, and then to small groups, before having a whole-class discussion. We outline their steps below and then offer sample questions that could be used with the reading ladder novels. Because the ladders are thematically arranged, all students—no matter what novel they read (different *content*)—can take part in a lengthy, critical discussion (*product*). Teachers should follow these steps:

1. Before students read the selected novel(s), prepare them for the themes or critical issues that the novels contain and that will be the focus of classroom discussions, writing assignments, and so on.

2. Have students read the novel(s).

3. Introduce the discussion web (see Figure 9.3) with the question(s) of interest in the middle of the diagram. Explain to students that they will have to construct support for both viewpoints by citing specific reasons from the text. Give students time to come up with at least two reasons for each viewpoint.

4. Pair each student with a partner to share and discuss their written ideas.

Ask them to continue to discuss reasons for each viewpoint and to add to their original list based on that discussion.

5. Pair each set of students with another set of partners (forming groups of four). Repeat step 4, directing students to revise and add to their original list of reasons. From this discussion and the textual evidence presented, have the group come up with a "conclusion," which they write in the box at the bottom of the web.

6. Each group then shares its conclusion with the rest of the class. Further discussion should take place (students are encouraged to revise their webs if necessary).

7. From their webs, and based upon how teachers differentiate instruction, students can write either a persuasive paragraph or a full persuasive essay.

Students in Lisa's young adult literature class brainstormed and came up with the following general questions related to the two themes of government regulation and control and humans playing God/man manipulating man:

1. Government Regulation and Control

   • Based on the novel(s) [you read], was there too much government control of its citizens?

   • Does the government have the right to use any means necessary to get information?

   • Should the government regulate what we watch on TV and have access to on the Internet?

2. Humans Playing God/Man Manipulating Man

   • Based on the novel(s) [you read], do you think that the way that humans manipulated one another made things worse than they were before?

   • In your book(s), the limits of science are tested; do you think that just because something is possible scientifically that we should do it?

   • Is genetic cloning a good thing to do?

Figure 9.4 shows a completed discussion web and written response composed by Kevin, Amy, and Jenny, based on their reading of *Little Brother*. As their written response shows, the discussion web helps students to generate justifications for both sides of the argument; this, in turn, helps them craft a more thorough response.

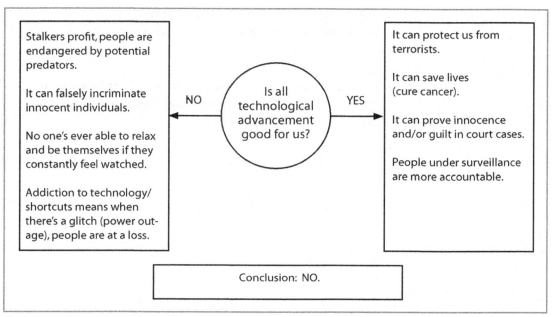

Stalkers profit, people are endangered by potential predators.

It can falsely incriminate innocent individuals.

No one's ever able to relax and be themselves if they constantly feel watched.

Addiction to technology/shortcuts means when there's a glitch (power outage), people are at a loss.

NO

Is all technological advancement good for us?

YES

It can protect us from terrorists.

It can save lives (cure cancer).

It can prove innocence and/or guilt in court cases.

People under surveillance are more accountable.

Conclusion: NO.

FIGURE 9.4. Sample web on the topic "Is all technological advancement good for us?"

After students completed the web, they prepared the following written response:

Technological advancement can be incredibly beneficial. The CIA's surveillance can protect us from terrorist attacks. Medical advancements in technology can make diagnosis and treatment more efficient and save lives before a disease has time to overrun a body. Perhaps technology will lead oncology researchers to a cure for cancer. Text message device records can prove guilt or innocence in court cases. Also, a huge benefit, people under surveillance are more likely to behave "well" because they become accountable for their actions.

However, even with all of the benefits of technological advancements, not all of them are good for us. The same people who have accountable behavior under surveillance may never be able to relax and be themselves because they constantly feel watched. Even beyond that, that feeling can progress to paranoia and insanity. The same technology used to "prove" guilt or innocence could falsely incriminate an innocent individual in the wrong place at the wrong time, or whose device was in the wrong place at the wrong time. In addition, stalkers can hack into or buy surveillance systems or spyware and people are opened up to potential predator attacks or invasions. Finally, advancements can cause a dependence (even addiction to) on technology and when there's a glitch in the system or a power outage, the system is handicapped. When the possibilities are thought out and the pros and cons weighed, not all technological advancements are necessarily benevolent to the people.

Use science fiction and fantasy-themed young adult novels, the concept of reading ladders, and discussion webs in your own classroom to get students talking about the role technology plays in our lives today.

Conclusion

As this book goes to press, we continue to juggle multiple young adult novels (we literally have stacks and stacks of YA books by our beds and in our offices) as we strive to stay abreast of new trends in the genre, prepare for upcoming courses and presentations, and search for that next gem of a book we can't wait to share with teachers and talk about with teens. We certainly are fans of the genre, and we'd love to hear from you if you're a fan, too! What are you currently reading? (We can't read them all!) We also love to get into classrooms where teens are reading young adult literature and conduct workshops for teachers, so let us know if you'd like us to come to you! We will!

We think it's important for teachers to collaborate and share ideas—ultimately, we see this book as a conversation we'd like to start with you; we'd love to talk to you about the ideas we present in this book. What questions do you have after reading? What strategies or activities did you try? How did it go? How would you modify them for your students? What do you think we missed or neglected? What do you need more of?

We invite you to start the professional conversation with us about young adult literature, differentiated reading instruction, and reading engagement. Let's help each other get teens excited about reading in our classrooms. Get in touch!

Susan L. Groenke, PhD
417 Bailey Education Complex
1122 Volunteer Boulevard
University of Tennessee
Knoxville, TN 37996
sgroenke@utk.edu
(865) 974-4242

Lisa Scherff, PhD
213 Carmichael Hall
Box 870232
The University of Alabama
Tuscaloosa, AL 35487-0232
lscherff@bamaed.ua.edu
(205) 348-5872

References

Professional Resources

Albright, L. K., & Ariail M. (2005). Tapping the potential of teacher read-alouds in middle schools. *Journal of Adolescent and Adult Literacy, 48*(7), 582–591.

Alexander, J. (2005). The verse-novel: A new genre. *Children's Literature in Education, 36*(3), 269–283.

Allen, J. (1995). *It's never too late: Leading adolescents to lifelong literacy.* Portsmouth, NH: Heinemann.

Allington, R. L. (2006). *What really matters for struggling readers: Designing research-based programs* (2nd ed.). Boston: Pearson/Allyn and Bacon.

Allington, R. L. (2009). *What really matters in fluency: Research-based practices across the curriculum.* Boston: Pearson/Allyn and Bacon.

Alvermann, D. E. (1991). The discussion web: A graphic aid for learning across the curriculum. *The Reading Teacher, 45*(2), 92–99.

Alvermann, D. E. (Ed.) (2002). *Adolescents and literacies in a digital world.* New York: P. Lang.

Alvermann, D. E., & Phelps, S. F. (1998). *Content reading and literacy: Succeeding in today's diverse classrooms* (2nd ed.). Boston: Allyn and Bacon.

Ammons, B., Bonds, C., & Figgs, L. (1999). *Differentiated literature circles.* Paper presented at the annual meeting of the National Association for the Gifted and Talented Conference, College of William and Mary, Williamsburg, VA.

Anderson, G. L., & Irvine, P. (1993). Informing critical literacy with ethnography. In C. Lankshear & P. McLaren (Eds.), *Critical literacy: Politics, praxis, and the postmodern* (pp. 81–104). Albany: State University of New York Press.

Anderson, L.W., & Krathwohl, D. R. (Eds.). (2001). *A taxonomy for learning, teaching, and assessing: A revision of Bloom's taxonomy of educational objectives.* New York: Longman.

Anderson, R. C., Hiebert, E. H., Scott, J. A., & Wilkinson, I. A. G. (1985). *Becoming a nation of readers.* Washington, DC: National Institute of Education.

Applebee, A. N. (1993). *Literature in the secondary school: Studies of curriculum and instruction in the United States*. Urbana, IL: National Council of Teachers of English.

Appleman, D. (2000). *Critical encounters in high school English: Teaching literary theory to adolescents*. New York: Teachers College Press.

Arnold, M., & Kunzel, B. (2007). Bold books for teenagers: Speculative fiction: Classroom must-reads. *English Journal, 97*(1), 118–122.

Ashcraft, C. (2006). "Girl, you better go get you a condom": Popular culture and teen sexuality as resources for critical multicultural curriculum. *Teachers College Record, 108*(10), 2145–2186.

Athanases, S. Z. (1998). Diverse learners, diverse texts: Exploring identity and difference through literary encounters. *Journal of Literacy Research, 30*(2), 273–296.

Atwell, N. (1998). *In the middle: New understandings about writing, reading, and learning*. Portsmouth, NH: Boynton/Cook.

Au, K., & Kaomea, J. (2008). Reading comprehension and diversity in historical perspective: Literacy, power, and native Hawaiians. In S. E. Israel & G. G. Duffy (Eds.), *Handbook of research on reading comprehension* (pp. 1197–1230). London: Routledge.

"Author profile: Walter Dean Myers." (2001). Retrieved April 12, 2008, from http://www.teenreads.com/authors/au-myers-walterdean.asp#view010605

Baker, R., & Zinsser, W. K. (Eds.). (1987). *Inventing the truth: The art and craft of memoir*. Boston: Houghton Mifflin.

Balfanz, R., McPartland, J., & Shaw, A. (2002, April). Re-conceptualizing extra help for high school students in a high standards era (ED-99-CO-0160). Paper commissioned for *Preparing America's Future: The High School Symposium*. Washington, DC: Office of Vocational and Adult Education.

Beach, R., Thein, A. H., & Parks, D. L. (2007). *High school students' competing social worlds: Negotiating identities and allegiances in response to multicultural literature*. Mahwah, NJ: Erlbaum.

Bean, T. W., & Harper, H. J. (2006). Exploring notions of freedom in and through young adult literature. *Journal of Adolescent and Adult Literacy, 50*(2), 96–104.

Bean, T. W., & Moni, K. (2003). Developing students' critical literacy: Exploring identity construction in young adult fiction. *Journal of Adolescent and Adult Literacy, 46*(8), 638–648.

Beers, G. K. (2003). *When kids can't read, what teachers can do: A guide for teachers, 6–12*. Portsmouth, NH: Heinemann.

Bickmore, S. T. (2008). It is inexcusable to deny *inexcusable* a place in the classroom. *The ALAN Review, 35*(2), 75–83.

Billmeyer, R., & Barton, M. L. (1998). *Teaching reading in the content areas: If not me, then who? Teacher's manual*. Aurora, CO: McREL.

Bishop, R. S. (1992). Multicultural literature for children: Making informed choices. In V. J. Harris (Ed.), *Teaching multicultural literature in grades K–8* (pp. 37–53). Norwood, MA: Christopher-Gordon.

Blau, S. D. (2003). *The literature workshop: Teaching texts and their readers.* Portsmouth, NH: Heinemann.

Block, C. C. (2004). *Teaching comprehension: The comprehension process approach.* Boston: Pearson/Allyn and Bacon.

Bloom, B. S. (1956). *Taxonomy of educational objectives: The classification of educational goals. Handbook 1: Cognitive domain.* New York: D. McKay.

Botzakis, S. (2009). Graphic novels in education: Cartoons, comprehension, and content knowledge. In D. A. Wooten & B. E. Cullinan (Eds.), *Children's literature in the reading program: An invitation to read* (3rd ed.) (pp. 15–22). Newark, DE: International Reading Association.

Brassell, D., & Rasinski, T. V. (2008). *Comprehension that works: Taking students beyond ordinary understanding to deep comprehension.* Huntington Beach, CA: Shell Education.

Britton, B. K., & Graesser, A. C. (1996). *Models of understanding text.* Mahwah, NJ: Lawrence Erlbaum.

Brown, J. (1998). Historical fiction or fictionalized history? Problems for writers of historical novels for young adults. *The ALAN Review, 26*(1). Retrieved May 22, 2008, from http://scholar.lib.vt.edu/ejournals/ALAN/fall98/brown.html

Bucher, K. T., & Hinton, K. (2010). *Young adult literature: Exploration, evaluation, and appreciation* (2nd ed.). Boston: Allyn and Bacon.

Bucher, K. T., & Manning, M. L. (2001). Taming the alien genre: Bringing science fiction into the classroom. *The ALAN Review, 28*(2), 41–45.

Buly, M. R., & Valencia, S. W. (2002). Below the bar: Profiles of students who fail state reading assessments . *Educational Evaluation and Policy Analysis, 24*(3), 219–239.

Burke, J. (2000). *Reading reminders: Tools, tips, and techniques.* Portsmouth, NH: Boynton/Cook.

Cai, M. (2008). Transactional theory and the study of multicultural literature. *Language Arts, 85*(3), 212–220.

Cart, M. (1996). *From romance to realism: 50 years of growth and change in young adult literature.* New York: HarperCollins.

Carter, B., & Abrahamson, R. F. (1990). *Nonfiction for young adults: From delight to wisdom.* Phoenix, AZ: Oryx Press.

Carter, J. B. (Ed.) (2007). *Building literacy connections with graphic novels: Page by page, panel by panel.* Urbana, IL: National Council of Teachers of English.

Cary, S. (2004). *Going graphic: Comics at work in the multilingual classroom.* Portsmouth, NH: Heinemann.

Christensen, L. (2000). *Reading, writing, and rising up: Teaching about social justice and the power of the written word.* Milwaukee: Rethinking Schools.

Cole, P. B. (2009). *Young adult literature in the 21st century.* Boston: McGraw-Hill Higher Education.

Compton-Lilly, C. (2009). Sociocultural consideration for students and classrooms: The case of Alicia Rodriguez. In C. Compton-Lilly (Ed.), *Breaking the silence: Recognizing the social and cultural resources students bring to the classroom* (pp. 1–10). Newark, DE: International Reading Association.

Crawford, P. (2004). A novel approach: Using graphic novels to attract reluctant readers and promote literacy. *Library Media Connection, 22*(5), 26–28.

Cunningham, P. (2006). Struggling readers: What if they can say the words but don't know what they mean? *The Reading Teacher, 59*(7), 708–711.

Cushman, K. (2003). *Fires in the bathroom: Advice for teachers from high school students.* New York: New Press.

Daniels, H. (1994). *Literature circles: Voice and choice in the student-centered classroom.* York, ME: Stenhouse.

Davis, P. (Director). (1974). *Hearts and minds* [Motion picture]. United States: BBS Productions.

DeCourcy, D., Fairchild, L., & Follet, R. (2007). *Teaching* Romeo and Juliet: *A differentiated approach.* Urbana, IL: National Council of Teachers of English.

Dickson, R., DeGraff, J., & Foard, M. (2002). Learning about self and others through multigenre research projects. *English Journal, 92*(2), 82–90.

Donelson, K. L., & Nilsen, A. P. (2004). *Literature for today's young adults* (7th ed.). Boston: Pearson/Allyn and Bacon.

Dredger, K. (2008). Incorporating student choice: Reflective practice and the courage to change. *English Journal, 98(1),* 29–35.

Dressel, J.H. (2003). *Teaching and learning about multicultural literature: Students reading outside their culture in a middle school classroom.* Newark, DE: International Reading Association.

Duthie, J. (1986). The Web: A powerful tool for the teaching and evaluation of the expository essay. *The History and Social Science Teacher, 21*(4), 232–236.

Elbow, P. (1973). *Writing without teachers.* New York: Oxford University Press.

Farmer, M., & Soden, J. A. (2005). The seven Cs of comprehension. *Voices from the Middle, 13*(2), 20–23.

Faust, M . (2000). Reconstructing familiar metaphors: John Dewey and Louise Rosenblatt on literary art as experience. *Research in the Teaching of English, 35*(1), 9–34.

Fauth, R. C., Brady-Smith, C., & Brooks-Gunn, J. (2002). *Education encyclopedia: Poverty and education: Children and adolescents.* Retrieved October 31, 2009, from http://www.answers.com/topic/poverty-and-education-children-and-adolescents

Finkle, S. L., & Lilly, T. J. (2009). Palestine: In graphic detail. *Classroom Notes Plus, 26*(3), 12–14.

Fisher, A. (2008). Teaching comprehension and critical literacy: Investigating guided reading in three primary classrooms. *Literacy, 42*(1), 19–28.

FitzPatrick, D. (2008). Constructing complexity: Using reading levels to differentiate reading comprehension activities. *English Journal, 98*(2), 57–63.

Freire, P. (1972). *Cultural action for freedom.* Harmondsworth, UK: Penguin.

Frey, N., & Fisher, D. (2004). Using graphic novels, anime, and the Internet in an urban high school. *English Journal, 93*(3), 19–25.

Galda, L., & Cullinan, B. E. (2002). *Cullinan and Galda's literature and the child* (5th ed.). Belmont, CA: Wadsworth/Thomson Learning.

Gallagher, K. (2004). *Deeper reading: Comprehending challenging texts, 4–12.* Portland, ME: Stenhouse.

Gallagher, K. (2006). *Teaching adolescent writers.* Portland, ME: Stenhouse.

Glasgow, J. N. (2001). Teaching social justice through young adult literature. *English Journal, 90*(6), 54–61.

Glasgow, J. N. (2002). Radical change in young adult literature informs the multigenre paper. *English Journal, 92*(2) 41–51.

Glenn, W. (2008). Gossiping girls, insider boys, A-list achievement: Examining and exposing young adult novels consumed by conspicuous consumption. *Journal of Adolescent and Adult Literacy, 52*(1), 34–42.

Goodnow, C. (2007, March 7). Teens buying books at fastest rate in decades. *Seattle Post-Intelligencer.* Retrieved October 27, 2009, from http://www.seattlepi.com/books/306531_teenlit08.html?source=mypi

Groenke, S. L. (2007). A different kind of censorship: Using *Gossip Girl* in the classroom to challenge traditional ideologies about female sexuality. *SIGNAL, 31*(1), 2–9.

Groenke, S. L., & Grothaus, M. (forthcoming). Learning synchronous chat technology-by-design in the high school English classroom. In S. Kajder & C. Young (Eds.), *Technology integration in the English classroom.* Charlotte, NC: Information Age.

Groenke, S. L., & Grothaus, M. (in press). Are we postmodern yet? Reading *Monster* with 21st century 9th graders. *Journal of Adolescent and Adult Literacy.*

Groenke, S. L., & Maples, J. (2008). Critical literacy in cyberspace? A case study analysis of one preservice teacher's attempts at critical talk about *Monster* in online chats with adolescents. *The ALAN Review, 36*(1), 6–14.

Groenke, S. L., & Maples, J. (2009). Small openings in cyberspace: Preparing preservice teachers to facilitate critical race talk. In S. L. Groenke & J. Amos Hatch (Eds.), *Critical pedagogy and teacher education in the neoliberal era: Small openings* (pp. 173–189). Dordrecht, Netherlands: Springer.

Guthrie, J. T., & Humenick, N. M. (2004). Motivating students to read: Evidence for classroom practices that increase reading motivation and achievement. In P. D. McCardle & V. Chhabra (Eds.), *The voice of evidence in reading research* (pp. 329–354). Baltimore: Brookes.

Guthrie, J. T., Rueda, R., Gambrell, L.B., & Morrison, D.A. (2009). Roles of engagement, valuing, and identification in reading development of students from diverse backgrounds. In L. M. Morrow, R. Rueda, & D. Lapp (Eds.), *Handbook of research on literacy and diversity* (pp. 195–215). New York: Guilford Press.

Harmon, J. (1998). "Lyddie" and "Oliver": Instructional framework for linking historical fiction to the classics[Electronic version]. *The ALAN Review, 25*(2), 16–20. Retrieved June 29, 2010, from http://scholar.lib.vt.edu/ejournals/ALAN/winter98/harmon.html

Hasbrouck, J. E., Ihnot, C., & Rogers, G. H. (1999). "Read naturally": A strategy to increase oral reading fluency. *Reading Research and Instruction, 39*(1), 27–38.

Heard, G. (1998). *Awakening the heart: Exploring poetry in elementary and middle school.* Portsmouth, NH: Heinemann.

Hillocks, G. (1980). Toward a hierarchy of skills in the comprehension of literature. *English Journal, 69*(3), 54–59.

Hopper, R. (2005). What are teenagers reading? Adolescent fiction reading habits and reading choices. *Literacy, 39*(3), 113–120.

Howard-Bender, K., & Mulcahy, C. M. (2007). Literature cyberlessons: Avenues for new literacies, critical literacy, and student engagement while reading. *The New England Reading Association Journal, 43*(1), 23–29.

Ivey, G., & Broaddus, K. (2001). "Just plain reading": A survey of what makes students want to read in middle school classrooms. *Reading Research Quarterly, 36*(4), 350–377.

Jacobs, D. (2007). More than words: Comics as a means of teaching multiple literacies. *English Journal, 96*(3), 19–25.

Jago, C. (2004). *Classics in the classroom: Designing accessible literature lessons.* Portsmouth, NH: Heinemann.

Johannessen, L. R., Kahn, E. A., & Walter, C. C. (2009). *Writing about literature* (2nd ed.). Urbana, IL: National Council of Teachers of English.

Jones, S., Clarke, L. W., & Enriquez, G. (2010). *The reading turn-around: A five-part framework for differentiated instruction.* New York: Teachers College Press.

Just Read Now! (N.d.). Discussion web. Retrieved July 13, 2010, from http://www.justreadnow.com/strategies/web/htm

Kaiser Family Foundation. (2005, January). *U.S. teen sexual activity* [PDF document]. Retrieved October 31, 2009, from http://www.kff.org/youthhivstds/upload/U-S-Teen-Sexual-Activity-Fact-Sheet.pdf

Kaywell, J. F. (Ed.) (1993). *Adolescent literature as a complement to the classics.* Norwood, MA: Christopher-Gordon.

Keene, E. O. (2007). The essence of understanding. In K. G. Beers, R. E. Probst, & L. Rief (Eds.), *Adolescent literacy: Turning promise into practice* (pp. 27–38). Portsmouth, NH: Heinemann.

King-Shaver, B., & Hunter, A. (2003). *Differentiated instruction in the English classroom: Content, process, product, and assessment.* Portsmouth, NH: Heinemann.

King-Shaver, B., & Hunter, A. (2009). *Adolescent literacy and differentiated instruction.* Portsmouth, NH: Heinemann.

Kirby, D., Kirby, D. L., & Liner, T. (2004). *Inside out: Strategies for teaching writing* (3rd ed.). Portsmouth, NH: Heinemann.

Kirby, D. L., & Kirby, D. (2010). Contemporary memoir: A 21st-century genre ideal for teens. *English Journal, 99*(4), 22–29.

Koenke, K. (1981). ERIC/RCS: The careful use of comic books. *Reading Teacher, 34*(5), 592–595.

Koplewicz, H. S. (2002). *More than moody: Recognizing and treating adolescent depression.* New York: G. P. Putnam's Sons.

Koukis, S. (2008). Concentric circles of interest: Widening student responses to M. T. Anderson's *Feed* through student book club discussions. In A. O. Soter, M. A. Faust, & T. Rogers (Eds.), *Interpretive play: Using critical perspectives to teach young adult literature* (pp. 55–66). Norwood, MA: Christopher-Gordon.

Landt, S. M. (2006). Multicultural literature and young adolescents: A kaleidoscope of opportunity. *Journal of Adolescent and Adult Literacy, 49*(8), 690–697.

Lee, C. D. (2001). Is October Brown Chinese? A cultural modeling activity system for underachieving students. *American Educational Research Journal, 38*(1), 97–141.

Lesesne, T. S. (2003). *Making the match: The right book for the right reader at the right time, grades 4–12.* Portland, ME: Stenhouse.

Lesesne, T. S. (2008, November 24). List from the ALAN keynote. Posting archived at http://professornana.livejournal.com/2008/11/24/

Lesesne, T. S. (2010). *Reading ladders: Leading students from where they are to where we'd like them to be.* Portsmouth, NH: Heinemann.

Lewis, C., & del Valle, A. (2009). Literacy and identity: Implications for research and practice. In L. Christenbury, R. Bomer, & P. Smagorinsky (Eds.), *Handbook of Adolescent Literacy Research* (pp. 307–322). New York: Guilford Press.

Lewison, M., Flint, A. S., & Van Sluys, K. (2002). Taking on critical literacy: The journey of newcomers and novices. *Language Arts, 79*(5), 382–392.

Louie, B. (2005). Development of empathetic responses with multicultural literature. *Journal of Adolescent and Adult Literacy, 48*(7), 566–578.

Lukens, R. J. (1999). *A critical handbook of children's literature* (6th ed.). New York: Longman.

Macrorie, K. (1988). *The I-search paper.* (Rev. ed. of *Searching Writing.*) Portsmouth, NH: Boynton/Cook.

Mason, P. A., & Schumm, J. S. (2003). *Promising practices for urban reading instruction.* Newark, DE: International Reading Association.

McCloud, S. (1994). *Understanding comics: The invisible art.* New York: HarperPerennial.

McDaniel, C. (2004). Critical literacy: A questioning stance and the possibility for change. *The Reading Teacher, 57*(5), 472–481.

McGill-Franzen, A. (2009). Series books for young readers: Seeking reading pleasure and developing reading competence. In D. A. Wooten & B. E. Cullinan (Eds.), *Children's literature in the reading program: An invitation to read* (3rd ed.) (pp. 57–65). Newark, DE: International Reading Association.

McNair, J. C. (2003). "But 'The Five Chinese Brothers' is one of my favorite books!" Conducting sociopolitical critiques of children's literature with preservice teachers. *Journal of Children's Literature, 29*(1), 46–54.

Mellor, B., O'Neill, M. H., & Patterson, A. H. (2000). *Reading stories: Activities and texts for critical readings.* Urbana, IL: National Council of Teachers of English.

Michaels, W. (N.d.) *Teachers notes (secondary) for* By the River [PDF document]. Downloaded October 21, 2009, from http://www.allenandunwin.com/_uploads/BookPdf/TeachersNotes/9781741143577.pdf

Miholic, V. (1994). An inventory to pique students' metacognitive awareness of reading strategies. *Journal of Reading, 38*(2), 84–86.

Miller, S. (2005). *Developing and promoting graphic novel collections.* New York: Neal-Schuman.

Milner, J. O., & Milner, L. F. M. (2003). *Bridging English* (3rd ed.). Upper Saddle River, NJ: Merrill/Prentice Hall.

Molino, A. C. (2007). Characteristics of help-seeking street youth and non-street youth. In D. Dennis, G. Locke, & J. Khadduri (Eds.), *Toward understanding homelessness: The 2007 national symposium on homelessness research.* Washington, DC: U. S. Department of Health and Human Services, U. S. Department of Housing and Urban Development.

Myers, K. L. (1988). Twenty (better) questions. *English Journal, 77*(1), 64–65.

National Coalition for the Homeless. (2008). *Homeless youth.* NCH fact sheet #13. Washington, DC. Retrieved June 29, 2010, from http://www.nationalhomeless.org/factsheets/youth.html

National Institute on Alcohol Abuse and Alcoholism. (2006). *Underage drinking: Why do adolescents drink, what are the risks, and how can underage drinking be prevented?* Retrieved November 4, 2009, from http://pubs.niaaa.nih.gov/publications/AA67/AA67.htm

National Institute of Child Health and Human Development. (2000). *Report of the National Reading Panel: Teaching children to read: An evidence-based assessment of the scientific research literature on reading and its implications for reading instruction.* Retrieved June 29, 2010, from http://www.nichd.nih.gov/publications/nrp/smallbook.cfm

Niday, D., & Allender, D. (2000). Standing on the border: Issues of identity and border crossings in young adult literature [Electronic version]. *The ALAN Review, 27*(2), 60–63. Retrieved October 25, 2009, from http://scholar.lib.vt.edu/ejournals/ALAN/winter00/niday.html

Nilsen, A. P., & Donelson, K. L. (2009). *Literature for today's young adults* (8th ed.). Boston: Pearson.

Noden, H. R. (1999). *Image grammar: Using grammatical structures to teach writing*. Portsmouth, NH: Heinemann.

Norton, B. (2003). The motivating power of comic books: Insights from *Archie* comic readers. *The Reading Teacher, 57*(2), 140–147.

Norton, D. E., Norton, S. E., & McClure, A. A. (2003). *Through the eyes of a child: An introduction to children's literature* (6th ed.). Upper Saddle River, NJ: Merrill/Prentice Hall.

NSTA standards for the education of teachers in science: Teaching through inquiry. (1998). In *NSTA standards for science teacher preparation version November 1998*. Retrieved October 11, 2009, from https://www.msu.edu/~haasdona/nsta.htm#3.0

Nunley, K. F. (2005). *Differentiating the high school classroom: Solution strategies for 18 common obstacles*. Thousand Oaks, CA: Corwin Press.

Ochoa, G., & Osier, J. (1993). *The writer's guide to creating a science fiction universe*. Cincinnati: Writer's Digest Books.

O'Connor, J. S. (2004). *Wordplaygrounds: Reading, writing, and performing poetry in the English classroom*. Urbana, IL: National Council of Teachers of English.

Ogle, D. M. (1986). K-W-L: A teaching model that develops active reading of expository text. *The Reading Teacher, 39*(6), 564–570.

Opitz, M. F., & Ford, M. P. (2008). *Do-able differentiation: Varying groups, texts, and supports to reach readers*. Portsmouth, NH: Heinemann.

Pedersen, D. (2002). Question and answer: Reading nonfiction to develop the persuasive essay. *English Journal, 91*(4), 59–63.

Perie, M., Grigg, W., & Donahue, F. (2005). *The nation's report card: Reading, 2005* (NCES 2006-451). Washington, DC: National Center for Education Statistics.

Pflaum, S. W., & Bishop, P. A. (2004, November). Student perceptions of reading engagement: Learning from the learners. *Journal of Adolescent and Adult Literacy, 48*(3), 202–213.

Pitcher, S. M., Albright, L. K., DeLaney, C. J., Walker, N. T., Seunarinesingh, K., Mogge, S., Headley, K. N., Ridgeway, V. G., Peck, S., Hunt, R., and Dunston, P. J. (2007). Assessing adolescents' motivation to read. *Journal of Adolescent and Adult Literacy, 50*(5), 378–396.

Postman, N., & Weingartner, C. (1969). *Teaching as a subversive activity* [PDF document]. Retrieved October 10, 2009, from http://www.sicsifim.unina.it/materiale/corsi/DM1_08/da_vincenzo.pdf

Probst, R. E. (1988). Dialogue with a text. *English Journal, 77*(1), 32–38.

Probst, R. E. (2004). *Response and analysis: Teaching literature in secondary school* (2nd ed.). Portsmouth, NH: Heinemann.

Putz, M. (2006). *A teacher's guide to the multigenre research project: Everything you need to know to get started*. Portsmouth, NH: Heinemann.

Rape, Abuse, and Incest National Network. (N.d.). *Who are the victims?* Retrieved October 31, 2009, from http://www.rainn.org/get-information/statistics/sexual-assault-victims

Rasinski, T. (2006). Issues and trends in literacy—Reading fluency instruction: Moving beyond accuracy, automaticity, and prosody. *The Reading Teacher, 59*(7), 704–707.

Rasinski, T. V. (n.d.). Assessing reading fluency. Pacific Resources for Education and Learning. Retrieved July 16, 2010, from http://www.prel.org/products/re_/assessing-fluency.htm

Rasinski, T. V., & Padak, N. (1996). *Holistic reading strategies: Teaching children who find reading difficult.* Englewood Cliffs, NJ: Merrill/Prentice Hall.

Reid, S., & Stringer, S. (1997). Ethical dilemmas in teaching problem novels: The psychological impact of troubling YA literature on adolescent readers in the classroom [Electronic version]. *The ALAN Review.* Retrieved November 5, 2009, from http://scholar.lib.vt.edu/ejournals/ALAN/winter97/w97-05-Reid.html

Reno, J. (2008, May 14). Generation R (R is for reader). *Newsweek.* Retrieved January 12, 2008, from http://www.newsweek.com/2008/05/13/generation-r-r-is-for-reader.html

Reynolds, M. (2004). *I won't read and you can't make me: Reaching reluctant teen readers.* Portsmouth, NH: Heinemann.

Richardson, J. S. (2000). *Read it aloud! Using literature in the secondary content classroom.* Newark, DE: International Reading Association.

Robb, L. (2009). *Assessments for differentiating reading instruction: 100 forms and checklists for identifying students' strengths and needs so you can help every reader grow.* New York: Scholastic.

Robertson, S. L. (1990). Text rendering: Beginning literary response. *English Journal, 79*(1), 80–84.

Romero, P. A., & Zancanella, D. (1990). Expanding the circle: Hispanic voices in American literature. *English Journal, 79*(1), 24–29.

Root, M. P. P. (Ed.) (1996). *The multiracial experience: Racial borders as the new frontier.* Thousand Oaks, CA: Sage.

Rosenblatt, L. M. (1978/1994). *The reader, the text, the poem: The transactional theory of the literary work.* Carbondale: Southern Illinois University Press.

Rosenblatt, L. M. (1982). The literary transaction: Evocation and response. *Theory into Practice, 21*(4), 268–277.

Rosenblatt, L. M. (1995). *Literature as exploration* (5th ed.). New York: Modern Language Association of America.

Roser, N., Martinez, M., Fuhrken, C., & McDonnold, K. (2007). Characters as guides to meaning. *The Reading Teacher, 60*(6), 548–559.

Ross, C. S. (1995). "If they read Nancy Drew, so what?" Series book readers talk back. *Library and Information Science Research, 17*(3), 201–236.

Samuels, S. J. (2002). Reading fluency: Its development and assessment. In A. E. Farstrup & S. J. Samuels (Eds.), *What research has to say about reading instruction* (3rd ed.) (pp. 166–183). Newark, DE: International Reading Association.

Scherff, L. (in press). Using young adult literature to promote comprehension with struggling readers. In L. A. Hall, L. D. Burns, & E. C. Edwards, *Empowering struggling readers: Practices for the middle grades*. New York: Guilford Press.

Scherff, L., Arteta, I., McGartlin, C., Stults, K., Welsh, E. M., & White, C. (2008). Teaching the memoir in English class: Taking students to *Jesus Land*. *The ALAN Review*, 69–78.

Schmitt, M. C. (1990). A questionnaire to measure children's awareness of strategic reading processes. *The Reading Teacher, 43*(7), 454–461.

Schneider, J. J., & Jackson, S. A. W. (2000). Process drama: A special space and place for writing. *The Reading Teacher, 54*(1), 38–51.

Schreiber, P. A. (1980). On the acquisition of reading fluency. *Journal of Reading Behavior, 12*(3), 177–186.

Shafer, G. (1999). Re-envisioning research. *English Journal, 89*(1), 45–50.

Shanker, J. L., & Ekwall, E. E. (2000). *Ekwall/Shanker reading inventory* (4th ed.). Boston: Allyn and Bacon.

Shor, I. (1987). *Critical teaching and everyday life*. Chicago: University of Chicago Press.

Slapin, B., & Seale, D. (Eds.) (1992, 1998). *Through Indian eyes: The Native experience in books for children*. Los Angeles: American Indian Studies Center, University of California.

Smith, M. W., & Wilhelm, J. D. (2002). *"Reading don't fix no Chevys": Literacy in the lives of young men*. Portsmouth, NH: Heinemann.

Smith, M. W., & Wilhelm, J. D. (2010). *Fresh takes on teaching literary elements: How to teach what really matters about character, setting, point of view, and theme*. New York/Urbana, IL: Scholastic/National Council of Teachers of English.

Spangler, S. (2009). Speaking my mind: Stop reading Shakespeare! *English Journal, 99*(1), 130–132.

Stallworth, B. J., Gibbons, L., & Fauber, L. (2006). It's not on the list: An exploration of teachers' perspectives on using multicultural literature. *Journal of Adolescent and Adult Literacy, 49*(6), 478–489.

Stover, L. T. (2000). Who am I? Who are you? Diversity and identity in the young adult novel. In V. R. Monseau & G. M. Salvner (Eds.), *Reading their world: The young adult novel in the classroom* (2nd ed.) (pp. 100–120). Portsmouth, NH: Boynton/Cook.

Sullivan, E. (2003). Up for discussion—Fiction or poetry? *School Library Journal, 49*(8), 44–45.

Sutton, R. (2001). An interview with Virginia Euwer Wolff. *The Horn Book*. http://www.hbook.com/magazine/articles/2001/may01_wolff_sutton.asp

Thomson, J. (1987). *Understanding teenagers' reading: Reading processes and the teaching of literature*. New York: Nichols.

Tomlinson, C. A. (1999). *The differentiated classroom: Responding to the needs of all learners.* Alexandria, VA: Association for Supervision and Curriculum Development.

Tomlinson, C. A. (2001). *How to differentiate instruction in mixed-ability classrooms* (2nd ed.). Alexandria, VA: Association for Supervision and Curriculum Development.

Tovani, C. (2000). *I read it, but I don't get it: Comprehension strategies for adolescent readers.* Portland, ME: Stenhouse.

Tway, E. (Ed.). (1981). *Reading ladders for human relations* (6th ed.). Washington, DC: American Council on Education.

US Secret Service and US Department of Education. (May 2002). The Final Report and Findings of the Safe School Initiative: Implications for the Prevention of School Attacks in the United States. Retrieved September 27, 2010, from http://www. secretservice.gov/ntac/ssi_final_report.pdf

Van Sickle, V. (2006). Subcategories within the emerging genre of the verse novel [Electronic version]. *The Looking Glass: New Perspectives on Children's Literature, 10*(3). Retrieved June 29, 2010, from http://www.lib.latrobe.edu.au/ojs/index. php/tlg/article/view/74/88

Vardell, S. (2007, April 19). Support teen literature day. Message posted to http:// poetryforchildren.blogspot.com/2007/04/support-teen-literature-day.html

Versaci, R. (2001). How comic books can change the way our students see literature: One teacher's perspective. *English Journal, 91*(2), 61–67.

Ward, T. B. (2008). Culturally situated response and narrator reliability: *Monster, Speak,* and *The First Part Last.* In A. O. Soter, M. A. Faust, & T. Rogers (Eds.), *Interpretive play: Using critical perspectives to teach young adult literature* (pp. 67–84). Norwood, MA: Christopher-Gordon.

Weiner, S. (2006). *The 101 best graphic novels* (2nd ed.). New York: NBM.

Whitworth, M. (2008). Judy Blume's lessons in love. *Telegraph.* Retrieved January 20, 2009, from http://www.telegraph.co.uk/culture/books/3670951/Judy-Blume%27s-lessons-in-love.html

Wilhelm, J. D. (2002). *Action strategies for deepening comprehension.* New York: Scholastic Professional Books.

Wilhelm, J. D., & Edmiston, B. (1998). *Imagining to learn: Inquiry, ethics, and integration through drama.* Portsmouth, NH: Heinemann.

Willis, A. I., & Parker, K. N. (2009). "O say, do you see?" Using critical race theory to inform English language arts instruction. In C. Compton-Lilly (Ed.), *Breaking the silence: Recognizing the social and cultural resources students bring to the classroom* (pp. 34–48). Newark, DE: International Reading Association.

Wolsey, T. D., & Lapp, D. (2009). Discussion-based instruction in the middle and secondary school classroom. In K. D. Wood and W. E. Blanton (Eds.), *Literacy instruction for adolescents: Research-based practice* (pp. 368–391). New York: Guilford.

Wood, K. D. (1984). Probable passages: A writing strategy. *The Reading Teacher, 37*(6), 496–499.

Worthy, J., Moorman, M., & Turner, M. (1999). What Johnny likes to read is hard to find in school. *Reading Research Quarterly, 34*(1), 12–27.

Yang, G. (2008). Graphic novels in the classroom. *Language Arts, 85*(3), 185–192.

Zemelman, S., & Daniels, H. (1988). *A community of writers: Teaching writing in the junior and senior high school.* Portsmouth, NH: Heinemann.

Zigo, D., & Moore, M. T. (2004). Science fiction: Serious reading, critical reading. *English Journal, 94*(2), 85–174.

Zimmer, T. V. (2009). Teacher's guide for *Satchel Paige: Striking out Jim Crow.* Retrieved November 5, 2009, from http://www.cartoonstudies.org/books/paige/guide.html

Zutell, J., & Rasinski, T. V. (1991). Training teachers to attend to their students' oral reading fluency. *Theory into Practice, 30*(3), 211–217.

Young Adult Novels

Abdel-Fattah, R. (2008). *Does my head look big in this?* New York: Scholastic.

Alexander, E., Nelson, M., & Cooper, F. (2007). *Miss Crandall's school for young ladies and little misses of color: Poems.* Honesdale, PA: Wordsong.

Alexie, S. (2007). *The absolutely true diary of a part-time Indian.* New York: Little, Brown.

Alvarez, J. (2002). *Before we were free.* New York: A. Knopf.

Alvarez, J. (2008). *Once upon a quinceañera: Coming of age in the USA.* New York: Plume.

Alvarez, J. (2009). *Return to sender.* New York: Alfred A. Knopf.

Anderson, L. H. (2009). *Wintergirls.* New York: Viking.

Anderson, M. T. (2004). *Feed.* Cambridge, MA: Candlewick Press.

Anderson, M. T. (2006). *The astonishing life of Octavian Nothing, traitor to the nation.* Vol. 1: *The pox party.* Cambridge, MA: Candlewick Press.

Anonymous. (1972). *Go ask Alice.* New York: Avon.

Appelt, K. (2004). *My father's summers: A daughter's memoir.* New York: Henry Holt.

Applegate, K. (2008). *Home of the brave.* New York: Square Fish.

Armstrong, J. (2003). *Shattered: Stories of children and war.* New York: Dell, Laurel-Leaf.

Atkins, J. (2010). *Borrowed names: Poems about Laura Ingalls Wilder, Madam C. J. Walker, Marie Curie, and their daughters.* New York: Henry Holt.

Beah, I. (2008). *A long way gone: Memoirs of a boy soldier.* New York: Farrar, Straus & Giroux.

Bennett, V. (2007). *Angelmonster.* Cambridge, MA: Candlewick Press.

Bernier-Grand, C. T. (2007). *Frida: Viva la vida! Long live life!* New York: Marshall Cavendish Children.

Bernier-Grand, C. T., & Diaz, D. (2009). *Diego: Bigger than life.* New York: Marshall Cavendish Children.

Blume, J. (1975/2007). *Forever. . .* New York: Pocket Books.

Blundell, J. (2009). *What I saw and how I lied.* London: Scholastic.

Booth, C. (2007). *Tyrell.* New York: Scholastic.

Brisson, P. (2010). *The best and hardest thing.* New York: Viking.

Bryant, J. (2009). *Kaleidoscope eyes.* New York: Alfred A. Knopf.

Bryant, J., & Sweet, M. (2008). *A river of words: The story of William Carlos Williams.* Grand Rapids, MI: Eerdmans Books for Young Readers.

Buckhanon, K. (2006). *Upstate.* New York: St. Martin's Griffin.

Burg, A. E. (2009). *All the broken pieces: A novel in verse.* New York: Scholastic Press.

Burgess, M. (1999). *Smack.* New York: Avon Tempest.

Canales, V. (2005). *The tequila worm.* New York: Wendy Lamb Books.

Carlson, L. M. (Ed.). (2005). *Moccasin thunder: American Indian stories for today.* New York: HarperCollins.

Carlson, L. M. (Ed.) (2005). *Red hot salsa: Bilingual poems on being young and Latino in the United States.* New York: Henry Holt.

Carman, P. (2009). *Patrick Carman's Skeleton Creek.* New York: Scholastic Press.

Carmi, D. (2002). *Samir and Yonatan.* New York: Scholastic Signature.

Carvell, M. (2005). *Sweetgrass basket.* New York: Dutton Children's Books.

Cassidy, A. (2007). *Looking for JJ.* Orlando, FL: Harcourt.

Chaltas, T. (2009). *Because I am furniture.* New York: Viking.

Chambers, A. (2004). *Postcards from no man's land.* New York: Speak.

Childress, A. (1974/2000). *A hero ain't nothin' but a sandwich.* New York: Avon.

Collins, S. (2008). *The hunger games.* New York: Scholastic Press.

Collins, S. (2009). *Catching fire.* New York: Scholastic Press.

Cormier, R. (1974/2000). *The chocolate war.* New York: Random House.

Coy, J. (2007). *Crackback.* New York: Scholastic.

Creech, S. (2001). *Love that dog.* New York: Scholastic.

Crutcher, C. (2007). *Deadline.* New York: HarperTeen.

Curtis, C. P. (2009). *Elijah of Buxton.* New York: Scholastic.

Daly, M. (1942/1985). *Seventeenth summer.* New York: Simon Pulse.

Davis, S., Jenkins, G., Hunt, R., & Draper, S. (2006). *We beat the street: How a friendship pact led to success.* New York: Puffin Books.

de la Peña, M. (2008). *Mexican whiteboy.* New York: Delacorte Press.

Desai Hidier, T. (2003). *Born confused.* New York: Scholastic Press.

Doctorow, C. (2008). *Little brother.* New York: Tor Teen.

Donnelly, J. (2004). *A northern light.* Orlando, FL: Harcourt.

Dowell, F. O. (2008). *Shooting the moon.* New York: Atheneum Books for Young Readers.

Downham, J. (2007). *Before I die.* Oxford: David Fickling.

Draper, S. M. (2008). *Copper sun.* New York: Atheneum Books for Young Readers.

Draper, S. M. (2009). *November blues.* New York: Simon Pulse.

Duncan, L. (1999). *I know what you did last summer.* New York: Bantam Doubleday Dell Books for Young Readers.

Ellis, A. D. (2010). *Everything is fine.* New York: Little, Brown.

Ellis, D. (2001). *The breadwinner.* Toronto: Groundwood Books.

Ellis, D. (2002). *Parvana's journey.* Toronto: Groundwood Books.

Ellis, D. (2003). *Mud city.* Toronto: Groundwood Books.

Ellis, D. (2009). *Children of war: Voices of Iraqi refugees.* Toronto: Groundwood Books.

Engle, M. (2006). *The poet slave of Cuba: A biography of Juan Francisco Manzano.* New York: Henry Holt.

Engle, M. (2008). *The surrender tree: Poems of Cuba's struggle for freedom.* New York: Henry Holt.

Engle, M. (2010). *The firefly letters: A suffragette's journey to Cuba.* New York: Henry Holt.

Farmer, N. (2004). *The house of the scorpion.* New York: Simon Pulse.

Ferguson, A. (2006). *The Christopher killer: A forensic mystery.* New York: Viking/Sleuth.

Filipović, Z. (1994/2006). *Zlata's diary: A child's life in wartime Sarajevo.* New York: Viking.

Filipović, Z., & Challenger, M. (Eds.). (2006). *Stolen voices: Young people's war diaries, from World War I to Iraq.* New York: Penguin Books.

Flake, S. (2007). *Money hungry.* New York: Jump at the Sun/Hyperion Paperbacks for Children.

Fletcher, C. (2008). *Ten cents a dance.* New York: Bloomsbury.

Frank, A. (1953). *Anne Frank: The diary of a young girl.* New York: Pocket Books.

Frost, H. (2003/2007). *Keesha's house.* New York: Farrar, Straus and Giroux.

Frost, H. (2008). *Diamond willow.* New York: Farrar, Straus and Giroux.

Frost, H. (2009). *Crossing stones.* New York: Farrar, Straus and Giroux.

Gallo, D. R. (Ed.). (2007). *First crossing: Stories about teen immigrants.* Cambridge, MA: Candlewick Press.

Gantos, J. (2002). *Hole in my life.* New York: Farrar, Straus and Giroux.

Garden, N. (1992). *Annie on my mind.* New York: Farrar, Straus and Giroux.

Giles, G. (2007). *What happened to Cass McBride? A novel.* New York: Little, Brown.

Gipi. (2007). *Notes for a war story.* New York: First Second.

Glaser, L., & Nivola, C. A. (2010). *Emma's poem: The voice of the Statue of Liberty.* Boston: Houghton Mifflin Books for Children.

Goodman, A. (2008). *The other side of the island.* New York: Razorbill.

Grandits, J. (2004). *Technically, it's not my fault.* New York: Clarion Books.

Grandits, J. (2007). *Blue lipstick: Concrete poems.* New York: Clarion Books.

Green, J., & Levithan, D. (2010). *Will Grayson, Will Grayson.* New York: Dutton.

Grimes, N. (2003). *Bronx masquerade.* New York: Speak.

Grimes, N. (2005). *Dark sons.* New York: Jump at the Sun.

Hemphill, S. (2007). *Your own, Sylvia: A verse portrait of Sylvia Plath.* New York: Alfred A. Knopf.

Hemphill, S. (2010). *Wicked girls: A novel of the Salem witch trials.* New York: Balzer & Bray.

Hesse, K. (2003) *Witness.* New York: Scholastic Press.

Hesse, K. (2005). *Aleutian sparrow.* New York: Aladdin Paperbacks.

Hesse, K. (2005). *Out of the dust.* New York: Scholastic.

Hiaasen, C. (2002). *Hoot.* New York: Alfred A. Knopf.

Hiaasen, C. (2010). *Scat.* New York: Alfred A. Knopf.

High, L. O. (2004). *Sister slam and the poetic motormouth.* New York: Bloomsbury.

High, L. O. (2008). *Planet pregnancy.* Asheville, NC: Front Street.

Hinton, S. E. (1967/1997). *The outsiders.* New York: Puffin Books.

Hopkins, E. (2004). *Crank.* New York: Margaret K. McElderry Books.

Hopkins, E. (2007). *Impulse.* New York: Margaret K. McElderry Books.

Hosseini, K. (2007). *The kite runner.* New York: Riverhead Books.

Hosseini, K. (2008). *A thousand splendid suns.* New York: Riverhead Books.

Hyde, C. R. (2000). *Pay it forward: A novel.* New York: Simon & Schuster.

Jansen, H. (2006). *Over a thousand hills I walk with you.* Minneapolis: Carolrhoda Books.

Jaramillo, A. (2008). *La linea.* New York: Square Fish.

Jiang, J. L. (1997). *Red scarf girl: A memoir of the cultural revolution.* New York: Scholastic.

Jimenez, F. (1997/2000). *The circuit: Stories from the life of a migrant child.* New York: Scholastic.

Jimenez, F. (2001). *Breaking through.* Boston: Houghton Mifflin.

Johnson, A. (2003). *The first part last.* New York: Simon & Schuster Books for Young Readers.

Johnson, L. (2009). *Muchacho: A novel.* New York: Alfred A. Knopf.

Kadohata, C. (2006). *Kira-kira.* New York: Aladdin Paperbacks.

Kass, P. M. (2006). *Real time.* Boston: Graphia.

Kelly, J. (2009). *The evolution of Calpurnia Tate.* New York: Henry Holt.

Kerr, M. E. (1995). *Deliver us from Evie.* New York: HarperTrophy.

Key, W. (2008). *Alabama moon.* New York: Square Fish.

Kim, D. K. (2004). *Same difference and other stories.* Marietta, GA: Top Shelf.

Koertge, R. (2001). *The brimstone journals.* Cambridge, MA: Candlewick Press.

Koertge, R. (2006). *Shakespeare bats cleanup.* Cambridge, MA: Candlewick Press.

Koertge, R. (2010). *Shakespeare makes the playoffs.* Cambridge, MA: Candlewick Press.

Laird, E., & Nimr, S. (2006). *A little piece of ground.* Chicago: Haymarket Books.

Lawson, J., & Morstad, J. (2010). *Think again.* Toronto: KCP Poetry.

Lester, J. (2005). *Day of tears: A novel in dialogue.* New York: Hyperion Books for Children.

Levithan, D. (2006). *The realm of possibility.* New York: Knopf.

Lockhart, E. (2008). *The disreputable history of Frankie Landau-Banks: A novel.* New York: Hyperion.

Lowry, L. (1993). *The giver.* New York: Bantam Doubleday Dell Books for Young Readers.

Lutes, J., & Bertozzi, N. (2007). *Houdini: The handcuff king.* New York: Hyperion.

Lynch, C. (2007). *Inexcusable.* New York: Simon Pulse.

Magoon, K. (2009). *The rock and the river.* New York: Aladdin.

Marchetta, M. (1992/2006). *Looking for Alibrandi.* New York: Alfred A. Knopf.

Marchetta, M. (2004). *Saving Francesca.* New York: Alfred A. Knopf.

Marchetta, M. (2008). *Jellicoe road.* HarperTeen.

Martinez, V. (1996/2004). *Parrot in the oven: Mi vida: A novel.* New York: HarperTrophy.

Mazer, H. (2002). *A boy at war: A novel of Pearl Harbor.* New York: Aladdin Paperbacks.

McCaughrean, G. (2007). *The white darkness: A novel.* New York: HarperTempest.

McCormick, P. (2006). *Sold.* New York: Hyperion.

McCormick, P. (2009). *Purple heart.* New York: Balzer & Bray.

McDonald, J. (2000). *Project girl.* Berkeley: University of California Press.

McDonald, J. (2006). *Chill wind*. New York: Farrar, Straus and Giroux.

Meminger, N. (2009). *Shine, coconut moon*. New York: Margaret K. McElderry Books.

Mora, P. (2010). *Dizzy in your eyes: Poems about love*. New York: Alfred A. Knopf.

Mosley, W. (2006). *47*. New York: Little, Brown.

Myers, W. D. (1988/2008). *Fallen angels*. New York: Scholastic.

Myers, W. D. (2000). *Monster*. New York: Scholastic.

Myers, W. D. (2002). *Patrol: An American soldier in Vietnam*. New York: HarperCollins.

Myers, W. D. (2008). *Here in Harlem: Poems in many voices*. New York: Holiday House.

Myers, W. D. (2009). *Sunrise over Fallujah*. New York: Scholastic.

Myers, W. D. (2009). *Dope sick*. New York: HarperTeen/Amistad.

Na, A. (2002). *A step from heaven*. New York: Speak.

Naidoo, B. (2005). *Making it home: Real-life stories from children forced to flee*. New York: Puffin Books.

Nelson, J. (2010). *The sky is everywhere*. New York: Dial Books.

Nelson, M. (2001). *Carver, a life in poems*. Asheville, NC: Front Street.

Nelson, M. (2004). *Fortune's bones: The manumission requiem*. Asheville, NC: Front Street.

Nelson, M. (2005/2009). *A wreath for Emmett Till*. Boston: Graphia.

Nelson, R. A. (2005). *Teach me: A novel*. New York: Razorbill.

Novgorodoff, D., Ponsoldt, J., & Percy, B. (2009). *Refresh, refresh: A graphic novel*. New York: First Second.

Nye, N. S. (1999). *Habibi*. New York: Simon Pulse.

Osa, N. (2005). *Cuba 15: A novel*. New York: Delacorte Press.

Park, L. S. (2002). *When my name was Keoko*. New York: Yearling.

Paulsen, G. (1987). *Hatchet*. New York: Bradbury Press.

Pearson, M. E. (2008). *The adoration of Jenna Fox*. New York: Henry Holt.

Peet, M. (2008). *Tamar: A novel of espionage, passion, and betrayal*. Cambridge, MA: Candlewick Press.

Perdomo, W., & Collier, B. (2010). *Clemente!* New York: Henry Holt.

Porcellino, J. (2008). *Thoreau at Walden*. New York: Hyperion.

Porter, C. R. (2000). *Imani all mine*. Boston: Houghton Mifflin.

Pyle, K. C. (2007). *Blindspot*. New York: Henry Holt.

Riverbend. (2005). *Baghdad burning: Girl blog from Iraq*. New York: Feminist Press at the City University of New York.

Rodriguez, L. J. (2005). *Always running: La vida loca: Gang days in L. A*. New York: Touchstone.

Rosoff, M. (2006). *How I live now.* New York: Wendy Lamb Books.

Ryan, P. M., & Sis, P. (2010). *The dreamer.* New York: Scholastic Press.

Rylant, C. (1993/2004). *I had seen castles.* Orlando, FL: Harcourt.

Rylant, C. (2006). *God went to beauty school.* New York: HarperTempest.

Sachar, L. (2000). *Holes.* New York: Dell Yearling.

Sandell, L. A. (2007). *Song of the sparrow.* New York: Scholastic Press.

Satrapi, M. (2004). *Persepolis: Story of a childhood.* New York: Pantheon.

Scheeres, J. (2005). *Jesus land: A memoir.* New York: Counterpoint.

Schlitz, L. A. (2007). *Good masters! Sweet ladies! Voices from a medieval village.* Cambridge, MA: Candlewick.

Shakur, T. (2009). *The rose that grew from concrete.* New York: MTV Books.

Shange, N. (2009). *We troubled the waters: Poems.* New York: Amistad.

Singer, M., & Masse, J. (2010). *Mirror mirror: A book of reversible verse.* New York: Dutton Children's Books.

Smith, C. (2007). *Twelve rounds to glory: The story of Muhammad Ali.* Cambridge, MA: Candlewick Press.

Smith, C. L. (2001). *Rain is not my Indian name.* New York: HarperCollins.

Smith, C. R., & Evans, S. (2010). *Black Jack: The ballad of Jack Johnson.* New York: Roaring Brook Press.

Smith, K. (2006). *The geography of girlhood.* New York: Little, Brown.

Smith, S. (2009). *Flygirl.* New York: Scholastic.

Sones, S. (2003). *What my mother doesn't know.* New York: Simon Pulse.

Sones, S. (2008). *What my girlfriend doesn't know.* New York: Simon Pulse.

Soto, G. (2006). *Buried onions.* Orlando, FL: Harcourt.

Spiegelman, A. (1973/1986). *Maus: A survivor's tale.* Vol. 1: *My father bleeds history.* New York: Pantheon Books.

Spires, E. (2009). *I heard God talking to me: William Edmondson and his stone carvings.* New York: Frances Foster Books.

Stassen, J. P. (2006). *Deogratias: A tale of Rwanda.* New York: First Second.

Stine, C. (2006). *Refugees.* New York: Laurel-Leaf Books.

Stratton, A. (2004). *Chanda's secrets.* Toronto: Annick Press.

Sturm, J., & Tommaso, R. (2007). *Satchel Paige: Striking out Jim Crow.* New York: Jump at the Sun.

Taylor, M. D. (1976/2003). *Roll of thunder, hear my cry.* London: Puffin.

Taylor, S. S., & Towle, B. (2010). *Amelia Earhart: This broad ocean.* New York: Disney/Hyperion Books.

Testa, M. (2003). *Almost forever.* Cambridge, MA: Candlewick Press.

Tohe, L. (1999). *No parole today.* Albuquerque, NM: West End Press.

Vaughan, B. K., & Henrichon, N. (2006). *Pride of Baghdad.* New York: Vertigo.

Volponi, P. (2006). *Black and white.* New York: Speak.

Volponi, P. (2007). *Rooftop.* New York: Speak.

Volponi, P. (2008). *Hurricane song.* New York: Viking.

Volponi, P. (2010). *Rikers High.* New York: Viking.

Von Ziegesar, C. (2002). *Gossip girl: A novel.* Boston: Little, Brown.

Wayland, A. H. (2004). *Girl coming in for a landing: A novel in poems.* New York: Dell Yearling.

Weatherford, C. B. (2007). *Birmingham, 1963.* Honesdale, PA: Wordsong.

Weatherford, C. B. (2008). *Becoming Billie Holliday.* Honesdale, PA: Wordsong.

Westerfeld, S. (2005). *Uglies.* New York: Scholastic.

Wiesel, E. (1982). *Night.* New York: Bantam Books.

Wild, M. (2004). *Jinx.* New York: Simon Pulse.

Wild, M. (2006). *One night.* New York: Laurel-Leaf Books.

Williams, C. L. (2010). *Glimpse.* New York: Simon & Schuster Books for Young Readers.

Williams-Garcia, R. (1998). *Like sisters on the homefront.* New York: Puffin Books.

Williams-Garcia, R. (2009). *Jumped.* New York: HarperTeen.

Wolf, A. (2004). *New found land: Lewis & Clark's voyage of discovery.* Cambridge, MA: Candlewick Press.

Wolff, V. E. (1994). *Make lemonade.* New York: Scholastic.

Wolff, V. E. (1999). *Bat 6: A novel.* New York: Scholastic.

Wolff, V. E. (2002). *True believer.* New York: Simon Pulse.

Woodson, J. (2001). *Miracle's boys.* New York: Scholastic.

Woodson, J. (2003). *Locomotion.* New York: G. P. Putnam's Sons.

Woodson, J. (2008). *After Tupac and D Foster.* New York: Puffin Books.

Wyatt, M. (2009). *Funny how things change.* New York: Farrar, Strauss & Giroux.

Yang, G. L. (2006). *American born Chinese.* New York: First Second.

Zarr, S. (2008). *Story of a girl.* Boston: Little, Brown.

Zimmer, T. V. (2007). *Reaching for sun.* New York: Bloomsbury Children's Books.

Zusak, M. (2002). *Fighting Ruben Wolfe.* New York: Scholastic.

Zusak, M. (2006). *I am the messenger.* New York: Alfred A. Knopf.

Zusak, M. (2006). *The book thief.* New York: Alfred A. Knopf.

Index

adventure and mystery texts as support for, 120
data on, 122
importance of inference and prediction skills, 122–23
probable passage worksheet, 124–26, *125*
Reading Level Inventories, 126–29
Seven Cs of Comprehension, 123–26, *124*
conclude stage of comprehension, *124*
connect stage of comprehension, 123, *124*
consider stage of comprehension, 123, *124*
content differentiation
defined, 7
Donnelly's *A Northern Light*, 38, 44
lesson plan for Crutcher's *Deadline*, 24
control in the reading process, 111–12
converse stage of comprehension, *124*
Copper Sun (Draper), 34
Coretta Scott King award, 97
Cormier, Robert, 14
Coy, John, 17–19, *18–19*
Crackback (Coy), 17–19, *18–19*
Crank (Hopkins), 66, *68*
critical literacy, *102*, 104–6, *106–8*
critical theory. *See* theory
Crutcher, Chris, 2, 15, 17. *See also Deadline* (Crutcher)
Cullinan, B. E., 19–20
culturally neutral, generic, or specific texts, 95, 97

Daly, Maureen, 14
Daniels, H., 115
Deadline (Crutcher)
author role-play, 30–31
charting character change, 32–33, *33*
Coy's *Crackback* compared to, 17–19, *18–19*
differentiated instruction lesson plan (overview), 23–25
frontloading, 25–27
good angel/bad angel activity, 29
hotseating, 27–29, *28*, 31
tableaux, 29–30
DeCourcy, Delia, 8

del Valle, A., 99–100
diagonal reading, 132
dialogue, in multicultural texts, 96
dialogue with a text, 82–86, *83*, 101, *103–4*
difference and diversity, 93–94. *See also* multicultural literature
differentiated reading instruction (DRI)
assumptions, not making, 10
dialogue with a text, 83
instructional, independent, and advanced levels, 23
lesson plan for Crutcher's *Deadline*, 23–33
principles of, 6–10
resource guide, 12–13
whole class and, 5–6
See also content differentiation; process differentiation and product differentiation
Differentiating the High School Classroom (Nunley), 9
dimensional perspective on critical literacy, 105–6, *106–8*
director role, 62
Discussion Webs, 140–44, *141*, *143*
Disreputable History of Frankie Landau-Banks, The (Lockheart), 120, *121–22*, 127–29
disrupting the commonplace, 105, *106–7*
diversity. *See* multicultural literature
Doctorow, Cory, 135
Donelson, K. L., 17, 35, 119–20, 130
Donnelly, Jennifer, 34–35
Downham, Jenny, 15
dramatization and performance
choral reading with Burg's *All the Broken Pieces*, 60–66
hotseating with Crutcher's *Deadline*, 27–31, *28*
Draper, Sharon, 34
Dredger, Katie, 5
Duthie, J., 140

Earhart, Amelia, 114
elements of graphic design, 112, *117*
empathizing stage, 20
enjambment, 55
Enriquez, G., 10

ethical discussions, need for, 139–40
"everyone improves," 10
Evolution of Calpurnia Tate, The (Kelly), 34

Fahrenheit 451 (Bradbury), 134–35
Fairchild, Lyn, 8
fantasy, supernatural, and science fiction
    characteristics of, 130–31
    Discussion Web, 140–44, *141*, *143*
    ethical discussion, need for, 139–40
    hesitancy about, 130
    reading ladders, 132–39, *133*
    selection of, 131–32
Farmer, M., 123
Farmer, Nancy, 134, 138
Fauber, L., 94
Faust, M., 79
Feed (Anderson), 134, 135
feminist theory, 47
Ferguson, Alane, 119
Fitzpatrick, Declan, 126–27
Flint, A. S., 105–6
fluency
    choral reading and, 60
    definition and dimensions of, 52–54
    multidimensional fluency scale, 60–62
    phrases and, 58
Flygirl (Smith), 34
Follet, Robin, 8
Ford, M. P., 25
foregrounding, 55
Forever (Blume), 14
"Four Dimensions of Critical Literacy"
    (Lewison, Flint, and Van Sluys), 105–6,
    106–8
Frankenstein (Shelley), 134, 136–37
free verse, 56
Fresh Takes on Teaching Literary Elements
    (Smith and Wilhelm), 22
frontloading, 25–27
Fuhrken, C., 20

Galda, L., 19–20
Gallagher, Kelly, 32
Gantos, Jack, 78, *80–81*, *90–91*
generalization and evaluation level of
    comprehension, 128

Geography of Girlhood, The (Smith), 50,
    51–52
gestural design elements, 112, *117*
Gibbons, L., 94
Giles, Gail, 119
Giovanni, Nikki, 70
Giver, The (Lowry), 134, 136
Glasgow, J. N., 48
good angel/bad angel activity, 29
Goodman, Allegra, 136
Gossip Girl series (von Ziegesar), 3
Gothic literature, 130
government regulation and control
    theme, *133*, 134–36, 142
graphic and BioGraphic novels
    examples of, 113–15
    importance of, 111–13
    research papers and reading guides,
        115–17, *116–17*, *118*
Green, John, 15

habits, reading, 7
Hatchet (Paulsen), 119
Heard, Georgia, 56
Hemphill, Stephanie, 49
Hero Ain't Nothin' but a Sandwich, A
    (Childress), 14
Hesse, Karen, 49, 66, 67
Hiassen, Carl, 119
Hillock, George, 126
Hinton, K., 130–31
Hinton, S. E., 14
historical fiction
    evaluation and selection of, 35–36,
        36–37, 37–38
    importance of, 34–35
    modified jigsaw/literature circle roles
        activity, 38–43
    tiered assignments and Major Works
        Data Sheet, 44, *45–47*
history, distortions of, 96
Hole in My Life (Gantos), 78, *80–81*, 82,
    90–91
Holes (Sachar), 119
Hoose, Phillip, 77
Hoot (Hiassen), 119
Hopkins, Ellen, 49, 66, *68*
hotseating, 27–29, *28*, *31*

reviewing whole work stage, 21
Reynolds, Marilyn, 1
Robertson, S. L., 59
role-playing, 30–31
roles in literature circles, 38–43, 62
Romantic literature, 130
Romero, P. A., 94
Root, M. P. P., 99
Rosenblatt, Louise, 79–82, 88, 101
Roser, N., 20, 22
Ross, C. S., 3
roulette, linguistic, 60
rubric for choral reading, *66*
Rushdie, Salman, 70

Sachar, Louis, 119
Satchel Paige: Striking Out at Jim Crow
   (Sturm and Tommaso), 113, 114–15,
   116–17
scaffolding, 123, 126, 140
Scat (Hiassen), 119
Scheeres, Julia, 78, *80–81*, 92
science fiction. *See* fantasy, supernatural,
   and science fiction
Seale, D., 96
seasonal poems, 70–71
sections in verse novels, 57
selection of YA literature
   adventure and mystery novels, *121–22*
   difficulty of, 3
   historical fiction, 35–36, *36–37*, 37–38
   Jago's criteria for, 4
   matching appropriate texts to
      individual students, 8–9
   multicultural texts, 95–97, *98*
   for reading ladders, 132–33
   realistic novels, 17–19, *18–19*
   science fiction, 131–32
   verse novels, 50, *51–52*
   See also choice and self-selected texts
setting, *47*
Seven Cs of Comprehension, 123–26, *124*
Seventeenth Summer (Daly), 14
sexuality, teenage, 14–15
Shafer, G., 115
Shelley, Mary, 136–37
Skeleton Creek (Carman), 119

Slapin, B., 96
small-group, differentiated instruction
   choral reading and choral poems, 60,
      63, 67, 68, 69
   dialogue with a text, 85–86
   lesson plan for Crutcher's *Deadline*,
      27–31
   See also literature circles
Smith, Kirsten, 48, 50
Smith, Michael, 22, 32
Smith, Sherri, 34
social activity, reading as, 3
sociopolitical issues, focusing on, 106,
   107
Soden, J. A., 123
spatial design elements, 112, *117*
Spiegelman, Art, 111
Stallworth, B. J., 94
stereotypes, 96
story maps, 60, *61*
Story of a Girl (Zarr), 15
storytelling with laughter and tears
   adventure and mystery, *122*
   historical fiction, *19, 37*
   memoir, *81*
   multicultural texts, *98*
   in selection criteria, 4
   verse novels, *52*
Stover, L. T., 95, 97–99
Stratton, Alan, 15
Stringer, S., 16–17
structural generalization level of
   comprehension, 128
struggling or reluctant readers, 10, 111
student-centered learning, 6
Sturm, James, 113, 114–15, *116–17*, 117
success, standards of, 96
Sullivan, E., 49
summaries and précis, 39, 84–85
summarizer role, 39–40
supernatural fiction. *See* fantasy,
   supernatural, and science fiction
Sutton, R., 50
symbols, 40, *47*

tableaux, 29–30
Taylor, Sarah Stewart, 113, 114

Authors

SUSAN L. GROENKE is associate professor of English education at the University of Tennessee, where she teaches courses on young adult literature, English methods, and teacher inquiry. A former National Board Certified teacher, she taught at both middle and high school levels before pursuing her doctorate at Virginia Tech. She is coeditor of the book *Critical Pedagogy and Teacher Education in the Neoliberal Era: Small Openings* and is also editor of NCTE's *English Leadership Quarterly*.

LISA SCHERFF is associate professor of English education at the University of Alabama, where she teaches courses such as secondary methods, young adult literature, and advanced literacy. She received a PhD in reading education with a graduate certificate in educational policy from Florida State University. She is a former high school English and reading teacher, and her research focuses on equity issues in secondary literacy, teaching young adult literature, and teacher preparation, induction, and mentoring. Her book *Thirteen Years of School: What Students Really Think* was published by Scarecrow Education in 2005. She is coeditor (with Leslie S. Rush) of *English Education*.

This book was typeset in TheMix and Palatino by Barbara Frazier.

Typefaces used on the cover include Constantia Italic and Nueva Std.

The book was printed on 50-lb. Opaque Offset paper by Versa Press, Inc.